NONVERTS

NONVERTS

The Making of Ex-Christian America

Stephen Bullivant

OXFORD
UNIVERSITY PRESS

OXFORD
UNIVERSITY PRESS

Oxford University Press is a department of the University of Oxford. It furthers
the University's objective of excellence in research, scholarship, and education
by publishing worldwide. Oxford is a registered trade mark of Oxford University
Press in the UK and certain other countries.

Published in the United States of America by Oxford University Press
198 Madison Avenue, New York, NY 10016, United States of America.

Library of Congress Control Number: 2022021552

ISBN 978-0-19-758744-7

DOI: 10.1093/oso/9780197587447.001.0001

Printed by Sheridan Books, Inc., United States of America

CONTENTS

CONTENTS

ACKNOWLEDGMENTS

Thanks are due, above all, to the seventy or so nonverts who generously gave up their time and, in several cases, prudent inhibitions about meeting up with strangers in bars to contribute to this project. A great many of them, suitably pseudonymized, end up quoted in these pages—some at great length—and I hope they enjoy finding themselves herein. I hope too that they feel like they have been represented in a fair and sympathetic manner. Naturally, not everyone ended up being mentioned or quoted directly. But all, without exception, were crucial for informing my ideas, and contributed much to the conclusions I draw (for which I alone, naturally, am responsible). I shall remain ever grateful for their kindness and candor alike.

As well as meeting around fifty of *Nonverts'* participants myself, I also had the assistance of two excellent researchers: Dr. Jacqui Frost and the late Dr. Tommy Coleman, who conducted interviews for me in Minnesota and Tennessee, respectively. News of Tommy's untimely death reached me in December 2021, as I was in the midst of making the final edits to this manuscript. This book is dedicated to him.

Many others contributed to this project in all kinds of ways. The work was made possible by the generosity of the John Templeton Foundation, which funded the research as part of the "Understanding Unbelief" project (grant no. 6024), led by my long-time "nonreligion" colleagues, collaborators, and compadres Drs. Lois Lee, Jon Lanman, and Miguel Farias (plus me).

My agent, Alice Martell at the Martell Agency, and editor, Theo Calderara at Oxford University Press, have been enthusiastic supporters of the book, not least in their encouraging swiftness in signing up me (Alice) and it (Theo). I hope they end up feeling that the gamble paid off.

A great many others, from all the many areas of my personal and professional life, deserve mention here too, including Claire Berlyn, Zofia Kicinova, Dr. Aprilfaye Manalang, Dr. Josh Bullock, Dr. David Bullivant, Norma Bullivant, Deacon Tom Gornick, Mary-Jo Gornick, Rod Dreher, Fr. Hugh Somerville-Knapman, Dr. Ryan Cragun, Brandon Vogt, Lizzie Ruse, Roz Mackraz Dieterich, Rev. Dr. David Poecking, Jordan Summers Young, Dr. Luke Arredondo, Elena Arredondo, Rev. Dr. Ryan Burge, Bernadette Durcan, Tim Kinnear, Dr. Jacob Phillips, the staff and "regulars" of The Penny Black, and Andrew Tucker.

The bulk of this book was written during the Covid-19 pandemic. I am indebted to Charles Tanqueray and James Beam for providing unfailing sources of comfort and resilience. My wife, Dr. Joanna Bullivant, has been characteristically wonderful throughout, triumphing over all the additional trials we've experienced over the past few years as she always does. Our four children, ever mindful of the need to maintain a proper work-life balance, have nobly kept us both from working for too long at any one time. Daddy loves them very much indeed.

NOTE ON SOURCES AND REFERENCING

Please note that where I have quoted directly from my interviewees, I have occasionally "tidied" the transcripts for ease of reading. I have kept these changes to a minimum, however, and have been careful to preserve both original meaning and personal, idiomatic style.

Where possible, I have given page references for works cited. However, in several cases, I read the books on Kindle or listened to them as audiobooks. In these cases, rather than give generally unhelpful references to "location" or "timestamps," I have simply indicated the chapter instead.

All web links given in the endnotes were correct as of October 2021.

None the Up and Up

"You British?"

"Yeah. I live near London," I reply, handing over my passport.

"You're the third Brit we've had in today."

"We're preparing for Brexit," I joke. He nods thoughtfully, with solemn affirmation.

"Y'all'll need it."

"It," in this case, isn't political wisdom, or prayer, or a stockpile of food or medicine (though, in the event, all three would have been prescient advice). The "it" I am apparently in need of today is firearms training.

I don't know whether southern Louisiana is renowned for its gun ranges, but I can honestly say I've never been to a nicer one. The people are warm and welcoming. Safety and responsibility are emphasized at all times. Even the T-shirts emblazoned with "LOVE" spelled out with weaponry—the "O" is a grenade; the "E" looks, to my as-yet-untrained eye, like an upended Kalashnikov—are neatly arranged and reasonably priced.

I'm here as the guest of John, a professional in his early thirties and an ambassadorial firearms enthusiast: "always interested to expose people with no experience with guns to the gun culture, especially if they are from another country." We meet at a coffee shop on the other side of town before driving over in our own vehicles. I got lost in traffic on the way, but I know I'm in the right place when I spy John's "Taxation is Theft" bumper sticker in the parking lot. John, evidently a regular, is inside chatting with the staff. With him are the guns he has carefully chosen for my afternoon's education: two pistols and an AR-15 semiautomatic.

John is the second new person I've met in town, and I like him a lot. He's earnest and erudite, laying great store by evidence, facts, and rational argument: "pro-science," albeit not to the extent of "venerating" its findings uncritically, and getting a "giant science boner"—all his phrases—about it. Our conversation flows freely: from the ideas of Epicurus to the sex lives of octopuses, right through to the future of climate change, the societal implications of artificial intelligence, and what transferable skills a modern time-traveler might have in the ancient Roman job market. ("Because we know that germs are a thing and that if you boil all your instruments and wash stuff . . . So that would be John in ancient Rome: just a weird doctor who had a funny accent from the future.") Since he tells me he's "the kind of person who thinks before he speaks," these are clearly the kinds of things he's thought a great deal about.

Compared to his real pet topics, though, these are merely the byproducts of wide reading and idle musing. What *really* interests John are politics, guns, and, well, the politics of guns. "I used to be a Republican," he later tells me over email, "when I thought I knew more than I did." An enthusiastic Bush voter in 2004, he only "grudgingly" supported McCain four years later "because I was so concerned about Obama." Those fears softened over time when "Obama didn't do all the 'extreme' far-left stuff that I had allowed Republican talking points to scare me about." Lesson learned, John bought his AR-15 just before the 2016 election, "as I was sure that Hillary would win, talk about gun control, and cause another

Obama-era panic-buying situation and drive prices up." The Trump years, though "a total shit-show," at least provided a much needed "shake-up." Ultimately, though, John perceives little difference between red and blue: "The status quo on so many things remains the same regardless of who is in power. You get unchecked spending, huge deficits, and constant warfare. You just get it with or without abortions." He's voted Libertarian since 2012.

* * *

I don't know whether southern Louisiana is renowned for its heavily inked, polyamorous bisexuals with long-standing penchants for the BDSM and "Leather" subcultures, who have the title "Reverend" on their business cards. But it should be. Because Judy, my other new friend in town, is an engaging example of the genre.

Now in her late forties, she has seen a fair bit of life—and, more than once, come perilously close to losing it. "In my very early 20s, I nearly died from an overdose. Then when I was getting clean and struggling with that, I was the victim of intimate partner assault and he nearly killed me." Left to die in a pool of her own blood and struggling to breathe with broken ribs, she somehow survived the night. A friend turned up the next day, called 911, and got her to the ER just in time.

Such traumas would have broken a weaker person. Or if not, they might at least have soured their outlook on the world. Not so Judy. She describes her life's mission as being one of "purposeful mindfulness. My focus is to make sure that I and the people around me experience as much love and joy and kindness as they can. Because there's just not enough of it going around." Central to her own practice of this are what she terms "little adventures": "People, I think, spend a lot of time coveting things that are bigger, better, more awesome, more amazing. They want the experience with capital letters: *The Experience*. But I would much rather have a life built on little memories, little adventures." Chief among these are ones shared with her husband and boyfriend, plus their own other partners—and so-called step-children: "Our tribe is incredibly intertwined and involved with each other, each other's lives, not necessarily romantically but just . . . If I died right now, those little adventures would be enough to have zero regrets for the choices in my life."

Beyond her own tribe, "Reverend Judy"—she was ordained online by the Universal Life Church, joining such fellow clergy as Adele and Stephen Colbert—works part-time as a wedding officiant, specializing in LGBTQ ceremonies.[1] Even in this city, which Judy and others stress is a *long* way, culturally speaking, from cosmopolitan New Orleans, this is a growing market.

Judy started formally blessing same-sex couples some fifteen years ago, around the same time Louisianans voted four-to-one to amend the state constitution to ban same-sex marriage. Since the US Supreme Court legalized it, however, Judy has regularly performed such weddings. "Blessings" remain popular at the annual city Pride event, with many keen publicly to "reaffirm their coupleness." These all help Judy's mission to "leave as many positive, impactful memories and footprints as I possibly can." So too, I expect, does her other job: running a bar. She sums up her philosophy with a nod to neopaganism: "All of those things absolutely give my life meaning. The fact that—to borrow one from the Wiccans—I've done no harm."

In politics (I bring it up; she doesn't) Judy also zigs where others zag. Regarding the two-party system to be "fundamentally broken, painfully broken," she prefers to support whichever candidate best matches her "fairly liberal set" of issues. In practice, that ends up making it "absolutely, absolutely imperative" for her to vote Democrat, even if that usually means—as it did in 2016—supporting a "political candidate who really does not represent me as an individual." When we spoke in summer 2018, she was "actually cautiously optimistic" for 2020, "because I am seeing lots of grassroots and lower level elections going to Democrats in surprising upsets." Meanwhile, she adds grimly, "the dumpster is burning . . ."

* * *

For all their contrasts, John and Judy have two very important things in common with each other—and moreover, with tens of millions of their fellow Americans. The first is that neither the straitlaced semiautomatic stockpiler nor the ebulliently mohawked progressive regards themselves as belonging to a religion. They are, in the media's now-ubiquitous terminology, religious "nones."

For her part, on surveys Judy normally opts for "no religion." If pushed and in the right kind of mood, she might gloss this with "conscientious objector, because it gets a laugh," or else simply identifies as "atheist" or "agnostic." Though the former is nearer to her actual position, she admits to some ingrained discomfort with the term itself: "Even now I struggle to identify myself as an atheist, although technically I suppose that I am one. But my first thought when I hear the word is bereft. Bereft of belief, bereft of faith, bereft of consolation and comfort." This instinctive, Pavlovian response soon gives way, however. "My second thought when I think of atheism is freethought and freedom."

John is just straight-up nonreligious: if the survey has a dedicated "atheist" tick-box, all the better. He used to identify as an agnostic, but after "doing more reading on the topic" he took the plunge: "Now I associate agnosticism with just not thinking about it enough at all." Where once he linked atheism to the "hypothetical militant atheist archetype," now he simply sees it as "just the default" for folks like him (i.e., "sceptical"). Like a lot of the people we'll meet in the coming pages, however, as comfortable as John is personally with identifying with the A-word, "I find that saying 'not religious' in mixed company is a way safer bet than saying 'atheist' because some people might hear 'atheist' and think that I'm actively trying to ruin their fun with their belief and their religion, and I'm not."

The second main thing they have in common is that both were brought up, albeit to different degrees, "in" a religion. That is to say, they are not simply nones, but what I call "nonverts": think "converts," but going *from* a religion to having none.

For John, growing up with religion amounted to little more than being baptized as a baby "for family reasons." His own parents were functionally nonreligious—"they just never even brought it up." His only memories of church are being taken, maybe twice, "because we were staying with dad's parents that weekend and it was awkward not to pretend." This meager experience did little to whet his appetite. Predictably enough, religion never really took.

Judy's upbringing was toward the opposite end of spectrum. Though she describes her stepfather as "a kind of lapsed Italian Catholic," her mother was and is notably pious in a traditionalist Catholic mold. Though never a fan of her mom's Masses in Latin, Judy was nonetheless "incredibly, painfully devout." Most unusually for a middle-schooler in the 1980s, she had even "gone as far as speaking to the Mother Superior at the convent here, making a fairly informal pledge to join as soon as I graduated: to take vows, or at least to try the convent." For reasons we'll cover later, this didn't last too long. By the age of sixteen, she had already dropped out of church more or less completely: no youth group, no Sunday school, no Mass. She retained a "lapsed Catholic" identity into her mid-twenties, marrying in the church for cultural and family reasons, while exploring various other spiritual paths: "I played around with nature religions for a while, paganism and Wicca. Buddhism as well; I'm a fan. If you had to pick one—it's not really a religion exactly—but if you had to pick one, I'm a big fan of that." Ultimately, she realized that she didn't have to pick one at all. "The idea of mystical spiritualism was very comforting for a long time. I don't need it though. And I think that maybe that's age, maybe that's study, maybe it's just life experience, I don't know. I just don't see it."

"Nonverts" may be a new coinage, and admittedly something of an etymological abomination. But the *reality* it points to, I'm convinced, is indispensable for properly making sense of the present, recent past, and long-term future of American religion. As I hope to show, nonverts are the key to understanding much of the so-called rise of the nones, how and why it happened, who they are exactly, and *what it all means* for the present and future of America. If that sounds like a lot—well, it is. But then, as we're about to see, there are a whole lot of nones, and a whole lot of those nones were once religious. And they are in the process of fundamentally and decisively changing the face of American society.

* * *

The fact is, in today's USA, Judy and John are in very good company. Nones account for roughly one in four American adults, or about *59 million* people. And as you might already suspect, they are far more diverse than popular stereotypes might have you believe. Furthermore, barring some Great Millennial Revival, this proportion is set to grow and grow for the foreseeable future. According to the biennial General Social Survey, in 2018 a third of 18-to-29-year-olds cited "no religion" as their personal "religious preference." The

2021 data are even more striking, with 30% of all adults and 44% of 18-to-29-year-olds identifying as nones. But for reasons I'll explain in detail in Chapter 3, there are good reasons (Covid, for one) for being cautious about these figures. Lest you think that that's just what late-teens and twenty-somethings are like, and that they'll all come altar-calling back when they grow up a bit . . . well, the signs aren't remotely favorable.

Figure 1.1 makes this point more clearly and concisely than I can in words. It shows just how rapidly the nonreligious share of the US population has expanded over the past twenty to thirty years. It also shows how young adults affirm "no religion" at double or triple the rate that the same age group did in any year between 1972 and 1994, when the "none" population first began to rise. Significantly,

Figure 1.1. Proportions of all US adults, and US adults under 30, with no religious affiliation, over time.

Source: *General Social Survey (1972–2018; weighted data)*

this wasn't simply a function of nones entering adulthood. That was certainly a part of it. But for reasons not immediately obvious, claiming no religion was becoming increasingly popular in other age groups, too.

Attempting to make sense, at a deep level, of how this has come about, and why it did so *when* it did is one of the overriding concerns of this book. It's a complex tale. America is, after all, a big, diverse, and fascinating place—and religion is a bigger, more diverse, and more fascinating topic in the United States than in most other countries. So too, therefore, is the story of how large swathes of Americans have lost, or at least substantially downsized, their religious believing, behaving, and belonging.

One major clue lies in the simple fact that, like Judy and John, a clear majority of America's nones haven't always felt this way. They are nonverts. That is, they used to be—and saw themselves to be—religious "somethings." In most cases, this was the "something" they were brought up as. Others may well have been various kinds of religious "somethings" along the road to becoming nones. Judy, for example, is one of America's roughly 16 million nonverts who say they were brought up Catholic. Add to them something like 7.5 million ex-Baptists, 2 million ex-Methodists, 2 million ex-Lutherans, and 1 million each of ex-Episcopalians and ex-Presbyterians. Another 2 million nones were brought up in non-Christian religions, just over half of whom say they were raised Jewish. All in all, only 30% of America's religiously unaffiliated adults say they were brought up as nones: roughly the same proportion who were cradle Catholics, and rather less than the percentage raised as some kind of Protestant (see Figure 1.2). That adds up to around 41 million nonverts. To put that figure in perspective, it's roughly equal to the adult populations of California and Pennsylvania, the nation's first and fourth most populous states, *combined*.

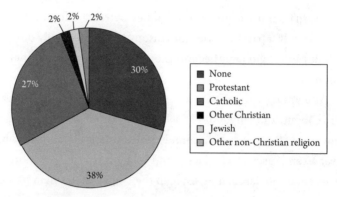

Figure 1.2. Religious upbringing of US adults with no religion.
Source: General Social Survey (2018; weighted data)

But why, exactly, is this so important?

First off, large-scale religious change tends to happen gradually. Throughout history, most people, most of the time, have kept whatever religion they happened to be brought up in. People *do* convert—or "switch"—from one religious or denominational identity to another, but even rare periods of "mass conversion" typically only affect hundreds, or perhaps thousands, of people. No doubt there are exceptions to this general rule, but if so, then they are just that—exceptions. Instead, even the most dramatic examples of religious growth or decline tend to occur over many generations. Birth and retention rates are often key here: hence the growing numbers, generation by generation, of the Amish or Haredi Jews (neither of whom attract especially many converts). Even a fairly modest-looking rate of increase, when sustained over a long period, can very quickly add up, as anyone with a mortgage or student loan will know all too well. Immigration helps too, especially if those immigrants themselves have lots of children. This playbook certainly served Catholics and Mormons well, for example, in previous generations.[2]

But the rise of the nones is not due to a sudden influx from more secular shores. Nor is it down to nonreligious parents typically raising quivers full of nonreligious babies. Instead, it's primarily due to a vast, wholly unprecedented "mass nonversion" of millions upon millions of Americans who were raised religious. Indeed, if this book contains any single, summarizable argument it is that the USA is in the midst of a social, cultural, and religious watershed—one that today's Americans are not merely living *through*, but millions have actively *lived out* in their own stories. This shift, while in many (not all) cases a very gradual one from the perspective of an individual lifetime, has manifested itself at the national level very swiftly indeed. It was less than twenty years ago that major newspapers started reporting on "the rise of the nones": the earliest example I can find is from December 2003 by Dan Lattin, titled "Living the Religious Life of a None." (Pleasingly, this also includes the "no, not *nuns*" joke that has been used in every church PowerPoint presentation on "mission and outreach" ever since. I hope Lattin gets royalties.) Fast-forward eighteen years, and none-specific headlines appear atop everything from earnest political think-pieces to such relatable *Buzzfeed* listicles as "21 Awkward Situations That'll Make Non-Religious People Cringe."

Second—and relatedly—by foregrounding nonverts specifically, over and above nones-in-general, I'm attempting to stress something significant that is often overlooked. Sociologists have been aware for some years that "ex-" identities are not simply descriptions of people's *pasts*: in many subtle and not-so-subtle ways, they influence people's current personalities, beliefs, feelings, circumstances, relationships, and a great deal else.[3] In truth, and as is often the case, the sociologists are late in catching up on what common sense screams at us. For example, an ex-girlfriend or ex-wife is in a special class of woman, forever different from all those other women who are not now, *and never were*, one's love interests. This has potentially very concrete personal and social ramifications if one does not properly recognize, and act in due accordance with, this "social fact."[4] Similarly, to be a "recovering alcoholic" is a statement about both past *and* present. And it's worlds apart from being a lifelong teetotaler, though both don't currently drink alcohol. The roles and relationships we *used to* have can exert powerful sway over our current selves. And the way we feel about our past covers a wide spectrum of emotions—loss, longing, affection, alienation, liberation, trauma, regret, anger, gratitude—in any manner of conflicting combinations. As we shall see, this is often very much the case when it comes to people's ex-religious identities, too.

* * *

Of course, what it means for an individual to go from being a Christian to being "nonreligious" diverges greatly from what it means for a whole country to go from being a predominantly Christian nation—the "city on a hill" so beloved of Winthrop and Reagan—to . . . well, it's going to be interesting to find out. Accordingly, this book operates on two levels. Very much to the fore will be the individual experiences of American nonverts. Just like classical conversion stories, each person's nonversion narrative is unique to them. Yet also like converts' testimonies, when one has listened to enough of them, common causes and influences, trends, and tropes do start to emerge. These do not manifest themselves in a set number of predefined paths, such that if a person has or does A, B, and C, then she will inevitably wind up at point Z. But one tends to see the same palette of experiences, albeit endlessly remixed, cropping up again and again. This is most apparent, not surprisingly, among people who started out in the same kind of religion to begin with. As we shall see, nones who were brought up as evangelicals, for all their internal diversity, make up a relatively coherent group when compared to ex-Catholics, ex-Mormons, or ex-mainliners: further proof of the ongoing significance of American denominationalism.[5] Likewise, an ironically ecumenical federation of ex-Christians—"that they may all be none" (with apologies to John 17:21)—would tend to have more in common with each other than they would with similar coalitions of ex-Jews or ex-Muslims. Reaching the point where you no longer identify with any religion, even nominally, will naturally be a rather different journey if you were brought up in a Black Pentecostal family in the Sunbelt than if you were raised a middle-of-the-road Episcopalian in New England. But it won't *just* be the starting point and route that are different. So too, in all likelihood, will the destination be. That is, your personal brand of nonreligiosity—your "noneness"—will be very different from that of your WASP-ish doppelgänger.

Alongside chapters focusing on individuals, I'll also sketch out the big picture. I say big, but I really mean huge: more or less the whole canvas of US social, cultural, religious, economic, and political life, both now and over the past thirty, fifty, or eighty years. Obviously, we will have to be very selective. This big picture is necessary for two reasons. In the first place, *Homo sapiens* is "by nature a social animal."[6] Our lives are not self-contained. They are intimately bound up with the lives of our families, friends, neighbors, and co-workers, obviously enough. But they are also enmeshed, in a million subtle ways, with individuals, groups, and movements that we have perhaps never met. Our lives are shaped by everything from the global economy to our social media feeds: everything, that is, that makes up our cultural backdrop. While our own ideas, attitudes, emotions, and actions are not simply the products of all these inputs, we are constantly influenced in all manner of ways. And we too, in turn, influence others.

Scholars have long noted the importance of one's family, one's peer group, the local or regional religious "microclimate," and the wider culture in affecting a person's becoming and/or remaining religious. It is easier to end up a Jehovah's Witness if one's parents consciously bring you up as one than it is if they bring you up as a Hare Krishna.[7] Falling in with a new crowd is a clear predictor of conversion to new religious movements and mainstream religions alike.[8] It feels much more easy and natural to be a "Bible-believing" Christian in Texas than it does in the Pacific Northwest.[9] If all this is true for the acquiring and maintaining of religious identities, it should apply equally to the drifting, weakening, losing, and discarding of them, too. And it does. What I mean is that each of the myriad, unique narratives plays out, and only makes sense within, a much bigger social and cultural landscape. Each nonvert has, if you like, his or her own personal subplot within some epic saga.

This particular saga has a logic and significance all its own. We already know that religion, and the loss of it, *matters* to people. This can take many forms: in the pages that follow are stories of loss and gain, comedy and tragedy, pain and joy, devastation and liberation. It is not only religious people to whom it matters, either. The mini-industry of "New Atheist" books, blogs, YouTube channels, and meet-up groups (on which more later) that began about fifteen years ago is proof enough that there are many committed nonreligious folks for whom religion matters a great deal. One has to think something is very important indeed to devote one's time, energy, and resources to fighting it. (That is not, I might add, a veiled claim that such devoted secularists are themselves, in their deepest Freudian psyches, secretly religious. One can devote one's whole life to fighting something—whether malaria, the New World Order, or the improper use of apostrophes—without secretly being in love with it.)

This importance of religion is not, moreover, confined to the private sphere. The various roles that religious groups have played in US political debates, often on both sides, are well known. Recent years have also seen the growing prominence of *nonreligious* political influencers—the Freedom from Religion Foundation, the Secular Coalition for America, the American Humanist Association—riding the rising tide of nones and, indeed, receiving a newly warm reception from politicos keen to court this demographic (whether they will be as politically successful as their conservative religious counterparts very much remains to be seen).[10] Outside of the Beltway Bubble, (non)religious identities correlate in complex ways with all manner of concrete concerns. One's religious identity, or lack thereof, can be a good predictor not only of one's beliefs, attitudes, and values on a wide range of topics, but also with such very practical things as health outcomes, happiness levels, and suicide rates.[11] Cause and effect can be very difficult to prove, or even guess at. But this doesn't affect our basic point. Either religion itself matters, or it is intimately bound up with other things that matter. Either way, the kinds of major religious changes afoot in America surely augur significant shifts of other types, too.

* * *

In the following chapter, we'll embark on the first of four denominational "deep dives," exploring nonversion in contemporary Mormonism. Analogous chapters on mainline Protestantism, evangelicalism, and Catholicism will follow. These chapters will aim to show that for all the talk of the "nones," and as much as they may have in common, it makes no more sense to talk about them as an undifferentiated mass than it would to talk about, say, Christians that way. The label "none" masks a great deal of diversity. By looking, rather, at "nonverts," these chapters will demonstrate that the factors pushing people toward nonversion vary considerably depending on the religious tradition they are leaving, and that those factors linger long after they have left the fold. Alternating with these will be broader, thematic chapters exploring "who" precisely America's nones and nonverts are, how and why nonreligiosity rapidly grew—*seemingly* out of nowhere—and what I'm calling the "Ex Effect," meaning how what you used to be affects who you are. The final chapter will conclude with some speculation about the likely future of post-Christian America. Before all that, though, a word or two about the types of evidence that *Nonverts* is based upon.

In the years just prior to the pandemic, I had the pleasure of flying and driving around several states—Florida, Illinois, Louisiana, New York, Oregon, Pennsylvania, Texas—interviewing nones of all backgrounds, ranging in age from eighteen (a Black, former Seventh-day Adventist man, in New York City) to seventy-eight (a White, ex-Methodist woman, in Portland, Oregon). Two research assistants also conducted interviews for me, in Minnesota and Tennessee. Participants were recruited through various channels, including existing personal networks and online message boards. All in all, we recorded detailed interviews, ranging from forty minutes to a couple of hours, with seventy people. To preserve their anonymity, names and other reasonable identifying characteristics have been changed or omitted. Naturally, I hope my portrayal of them is sufficiently faithful that they are still able to recognize themselves where and when they feature in these pages.

In addition to the rich three-dimensionality one only gets from qualitative study, this book also presents quantitative data from high-quality, nationally representative social surveys. Most of these come from my own analyses of the biennial General Social Survey (GSS), administered by the National Opinion Research Center at the University of Chicago. Though drawing most heavily from the 2018 wave, I will occasionally make use of the full dataset going back to 1972. Other leading data sources, for example the regular surveys done by Pew, Gallup, or the Public Religion Research Institute (PRRI), will also appear where useful. But the GSS, for good though boring reasons, will be our go-to data.[12] Unless otherwise stated, assume that any statistics cited are from there.

Finally, I have been researching and writing about American and European nonreligiosity, in all its myriad types and shades, for around fifteen years. Over roughly this same period—not that I'm claiming any credit—the interest of other sociologists, psychologists, anthropologists, and historians has grown immeasurably.[13] There has suddenly arisen a wealth of pioneering research probing all manner of nonreligious phenomena, big and small. One of my hopes for this book is to bring some of this fascinating and innovative work, much of it buried behind journal paywalls or in expensive academic books, to a wider audience. Naturally, the evidence, ideas, and arguments put forward here reflect, build upon, and (not infrequently) disagree with this body of scholarship. In the interests of readability, citations, suggestions for further reading, technical discussions, and personal tangents have mostly been confined to the endnotes. They are there for the benefit of readers who like or need these kinds of academic accoutrements. Others may simply allow their eyes to skim over the little numbers floating in the text, safe in the knowledge that they're mainly missing out on bibliographic details and dad jokes.

When the Saints Go Marching Out

"I was brought up very, very Mormon."

"And how would you identify now, say on a survey?"

"If there was a blank space I'd write 'Angrily and unfortunately atheist.'" He laughs. "Yeah, I don't like atheism."

"Well, that seems like a good place to start . . ."

Brandon, a medical student in his late twenties, sips his pint of craft beer: eloquent testimony to how very, very far he's come from being very, very Mormon. He tells me about his "astoundingly Mormon" hometown in southern Idaho—the middle of America's middle America—where every street in his neighborhood was named after a character from the Bible. With his parents active in their local ward, there were no clear distinctions between church, family, and social life: "it was all under the same umbrella." Even at his secular public high school, a free-study period was allocated in each day's timetable to allow its majority-Mormon students to troop off for religious instruction at the purpose-built seminary across the street.[1] So complete was this LDS bubble in which Brandon and his four siblings were raised that he was nine or ten years old before he knowingly met a non-Mormon. A new boy moved into the neighborhood, and Brandon vividly recalls a "moment of shock" at discovering his wildly exotic religion: *Christian*. "I rang my parents.

It blew my mind that not everyone in the world is Mormon. It was staggering."

* * *

This must seem like an odd place to start, among the Mormons of small-town Idaho. And it is, in a few ways. First, while this book is not *only* interested in former Christians—in the fullness of time we'll meet nones who were raised as Muslims, Jews, and Buddhists—an overarching theme is indeed the waning, and in many cases waned-ness, of "Christian America" considered as a totality. Foregrounding Mormons,[2] whom many Americans don't even count as Christians in the first place, is perhaps a little idiosyncratic. Second, Mormons make up only a small proportion of the American population—perhaps no more than 2%. This fact is, moreover, surely exaggerated by the Latter-day Saints' historical concentration in the western and mountain states. One could go one's whole life in large swathes of the South, Midwest, and Northeast without ever knowingly meeting a Mormon beyond awkwardly avoiding a missionary's eye on the subway. Brandon's near-opposite experience is thus wholly unrelatable for the vast majority of readers. Finally, of all well-known religious groups in the United States, the LDS Church has been among the most resilient. While many churches have been hemorrhaging members, especially younger ones, the Mormons have not.[3] "Mormon envy" is a genuine thing within church circles, not least among those concerned for keeping young adults believing and committed—and with good reason.[4] How many eighteen-year-olds do you suppose are willing to spend two years, working twelve-hour days, six days a week, traipsing the sidewalks of Wherever-They're-Sents-ville in the hope of converting just one or two strangers to the life-changing joys of the United Methodist Church? Yet thousands of Mormons set out on such missions each year.

It is certainly true that, at the deep level of doctrine, Mormonism differs greatly from traditional Christianity. LDS understandings of the nature of God, and thus of such core topics as the Trinity, sin, and salvation, are a long way from those broadly held in common by Catholic, Orthodox, and (most) Reformed churches. The Saints' distinctive doctrines are not, moreover, merely "on the books." Unlike many members of other denominations, Mormons typically know what their church teaches, and explicitly agree with it.[5] That said, Mormonism's own self-understanding has always been that it is a *restoration* of true Christianity. The person of Jesus Christ is clearly front and center within LDS practice and belief, both as a cosmic figure and as a real-life person who walked the Earth. (Indeed, who walked rather more of it than is typically allowed within traditional Christianity, since Mormons believe that Jesus visited North America.) Accordingly, Mormons overwhelmingly regard themselves as Christians—and roughly half the US population agrees—though as young Brandon's experience suggests, even they admit a distinction between *Mormon* Christians and the other sort. Furthermore, it is certainly true that the Latter-day Saints *look*, in practice, very much like an American Christian church. Through a sociological lens at least, if Mormonism *isn't* to be counted as some kind of Christian religion or denomination—bearing in mind the kaleidoscopic forms in which Christianity has existed—it is very hard to see what else it could be.

In fact, focusing on Mormonism serves as an ideal overture to the rest of *Nonverts*. Several themes, developed with much greater orchestration later on, can receive an introductory hearing. At the same time we can restrict our horizons, for the moment, to a single, small, and self-contained case study. If significant levels of nonversion are emerging in the small-town religious subcultures of Idaho and Utah—and they are—then it doesn't augur well for the nation's other denominations. Furthermore, this book aspires to say something true and interesting not just about Americans, but about America itself. Given the Latter-day Saints' peculiar place within US history and culture, this too qualifies them for attention here. Maybe if Paul Simon had wasted less time counting cars on the New Jersey Turnpike and headed instead to Provo, Orem, or Rexburg, he might have found more of what he was looking for.

Mormonism's sheer "Americanness" has struck an impressive lineup of cultural commentators, from the author of *War and Peace* to the creators of *South Park*.[6] The United States has a strong track record in birthing religious impulses and expressions, both new and renewed, and exporting them with remarkable success. Pentecostalism, Jehovah's Witnesses, Christian Science, Seventh-day Adventists, the Hare Krishnas, Scientology—all (re)born in the USA, and all now famous throughout the world. What sets Mormonism apart is that Joseph Smith's retooling of Christianity does not merely translate the biblical witness *for* the New World, it quite literally transports it there, with the resurrected Jesus visiting early inhabitants of the continent. Add to that Smith's own (to his followers) martyrdom barely ten miles from the Mississippi, and a pioneering history in the Old West that even today's ex-Mormons take an immense amount of pride in recounting, and you have a very American religion. ("Tell me about your family," I encourage self-described "stone-cold atheist" Norah, raised in 1960s Utah. "How about I start with my great-great-great-great-grandfather?" she offers, and promptly does.)

And yet, while deeply rooted in their native soil, the Saints' ambitions have long been thoroughly global. Again, one might say, not unlike America herself. My own hometown of Preston, northwest England, has a Mormon ward (est. 1837) that predates Salt Lake City's by a decade (est. 1847). LDS missionaries were baptizing in my local River Ribble—a mere creek compared to the Mississippi—a good two years before their compatriots even reached Nauvoo. Since the mid-1990s, there have been more Mormons outside the USA than inside it. This trend is only likely to continue.

Nevertheless, this "American religion" with its "All-American prophet" has a further affinity with its homeland. The LDS embrace of mainstream America's virtues and cultural values over the course of the twentieth century is one of history's greatest corporate rebrandings. From almost its earliest days until the late nineteenth century, the LDS Church was at war—often figuratively, sometimes literally—with surrounding communities and with local, state, and federal authorities. Utah only attained statehood in 1896 after six failed attempts, having disavowed the practice of "plural marriage" several years prior. Old memories died hard. Zane Grey's genre-defining Western *Riders of the Purple Sage*, published in 1912, could still trade effortlessly on the literary stereotype—established by such diverse writers as Jules Verne and Arthur Conan Doyle—of the barbarous Mormon polygamist, willing to murder any no-good Gentile who stood in his way. "Did you ever know or hear of a Gentile prospering in a Mormon community?" asks one of Zane Grey's characters.[7] It is hardly a ringing endorsement of the 45th state's newfound place within the Union.

Fast-forward a hundred years, to 2012 and a Mormon's credible run for president, ultimately winning twenty-four states and 47% of the popular vote. This was not, needless to say, the barnstorming run of a maverick firebrand. Romney's appeal, such as it was, was *precisely* the opposite. White, male, middle-aged, affluent; a calm, measured, "safe pair of hands"; a clean-living patriot and upholder

of traditional family values; fiscally, morally, sartorially conservative. "Mitt Romney: 'Boring' by Design?" asked *The Week* in 2011,
before answering unequivocally in the affirmative.[8] But here's the
important part: Romney's impeccable establishment credentials
did not, by 2012, confound popular Mormon stereotypes but
rather confirmed them. In many ways, he *was* the stereotype. True,
Romney didn't speak much of his religiosity on the campaign trail.
He didn't need to. It spoke for itself, loud and clear. Two of his
great-great-grandparents were among those first English converts,
baptized in the Ribble in 1837. Mitt himself, an alum of Brigham
Young University (like all five of his sons), has variously served the
church as missionary, bishop, and stake president, alongside an
impressive career of both business and public service. He was, in
short, the Very Model of a Modern Mormon Man. Commenting
on this "staggering" transformation of the Mormon brand, historian
Matthew Bowman notes astutely:

> From a looming threat to the American republic, a religion that
> Americans feared would inculcate the perversity of polygamy,
> the death of democracy, and raving heresy, Mormons have be-
> come at the dawn of the twenty-first century the living image
> of bland, middle-American tedium, so wed to awkward cultural
> conventionality that their strange beliefs seem a curious acces-
> sory rather than a serious challenge to American assumptions.[9]

Of course, Romney lost the 2012 election: well beaten
by a Democratic president embodying other "staggering"
transformations in many Americans' ideas of who they are and
ought to be. In 2016, moreover, the GOP successfully offered up
its own counter-offer to staid and stable respectability. More to the
point, the 2020 campaigns proved that *neither* party's competing

visions of America necessarily sit comfortably with the virtues and values Mormons have assiduously cultivated over the past century. This is something often felt, viscerally and instinctively, by younger generations of Mormons, raised with at least one foot in a surrounding culture for which (to cite some commonly cited issues) love, sex, marriage, or child-rearing are not the exclusive preserve of one man and one woman. This may turn out to be the great irony of Mormon mainstreaming. A religious group that suffered for affirming polyamory *before* it was cool may now be paying the price for championing the ideal of monogamous heterosexuality as (for many) it *ceases* to be.

* * *

Like most ex-Saints I've spoken with, Brandon remembers much about his upbringing with thankfulness and affection: "Great people, Mormons." Growing up was not all plain sailing, however. Aged 12, he returned from summer camp to learn that his best friend had been killed in a canoeing accident. His parents, "very stark, rugged folk," relayed this news in a bluntly matter-of-fact way. "They were like, 'Hey, come upstairs, we have something to tell you.' It was the first thing when I got home. They just said, 'Brett is dead.'" The funeral was, understandably enough, "really brutal, everything about it was just really dark in a way that I've only ever seen in Mormon communities." He and two friends, dressed in their Boy Scout uniforms, were brought up to the pulpit in front of perhaps 900 people to "sing one of the saddest hymns in the Mormon Church, all choked up at my dead best friend's funeral."

This "devastating" event, though not *the* moment that shattered his hitherto unquestioned faith, "was definitely a solid punch to it." It precipitated a period of intense spiritual turmoil. The Latter-day

Saints set great store in receiving a personal revelation, or testimony, which in the Book of Mormon's phrasing will "manifest the truth of it unto you, by the power of the Holy Ghost" (Moroni 10.4). Plagued by doubts and disquiet, Brandon thus set about doing "everything right" in pursuit of peace and reassurance.

> I would pray constantly, weeping and shaking. I would read the Book of Mormon and the Bible. I fasted once for three days when I was 15 or something. I remember after the three days, I walked up the stairs and I passed out, because I was so hungry. [He laughs, self-deprecatingly, at the memory.] It was that that pushed me over. It was that I followed that religion's logical conclusion, which is that God loves you to its extreme. Praying, doing everything right, and still not feeling any love—just this relentless, vapid indifference in my chest. So I came to realize that, like, OK, either God hates me, or he's indifferent. And either one of those, which were my experience, disproves the religion.

Reading this now, one suspects a medical professional might have drawn different conclusions from this bereaved early teen's pattern of behavior and feelings of "relentless, vapid indifference." (Though perhaps not. Brandon once visited a local doctor with severe chest pains: "His prescription for my heart pain was actually 'pray more.'") Regardless, one fateful day "in a very emo, dramatic moment, I tore my Book of Mormon, threw it in the closet, and I was just like, 'Fuck this.'" For some ex-religious folks, this type of symbolically transgressive, Rubicon-crossing moment can be one of liberation, even euphoria.[10] Not for Brandon—or rather, not yet. This sensation of having your faith, your whole world, "just die inside you" is "not something you would ever wish on anybody." The psychological, emotional, and physical toll of all this was traumatic enough. But living in a world where one's religious life is intimately bound up not just with one's family but with the whole wider community of friends, neighbors, and schoolmates—it could hardly fail to have wider repercussions. Teenagers' relationships with their parents can be turbulent at the best of times. Brandon's dad during this period was also his "Bishop," a senior pastoral and administrative role that rotates among a particular ward's upstanding, married men. This resulted, on the one hand, in his seeing little of his father, whose time was even more consumed with work and church responsibilities than it was normally. On the other hand, it also installed his dad as his chief religious and moral authority and confidant. Among a bishop's major responsibilities is interviewing the young people of his ward, one-on-one, and hearing their confessions.[11] On a semi-regular basis, therefore, Brandon would sit down with his father to be interrogated on the state of his soul. Unlike Catholic confessions, which are traditionally done anonymously and in the dark, "with Mormons it's a table like this, *with a fucking light.*" One imagines it wasn't an entirely comfortable experience for either party: "I'd sit at the table and he'd ask me . . .—well, you can fill in the blanks here. But when you're a 15-year-old . . ."

With tensions at home, ostracized as "trouble" within the close-knit Mormon community, unable to sleep properly, and assailed by suicidal thoughts, Brandon vowed to get the hell out at the first possible opportunity. He graduated from school early and managed to scrape together $2,000 working at a "nightmare hotel." By this time, moreover, he was an atheist, and rather relieved to be so. The idea that there *might not* be a God at all, as opposed to there being one who simply hated him, didn't occur until he was about sixteen—proof of the sheer taken-for-granted normalcy of believing in this "Mormon epicenter": "It sounds so silly now, but I had never even heard of it. I didn't even know there was such a thing as atheism."

Sitting in Pizza Hut with his one (also misfit) friend, "and he was just like, 'Y'know, what if there's not a God?' And I can still feel it, this weight lifting off my shoulders, and being like, 'Whoa, that makes a lot of sense. What if God doesn't hate me? What if the universe is actually just indifferent to me?' It was liberating."

So one morning, aged eighteen, he packed up his car and left for Oregon. Why Oregon exactly, he's got no real idea other than that "it seemed far away, in the corner." Twelve hours later, having driven through the pouring rain "oscillating between laughing and crying," Brandon arrived. No job, no friends, no regrets, and no bridges unburned: he deleted every single number from his phone, Pizza Hut pal included. He was free, finally, from the claustrophobic confines of God, religion, and close-knit community. Before the month was out, he had been recruited into a cult.[12]

"You know those moments when you want to take yourself seriously, when you think you're kind of smart? Well, something that makes me know I'm not smart—makes me know I'm a fucking idiot—is that I spent all this time leaving the Mormon Church. Then within thirty days I joined a cult." He laughs again, and swigs his beer. "When you grow up really, really Mormon I think it primes you to be gullible—and I don't mean that in a bad way. I mean it makes you innocent, open-minded, trusting of people. I'll probably go on to buy a timeshare after this. . . . My whole life is a fucking cliché."

"I dunno, man," I counter. "It seems pretty original to me."

* * *

"Remember, you're a born Mormon. There have been Mormons who turned heretic—damn their souls!—but no born Mormon ever left us yet."[13] Maybe that really was the case in the 1870s, when

Riders of the Purple Sage is set. But I doubt it; even the tightest flocks produce the occasional black sheep. Still, as previously noted, the Saints have historically done well in producing lots of Mormon babies, and then keeping them *as* Mormons into adulthood. While their zeal in seeking converts is well known—all those name-badged mini-Mitts going about in pairs—a very large contributor to Mormonism's meteoric growth has always been birth rate and retention. The same is true, or (as with Catholics) used to be, of several other religious groups.

Yet in recent decades, the Church's domestic growth rate has begun to slow noticeably. Precise, up-to-date rates are difficult to gauge from nationally representative surveys, since Mormons rarely show up in usable subsample sizes. There are two ways around this. The first is every so often to do a very large survey, with tens of thousands of respondents, allowing minority groups to appear in sufficient numbers. The second is simply to add together multiple years' worth of smaller surveys. While both methods come with difficulties attached, they can nevertheless give us a reasonable insight into the big picture. Fortunately for us, both have been tried. Data from the 2014 Pew Religious Landscape Survey, with a sample size of some 35,000 Americans, found that a third of those brought up Mormon no longer identify as such. The same year, sociologist Darren Sherkat published a very similar estimate of Mormon disaffiliation, derived from combining decades' worth of the General Social Survey. There is, moreover, good evidence that this rate is notably higher among those born in most recent decades.[14]

What proportion of these are genuine nonverts, rather than having converted to some other religious group, is a little trickier to divine with confidence. We end up dealing with ever-thinner slices of data—subsamples of subsamples—with ever fatter margins of error. However, my own analysis of Pew's data suggests that in 2014, around 18% of all cradle Mormons identified as either "nothing in particular" or with one of a handful of specifically nonreligious labels (i.e., atheist, agnostic, humanist). Among under-30s, the proportion rises to 29%. Precise percentages aside, in the words of LDS scholar and journalist Jana Riess: "we can say with confidence that Mormon retention is declining from one generation to the next, and that the LDS Church is losing a greater share of young adults than it has in the past [. . .] Mormonism is exceptional in many ways, but it is not able to wholly resist the larger forces at work in American religion."[15]

By the standards of most denominations, *only* losing three out of every ten born-and-raised by the time they've hit thirty is pretty good these days. By LDS standards, however, it is testimony to quite how irresistible those "larger forces" have become. To the sociologist's eye, Mormon customs and culture look precision-engineered to foster high levels of commitment.[16] Tight social networks of like-minded people tend to produce strong belief in, practice of, and commitment to their shared ideas or ideals: a truism that applies as much to CrossFit, Weight Watchers, or Amway as it does to religious or political movements. The LDS Church has traditionally done this very well, with Mormon-majority towns such as Brandon was brought up in being a case in point.[17] Even far outside of this so-called Jell-O Belt, indeed in far-flung places across the world, Mormons are adept at constructing proxies of these communities, with full programs of church and church-related meetings, events, service projects, and social groups, throughout the week: "this enormous structure built around" you, as Abigail, a lawyer and agnostic in her late thirties tells me over coffee. Conversely, several interviewees remarked on how easy it felt *not* being a Mormon once they'd stepped out of this world. Abigail herself recalls, as an important step in her own exit journey, a summer backpacking in Europe after high school. Even though she was accompanied by other Utahn LDS girls, "it was the first time that I was fully immersed with people from outside my small cultural worldview . . . going out and meeting these people who have all sorts of different life paths." Likewise, Cady contrasts her constant struggles against doubts when living in Utah ("I really wanted to believe, but I felt like I was tuned into the wrong radio station") to her atheism now feeling so easy and natural: "Right now it's something I'm very comfortable with; I'm surrounded by people my own age, with a wide range of belief systems. It's fairly easy to be a nonbelieving twenty-something in New York City."

As Christian Smith and colleagues put it, "the single most important measurable factor determining the religious and spiritual lives of teenagers and young adults is the religious faith, commitments, and practices of their parents."[18] Simply put, the more committed your parents are, then, on average, the more committed you'll likely turn out to be. Accordingly, the LDS norm of intense levels of religious practice, including as a family, ought to give them a strong advantage here. Also, there is some evidence that *dads'* religiosity is particularly influential. This is noteworthy in light of the high expectations placed on LDS fathers in overseeing their own family's religious faith, as well as taking on significant church "callings" over and above their domestic duties. To a degree, almost all young Mormons are "clergy kids" whose ordained fathers serve as part-time, unpaid ministers.[19]

Lastly, marriage between two members of the same faith is a good bet for (a) keeping both of them in, and (b) raising a next generation to do likewise. This is likely so for several reasons. One's life partner is, naturally, a huge influence over one's own views and values, religious or otherwise: marrying "within the fold" means mutual reinforcement. Both spouses will typically also be knitted into each other's family and social circles. If they are all on the same page, religiously speaking, this will in turn reinforce the faith's taken-for-grantedness. Their children don't receive mixed messages as to which religious path, if any, to go "all in" on. Their two main doses of religious example are complementary rather than competing. And once again, the LDS put a great deal of work into *encouraging* what social scientists insist on calling "religious homogamy." "Growing up it was like the best thing I could possibly do was marry a nice Mormon boy and raise nice Mormon babies," recalls Cady of her suburban Salt Lake upbringing. Since Heavenly Father helps those who help themselves, a good deal of LDS youth ministry is geared, implicitly and (often) explicitly, to helping young Mormons do just that. A clear example here are Singles Wards, where unmarried eighteen- to thirty-year-olds are assigned to a dedicated "parish" as the focus for their religious and social life. These are enough of a thing to have spawned a whole subgenre of rom-coms, which gently satirize the whole experience. In itself, this proves there to be a sufficiently large market of movie-goers, at least in Utah and the surrounding states, who find such topics relatable (and hence make such movies financially viable).[20]

At least in general outline, none of these retention strategies is unique to Mormonism. A keenness for young people to "marry in" and bring the ensuing babies up within the fold is so common in many religious and/or ethnic groups as to be a sitcom cliché. Nor are Mormons the only, or most successful, examples one might give: the Amish congregations of Pennsylvania, Ohio, and Indiana, or the Haredi Jewish communities of New York and some other major cities, all well outstrip the LDS in the close-knittedness of their communities and thus the retention of those brought up within. Nevertheless, within the broad cultural mainstream of American religious groups, the Saints have—up until now, at least—occupied a distinctive place.

* * *

"I figured out I was gay when I was twenty-three. My husband and I went to go see the midnight viewing of *Pirates of the Caribbean 2*. And there's a scene where Keira Knightley chains Johnny Depp to the ship secretly, by seducing him, right?"

"Yeah," I reply nonchalantly, as though this were the kind of thing strangers in cafes say to me all the time.

"So, during the scene of seduction, I realised that I would much rather be kissing Keira Knightley than Johnny Depp, who was supposedly the hottest man in the world. And I don't remember the rest of the movie because I was just like, "Wait, why do I think that?" And then, "Well, shit, that makes a lot of sense, that makes sense. *Okay*."

Elizabeth, now in her early thirties and in a longtime same-sex relationship, hails from northern Utah: "Everyone I knew was Mormon. I had absolutely no context outside of this. So, my whole framework of existence was based around the truth that was the Mormon Church." Aged eighteen, she headed off to Salt Lake City to start college. She met a guy online, "a Returned Missionary, faithful in the Church and all that stuff," and they got on well. So, as she puts it, "It all lined up: this is what God wants me to do." One chaste courtship later, they were married at the Mormon Temple. It was then that the plan began to unravel. Wedding-night "intimate relations and whatnot" didn't really work out; things were no better on their honeymoon. "I never really got in the mood and I couldn't really figure it out. This was what God wanted so, of course, now we're married, this is what he wants too. I couldn't really figure it out, but, like, I just went through the motions." Like Brandon having given no thought to atheism until a friend raised the idea in a Pizza Hut, Elizabeth had simply never encountered "gay" as something that people like her either were or could be. "I knew no gay people, I had no exposure to it. And gay people were "bad people." I was a good person, so I couldn't possibly be gay," she shrugs, amused by her naiveté. "I'd never had the idea like, "Oh, look, there is a happy gay person in a happy functional relationship. I could be like that." It just wasn't a *possibility*."

Tellingly, this moment of recognition didn't happen in a vacuum. She and her, "at this point, basically just best friend's" husband had settled away from Utah after their marriage. "I left everything I knew behind, all my friends, all the family, and everything. Starting out in a new place is very stressing. I got really depressed that first year." This was during the run-up to the 2004 election, as the US was becoming ever-deeper involved in Iraq. For the first time, Elizabeth became interested in politics. "Growing up, politics was always just 'Republicans are the good guys. Of course.' But now I saw, obviously, that the Republican Party had lied to people to get them to support a war, and that really just rubbed me the wrong way. I valued honesty super-highly, especially being religious. It was like, this is one of the tenets and key things of our faith."

It was the Sunday before the election day and I'm sitting in church. I was listening to one of the leaders, and he made a stupid joke. He said, "Oh, and in case you hadn't heard, they changed the voting dates this week. So, all Republicans will go vote on Tuesdays and Democrats are supposed to vote on Wednesdays." For me, all of a sudden, that made this connection in my brain that I wasn't really aware of. Because it connected religion and politics, and I saw how someone was lying, even just with a stupid joke. And all of a sudden, it made that connection. Something in my brain wasn't right, so I got up and I walked out. And I didn't go back.

* * *

Discomfort with a religion's stance on politics, or on questions around sex, gender, marriage, family, and relationships, is a common theme in nonversion accounts. While by no means specific to Mormonism—as we shall see when we meet our former Catholics and evangelicals—it is not surprising that it should feature heavily in ex-LDS testimonies. As noted earlier, over the course of the twentieth century the Saints have been firm upholders of "traditional family values." While the extent to which individual Mormons practice what their leaders preach is not *always* as straightforward as one might expect, it is nonetheless true that Mormons are more likely to be (heterosexually) married, less likely to be cohabiting, (slightly) less likely to be divorced, and tend to have more children than Americans in general.[21] This, coupled with LDS patriotism and their concentration in the largely rural, middle-American heartlands, has long made the Republican Party the Saints' natural home. Interestingly, however, the most recent cycles have somewhat undermined this easy fit between values-voting Mormons and the GOP. Though Romney decided against running in 2016, he ultimately emerged as the darling of #NeverTrump Republicans— that is, those unable, like Mitt himself, "as a matter of personal conscience" to vote for either main-party candidate.[22] (Another anti-Trump Mormon moderate, Evan McMullin, did in fact run as a third-party "protest" candidate, receiving more than 20% of the vote in Utah, just six points behind Hillary Clinton.) Romney was the only GOP senator to vote for Trump's impeachment in 2019, and the first to congratulate Biden on his electoral victory in 2020. True to form, his contempt for Donald Trump—Romney once described Trump's promises as "as worthless as a degree from Trump University"—is by no means a maverick position among committed Mormons. As noted in an October 2019 *New York Times* column, "the one religious faith that is the most heavily Republican is also somewhat disgusted with Trump. Barely half the members of the American-grown Church of Jesus Christ of Latter-day Saints approve of his presidency."[23]

These Mormons' never-Trumpery was partly motivated by his failures, in word and deed, to affirm conservative sexual and family norms. (It was not the only issue: the Saints are notably progressive on certain issues, including immigration. Growing numbers of Latino Mormons add to a powerful folk-memory of immigrant converts flocking to build the new Zion. A two-year mission, immersed in another country's language and culture, also lends a cosmopolitan *je ne sais quoi* not stereotypical of rural Westerners. Hence Newt Gingrich's infamous 2012 attack ad: "Just like John Kerry, [Romney] speaks French too.") This antipathy to Trump ought not be overstated, however: 69% of Mormons voted for Trump in 2020, a higher proportion than did so in 2016.

Then again, many other current and former Mormons like neither Trump nor the Church's traditional sexual and gender norms. Notably, a plurality of Mormon under-forties went for Biden in 2020. Cady, for example, our Utah-raised "nonbelieving twenty-something in New York City," mentions how increasing concern "about social issues in the Mormon Church, especially the position of women and LGBT issues," was a factor in her own gradual distancing. "None of that, like, confirmed for me that there would be some all-loving Being behind that institution."

Such qualms are felt most strongly by those for whom the Church's moral strictures are not abstract, but personal. Elizabeth, a lesbian herself, is an obvious example. For Mark, a divorced dentist in his early thirties, it was his flatmate's coming out that was the catalyst. "It really put it to the forefront for me, because I didn't know any gay people growing up. If you never deal with it, then the Church's teaching just is what it is. But when it comes into your life, and you experience it first-hand with people you know and love, it's like, 'No, I'm not going to like hold that against you. That'd be crazy.' So once I started going down that pathway [my Mormon belief] was over pretty quick." This pathway doesn't only apply to millennials, either. In Cady's family, her younger sister's coming out triggered the "marching out" of their hitherto-faithful mom and dad: "I think they'd always been strong proponents of LGBT acceptance and rights on a political level. So I think they already had the sense of 'if it was my kid, I wouldn't stick around.' And then it was their kid, so they didn't stick around."

Elizabeth's, Mark's, and Cady's qualms over their church's positions on sexuality and gender norms are widely shared among their twenties and thirties peers, but it is far from an LDS-only phenomenon. We are now a half-century on from the dawn of the sexual revolution, into which the postwar baby boomers came of age. The far-reaching cultural and legal changes that boomers experienced as radical and exciting, their grandchildren either simply take for granted or else regard as outdatedly retrogressive. Since the sixties and seventies, mainstream American norms concerning, say, divorce, sex outside marriage, homosexuality, and abortion have moved further and further from traditional Christian positions.[24] (Contraception, with the advent of the Pill, can also be added to this list, though with significant qualification. While many Protestant denominations began dropping their opposition to contraception in the 1930s, eugenics, not women's liberation, was the driving force.[25]) This was not a single, one-off realignment but rather the kickoff to an ongoing process of liberalization. Yesterday's progressive positions become today's bourgeois conformity and eventually tomorrow's retrograde conservatism.

These tectonic shifts, deciding what is or is not "OK in [insert current year]," have had all kinds of repercussions for American religion, politics, and society. Here, I want to highlight just one. Those brought up and socialized in Brandon's "Mormon epicenter," with its close-knit networks and normative "Christian family values," are *simultaneously* brought up and socialized into a wider American culture in which those values are increasingly foreign and, in some cases, actively resisted. This diffuse, wider culture is refracted in all sorts of ways: books, films, Netflix serials, television hosts' monologues; the conversations or social media updates of one's friends and co-workers; the outward projections of celebrities, Instagram influencers, or multinational corporations. How each individual resolves their dual citizenship in these two worlds can range very widely. Going all in, and doubling down in one direction, is an option, though often a high-cost one. Alternatively, the idea of a Mormon Spectrum has recently gained ground online, precisely to allow space for (fittingly) non-binary identities. Meanwhile, Mark now describes himself as religiously "nothing" though "almost ethnically Mormon basically." He's left the Church, has no "belief in divinity at all," is liberal on gay rights and "pro-abortion." And yet, he's straitlaced, fiscally conservative, partakes of neither curse words, tobacco, alcohol, nor caffeine, and all his non-dentist friends are "still pretty much Mormons." He is a paradox, a quintessentially Mormon none. A secular Saint.

The LDS Church is not the only religious body in contemporary America to have troubles with the "culture-fit" between its traditional norms and those of the wider society. Nor is theirs the only approach to navigating them, as the chapters that follow should amply demonstrate. The Mormon case is significant, however, as the clearest example of what one might call the "subcultural defense strategy." Later, we'll meet variants of this from both Catholic history and evangelical present, as well as a very clear counter-strategy from the mainline. Aside from certain immigrant subgroups *within* bigger denominations, it is hard to think of a better example of religious subculture maintenance from a sizable group *otherwise* significantly integrated into the US mainstream. (Again, while the Amish or Hasids are not actually walled off from American society, they have produced rather fewer movie stars, talk show pundits, athletes, best-selling novelists, or Grammy winners.) Furthermore, up until recently, Mormons seemed to be having very much more success than other Churches trying a similar tack. Sure, the road to "become saviors on Mount Zion" has, appropriately enough, always been an uphill one.[26] But it appears to be growing ever steeper.

* * *

"From the day I walked out the church—when I had that joke trigger something in my head—there was a couple of months of thinking, 'I'm supposed to be going to church, I'm supposed to be doing these things. Why am I not doing them? Why am I so bothered by this?' And then that finally allowed me to take the steps to research the history of the Mormon Church from *other* sources for the first time. And then once I started researching, then my whole belief in Mormonism fell apart in a couple of days. I was just like, There's no way this could be possibly true. I mean, thank goodness for the internet."

I scrawl "INTERNET" on my notepad, as I would on many other occasions over the course of this research. It's a point we'll be coming back to more than once. "And this was the first inkling you'd had?"

"Yes. When your whole world and everyone you know believes the thing, it's very hard to question it. So even though I was on the internet the whole time, I never really looked at anything because it's like, This is the truth. Everyone I know believes this is the truth, so it is the truth."

"So you literally got home one day and googled 'Mormon history' or whatever?"

"Yes, yes. And due to the wonderful thing called the internet, it easily unraveled. Then from that point to actually leaving, I think it was another six months before I sent in the formal request."

One does not simply leave the Church of Jesus Christ of Latter-day Saints. As befits an American, corporate faith, there's paperwork involved. Not all those who regard themselves as former Mormons go through it, despite easy how-to guides and proformas being readily available online. This could be for many reasons, though often cited is the fact that if you do, then—in effect—they go tell your parents what you did. As high-powered lawyer Abigail explains it:

> At the end of each year there's something called a "tithing settlement" where your mom and dad will go and meet with their bishop. He'll say, "Oh, blah blah, review of the year, how you doing? Everything good?" And he'll print out a copy of their records which will list mom and dad, then all their children "born in the covenant." And if you take your name off the record it will take them off. And since they only have X number of children they would notice that very quickly.

Abigail's parents are already well aware that she's far from being an orthodox, practicing Mormon, and they have been for a long time. Nevertheless, "out of respect for my dear father—it would just emotionally crush him—I would never do that while my parents are alive." She adds, "I'm not waiting for the minute they die, but I wouldn't be necessarily opposed to it later in life. Though while they can still find out about it I would never do it." For others, however, officially leaving feels like a necessary act: a meaningful statement about *who* they are, and what they're not. Elizabeth is one of them.

"I was all, 'Yes, I want the letter! I'm going to post this on my Facebook wall!' Y'know, *I escaped*." She laughs.

Tactful as ever, I mention to her the "family feelings" considerations raised by Abigail. She stops laughing.

"Mormonism teaches that if your kid leaves the church, you've failed as a parent. And so that makes it really hard. When you do the Temple marriage, if you follow your covenants then the promise is you will get to be with your family forever. And if people go astray from that, then you don't get to be with your family forever. So, one person leaving can destroy this whole beautiful, magical thing that they've sacrificed things for. So, I definitely understand it's a big thing. I basically wrote my parents a letter because I didn't know how else to tell them, and I just said, 'I'm leaving the church, I don't believe it. I'm sorry. I still love you.'"

"And?"

"My mum took it really, really bad. She constantly called me, emailed me, saying 'I can't believe you're doing this to our family. How could you?' It was just her lashing out in any way she knew how, because I was destroying their forever family. After a few months of basically constant harassment, I decided to cut off all contact. I just couldn't do it anymore. So, I moved, and I changed my number, so she had no way of contacting me. For about six months I didn't do anything, and then I wrote them a letter and so, we started writing letters back and forth. Eventually, we built things back up. In terms of religious stuff, we don't really talk about it too much."

Our time nearly up, I comment on just how hard and disorienting all this must have been. The radical break with the faith and values she'd grown up with; the estrangement from home and family—not to mention Keira Knightley interfering with her marriage. And all before she'd left her early twenties.

"Yes, it was very isolating."

"Either really scary or really exciting, or both?"

"Kind of both. But yes, it was really scary at first. Then, once I moved through those stages of grief, it really felt freeing. Because then, I could base my reality closer to what I felt was *actual* reality."

So began Elizabeth's new beginning. Needless to say, she had *a lot* of catching up to do: "I was so clueless about that sort of thing. And I was scared and nervous, even though I don't believe it anymore, it's still ingrained in you for so long."

Overcoming a lifetime's worth of prohibition and guilt, she steeled herself and took the plunge. As many others have found out before her, your first time isn't necessarily the most enjoyable.

"I remember sneaking over and getting a cup of black coffee and just trying it. And I was like, 'Oh.' Because one, it was office coffee and so probably terrible, and then, drinking it black for the first time. I just remember laughing at myself later. That is probably the worst way to go about trying coffee for the first time. But nowadays, my favorite thing is to get up early, have a cup of coffee, get the cat on my lap, and wake up slowly. It's a wonderful thing, and it's curious how religion made that a bad thing, I don't know. So now, I drink alcohol in moderation, and probably way too much coffee. But it's delicious, what can you do?"

None Specifics

It's a bright August morning in northern Florida. Kate and Grant, both in their mid-fifties, are busily preparing to head off to the coast; it's their wedding anniversary. But naturally, Southern hospitality being what it is, they'd be *only too delighted* to have a stranger turn up early to drink their coffee, stare in wonder at their backyard bird feeder, and turn their back porch into an interrogation room.

Kate's the talker of the two. Nearing the end of our freewheeling conversation, taking in her mainline upbringing in Georgia, a Pentecostal conversion that led to foreign missionary work, and then a turbulent period working in a scandal-hit megachurch, I put to her a standard survey question: "Do you regard yourself as belonging to or having a connection with a particular religion?"

"No. I would absolutely be a 'none.' I read and try and understand Buddhism and different things like that, but there is nothing that I would adhere to or call myself at all. I think the reason is that because I am such a personality of 'all or nothing.' I'm an alcoholic, for instance; I've been sober six years now."

"Congratulations," I say, though it never quite feels like the right thing *to* say.

Chuckling, she continues. "And that's why—everything I do is like that. With the religion thing, with the church, I just *had* to work there. I had to be in the very thick of it, in the trenches of it all. I just go all-in."

Now Kate is "all-in" at being "all-out." When it comes to having religion, she's fifteen years sober.

* * *

"None." "Nonreligious." "Nothing in particular." "Unaffiliated." Despite often being described as America's fastest-growing religious affiliation, such terms can feel a little awkward as personal labels. Several sociologists have argued that "none" and its brethren aren't genuine identities at all, just the artificial by-products of tick-box surveys.[1] To suppose one can speak of "nones" as a genuine grouping of Americans, this line of argument goes, is as silly as thinking that "Other (please specify)" is a real occupation.

There's some truth to this, to be sure. "The nones" *are* a very large, broad, and diffuse category. And they are, to a certain extent, a statistical convenience. As we will see in this chapter, many of those who end up counted within the "X% of nones" on handy infographics may not instinctively think of or describe themselves with this kind of label. That applies all the more, of course, to the "nonverts" among them. But the same is true of familiar abstractions like People of Color or LGBTQ. These are accepted as being useful and meaningful shorthands, precisely *because* they bring together a diverse collection of much more specific identity groups.

That said, people often do embrace allegedly empty categories like "none," "nothing," or "nonreligious." This is frequently true for those brought up and/or still living in deeply religious contexts. For Kate, the sheer fact of her *not* having a religious affiliation is "just for me a big deal. Maybe because of my past, maybe because if I had been a nonbeliever my whole life it wouldn't be a big deal. But I came from such a different place to this place that you have to think about it." For others, terms like "none" or "nothing" are not so much *statements* as, well, just an accurate description. "I would say 'no religion,'" Rick, an African American software engineer from New York, tells me matter-of-factly. "Because that's it. I mean I don't need to do the whole like 'Well I was raised a Baptist' deal. I'm just not religious."

Even for those preferring a more specific identity—atheist or agnostic, say—adopting a generic label can often be useful. Hassan, raised a Muslim in North Africa, sees himself as a "nonbeliever." But if asked, he normally prefers the evasive "I'm in no man's land": an answer which, given that apostasy is a capital crime in his native land, is not quite so tongue-in-cheek as it might come across. Less dramatically, unbelieving interviewees were often sensitive to the awkwardness that a blunt avowal of atheism might bring to a social or work setting. Hence for Sarah, working in local government in Minnesota's Twin Cities region:

> I don't bring up religion in a workplace environment, but if it were to come up, I'd just say I'm "nonreligious" because that's a little less . . . I mean it's a little bit more *workplace*. Even though I would like to come out and say "Hey, I'm atheist!" and use that decisive word, I don't want to bring it into the workplace.

Rick, meanwhile, is mindful of other forms of social repercussion: "In the past I've dated Black women, and they tend to be—in my personal observation—more religious. Minority women tend to be more religious. So, if I just go off the bat with 'Oh, I'm atheist,' they're going to be like, 'Ewwww, like I don't know if I want to hang out with this guy,' so . . ."[2]

For each of these nones, while the precise meaning and personal salience of so broad a label clearly varies, it is far from just a statistician's fiction. (Note too that broad labels like "Christian" or "Jewish" or "Buddhist" likewise obscure tremendous diversity.) As the British sociologist Lois Lee has put it: "generic nonreligious identifications are not merely imposed on people by social researchers but can be made and performed by them in their everyday lives." That is to say, "it is wrong to assume that the 'nones' are always nothings."[3] In America, this is likely becoming more the case simply because being a "none" has become a definite *thing* in the past decade or so, helped greatly by the term gaining common currency through media reports. Not incidentally, this is similar to how "evangelical" and "born-again Christian" suddenly became widely understood and embraced identities in the 1970s. It's not that such people didn't exist before, but now they had both a "brand" and the self-confidence that comes from headlines inducting them into a millions-strong movement.[4] People like to belong, even if only in "imagined communities." (This is true even among self-conscious nonconformists: the goths, emo kids, and AV clubbers are as much high school "tribes" as are the jocks and cheerleaders, if not more so.) And for Americans turned off by religion to varying degrees, "a quarter of the US population and growing" is a significant tribe to feel part of, even for those with little desire to seek and hang out with the others.

* * *

Digging a little deeper, it's worth considering quite what labels like "none" or "nonreligious" actually amount to when used in those "quarter of the US population"–type headlines. It is one thing to ride around the country, talking face-to-face with dozens upon dozens of such folks. But it is a very different thing to jump from these flesh-and-blood nones to making generalizations about roughly 59 million Americans. Who exactly are these people, and how do we count them? And more to the point, given this book's title and main thesis, what is distinctive about the "nonverts" among them?

Let's start out at the simplest and most basic level. It's quite common for surveys or polls to include questions about religion (though not the US Census, which, unlike those of other countries, doesn't feel it quite proper to ask). *Some* surveys are specifically designed for studying religious trends, and if so, they'll ask a lot of other detailed questions about religious identity, practice, and beliefs. Good examples are the periodic surveys put out by nonprofit "fact tanks" like the Pew Research Center or the Public Religion Research Institute (PRRI), or large-scale university-driven initiatives such as the Baylor Religion Survey or the American Religious Identification Survey (ARIS).

Mostly though, the people doing the surveys—and more to the point, those *paying* for them—aren't typically interested in religion directly. Their real interest is in politics or consumer trends or demographic shifts or whatever, but they often ask one or two religion-y questions anyway. Why do they do this when, in survey design, extra questions cost money? They do it for the simple reason that certain religious indicators, especially affiliation and regularity of church, synagogue, mosque, or Celebrity Center attendance, are significant characteristics with important implications for how people think, feel, and behave regarding other topics. The most obvious examples here are political opinions and voting behavior. Hence all those headlines, based on some poll or other, saying "Policy X favored by 80% of Catholics and Mormons," or "Candidate Y losing traction among Black Christian voters," or whatever.

Now, the standard religion question on a survey is some variant of "What is your religion?"—or (as per the GSS) "What is your religious preference?"—followed by a list of suggestions. These almost always begin with several types of Christian options, for example, Catholic, Protestant, Other Christian; or perhaps Catholic, Baptist, Methodist, Mormon,[5] and so on. There's several different ways to cut the denominational cloth, but we needn't worry too much about that just now.[6] These are followed by a handful of non-Christian religious options, certainly including Jewish and Muslim, plus perhaps one or more of Buddhist, Hindu, and Sikh. Then right at the bottom of the list you normally get an "Other (please specify)" option, and a "No religion" or "None" box. There might also be a "Don't know" or "Refuse to answer" box, but again, we needn't worry about those.

Helpfully, many surveys also ask the same people some version of (again, quoting the GSS wording) "In what religion were you raised?," typically followed by the same set of categories. This is hugely useful since, armed with these two questions, we can learn much about the overall dynamics of religious stasis or change in a society. We can see not only what numbers of people raised as an X end up leaving to join Y or Z, but also the numbers of cradle Ys or Zs who have moved in the other direction.[7]

As noted in Chapter 1, at the most basic level a none is essentially any person who ticks that "No religion" or "None" box on a survey. This same group is sometimes called "the unaffiliateds" or similar, because when asked to pick from a range of religious affiliations (Catholic or Muslim or Zoroastrian or whatever), they say they don't have one. However, this can lead to confusion since "unaffiliated" is more commonly used as a political label for those not registered with a particular party. The basic idea is, of course, the same. Independents. Free agents. Footloose and fancy-free. They don't align with any of the standard labels.

Often but not always, these nones are also taken to include people who tick the "Other (please specify)" box, then write in something like "humanist" or "atheist" or "agnostic" or "spiritual but not religious." Or maybe they've written in something like "I don't care if there's a god," or "I don't define myself by what I'm not," or "sensible" (all actual responses to one of my team's recent surveys).[8] There aren't normally many people who do this, but you tend to get a few. Since these are all reasonably regarded as being *nonreligious* answers to the question, they get usually get added to the nones, too. Other write-in options might pose trickier problems. I've devoted more time to worrying about Jedi Knights than I'd care to admit. Though that, too, is a topic that needn't distract us here. (Unless you *really* want it to, of course; that's the fun of endnotes.)[9] And naturally, a similar methodology applies to interpreting religious upbringing questions, too. That is, a "cradle none" is just someone who answers "no religion," or else one of a select group of other more or less straightforwardly nonreligious options ("unaffiliated," "secular," etc.) when asked how they were raised.

What all this amounts to is that, when you read a statistic like "23% of the US adult population are now religious nones," what that actually means is "Some people did a big, representative survey of American adults, and twenty-two people in every 100 answered 'no religion' when asked what religion they belonged to (and a further one in every 100 people we asked replied 'atheist' or 'agnostic' or 'I don't believe in dumb sky fairies')." Likewise, when I quote a statistic like "16% of the US population is actually a nonvert," this is a shorthand for "The good people at the GSS did a big, representative survey of American adults, and sixteen out of every 100 people picked one of the 'no religion' options when asked about their current religious affiliation, *but also* picked one of the religious options when asked how they were raised." And that's pretty much it.

Importantly, the fact that a person said or ticked or clicked "No religion" does not, in itself, tell us whether or not they believe in God. Whether or not they attend church. Whether or not they believe in Fate or Reincarnation or Astrology. Whether or not they've accepted Jesus Christ as their Personal Lord and Savior. Whether or not they attend synagogue every single Sabbath. Whether or not they pray. Whether or not, if they were raised in a religion, they got married in a church and will quite probably get their kids baptized. Whether or not they believe in Chupacabra, Cthulu, Bigfoot, or the Fouke Monster. Not identifying with a particular religion or denomination is *perfectly compatible* with all kinds of beliefs or attitudes or practices. (As of course is identifying *with* a particular religion or denomination. The fact that a person ticks the Catholic or Presbyterian box doesn't logically imply that they actually believe certain things or act in a certain way.)

Potentially, then, these nones are a very varied and diverse group of people. None-ness is, you might say, a very big tent. One ought to be cautious in making sweeping statements about someone based on a box they've ticked. Again, this is 59 million American adults we're talking here. There's no one type of none.

* * *

In fact, things get more complicated—and frankly, much more interesting—the more we dig into how these tick-box surveys, censuses, or polls work. Funnily enough, *how* you ask people about their religious identity can sometimes produce very different responses. In Britain, for example, if a survey question asks, "What is your religion?" then significantly fewer people answer "No religion" than they would to a question like, "What religion, if any, do you feel you belong to?" If you ask people, "Do you have a religion, yes or no?" and *then* ask the ones who say "yes" which religion they belong to, you get a different proportion of answers again.[10]

This is pretty weird. You might think that a person who is Lutheran would answer Lutheran more or less *however* you asked them what their religion was; as would a person who's a Jehovah's Witness or a Jain or, well, a Jedi. Likewise, people who are religiously unaffiliated would say so however you asked them. Slight changes in question phrasing shouldn't make a difference, should they? Yet they do. And in the social sciences, just as much as in the natural sciences, anomalies often end up alerting us to something very important. Religious identities, as with other kinds, are complex, multifaceted things. Sure there are plenty of people who are Catholics, who know they're Catholics, and will tell you that they're Catholics no matter how or when you ask them. There are also lots of people who have no religion, know they have no religion, and will tell you that they have no religion howsoever you inquire.

But this simply isn't true for lots of people: indeed, for a very large segment of the population of many Western countries. Lots of people have a very ambivalent, ambiguous sense of religious belonging. They might think, "My ancestors all came from Ireland during the potato famine, and of course I was baptized and did First Communion and all that, and we used to go to Mass at Christmas, Easter, and whenever Granny O'Gorman used to visit . . ." *But also,* "Still, we never used to pray or go to Mass as a family otherwise, and I've not been at all in the past twenty-odd years apart from for weddings and funerals, and to be honest, I'm not sure if I believe in a God with the way the world's going, and I certainly don't believe in one who is anti-choice—and besides, I really don't like the idea of putting my name to an organization that's covered up so many horrific crimes against kids. . . . " *And also,* "On the other hand, I *did* pray a Hail Mary when my daughter was in the hospital that time, and I guess it felt a bit odd when she didn't want a church wedding. And of course we always make a big thing of St. Patrick's Day, what with all the Guinness and dyeing the Chicago River green . . ."

Now, how do you distill all that down into a single tick-box answer on a survey asking, "What's your religion?" Are they Catholic or nonreligious? They're both, and neither. Or sometimes feel like one, and sometimes the other. Accordingly, it turns out that such people might answer one way, and might answer the other . . . and the likelihood of *which* they opt for seems to be swayed by, among other things, the precise way the question is asked. Personally, I like to think of them as "Schrödinger's Catholics."

The general phenomenon, however, is not simply a Catholic quirk. It's common among nonverts of all stripes, and is intimately bound up with the many ways in which people's pasts continue to color their presents—something we will see again and again throughout this book. That said, my hunch is that it's most evident in (or rather, *half-out* of) traditions with a strong sense of tribal or cultural belonging. Recall Mark the dentist's remarks on feeling both a religious "nothing" and "almost ethnically Mormon basically," for instance. America's Jews, among whom Jewishness is frequently a complex blend of practice, belief, tradition, ancestry, ethnicity, and community, are another good example.[11]

Sociologists have coined a name for these people: *liminal nones*. (Liminal means to be on the threshold, or perhaps better here, on the fence between two different identities. That is, they have one foot in the religion of their upbringing or family, and another in being nonreligious.) Importantly, it's worth noting that this doesn't simply mean that there's a chunk of nones in each survey who, in a different mood on a different day, might easily have checked a different box. It also follows that there's a good chunk of religiously affiliating folks who, in a different mood on a different day, might easily have ticked no religion instead. Liminality works both ways. (And there is also, of course, a good chunk of people who say they were raised nonreligiously who might, on a different day, tick one of the religious options. Obviously, there are different degrees of being raised religiously: where a weak, nominal, or culturally Christian upbringing ends, and a nonreligious one begins, is not always clear-cut.) This kind of ambivalence does not, obviously enough, lend it-self easily to precise measurement, though the general phenomenon is probably quite common.[12]

The upshot of all the above, added also to different surveys' methodologies and sampling strategies, is that there's a certain fuzziness around each "proportion of nones" statistic—mirroring, in large measure, the fuzziness that a great many individuals feel about their *own* (non)religious identity, past and present. Similar issues occur with other types of identity. The wording of race or eth-nicity questions can have a significant impact on the result one gets: "Hispanic" and "Latino/a" mean different things to different people (do people from Portuguese- or French-speaking Latin countries count as "Hispanic"? Is "Latino/a" its own race, and if so, is a Black woman from Puerto Rico a Latina or not?).[13] People who are mixed-race have long found single tick-box options irritating. Add to that the rapid growth of DNA testing, and hence of the kind of dilemmas faced by Cal, a Minnesotan twenty-something who told me he *used to* just tick the "Native" box and be done with it: "I took an ancestry thing, so now it's up in the air. I look at job forms, and I don't have anything that's 50% even. I have some Hispanic, some Native. I'm more German than anything, but like, I'm *brown*."

Our somewhat breezy tour of survey methodology has hopefully helped to explain quite how the very precise-seeming percentages of nones (or indeed nonverts), normally quoted by journalists di-rectly from the press releases of pollsters and academics, are arrived at. It should also have shown why each *single* figure ought to be understood for what it is: the combined product of both an actual empirical reality *and* the precise methods used to try and measure it. While there may be no single, perfect sampling strategy, and no Platonic Form of the Ideally Worded Question, that doesn't mean that there aren't better or worse methods. And it doesn't mean they aren't all measuring, even if with slightly differently calibrated instruments, real—and often important—things about society.

Figure 3.1 makes this point very clearly. This shows our trusty GSS figures (solid black line) for the overall proportion of nones in the US adult population, as last seen in Chapter 1. But it also shows the estimates arrived at in different years by other reputable survey programs, each using subtly different sampling strategies and question wording. For reasons we needn't go into here, whether a survey is conducted in person, online, or by telephone can also affect how a person might answer. Especially among the sorts of "liminal" populations we're concerned with here, it is therefore not surprising that different survey methodologies should produce a range of answers for the number of nones in any single year. Critically, the fact that each survey program is normally consistent in its methodology, aside from the occasional tweak in each wave, means that we can tell that the divergence between methodologies isn't due to random chance.

During the past decade, we have regular measurements from six separate surveys. Gallup's signature methodological blend reliably gives measurements at the low end of the range, while the Cooperative Congressional Election Survey (CCES) is equally dependable at the upper limits. Meanwhile, the others cluster closely together somewhere roughly in between. Crucially, all track the same underlying phenomenon—namely, the continuing rise of the nones—as occurring at roughly the same rate. Looking further

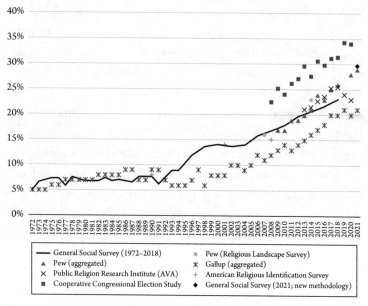

Figure 3.1. Proportions of all US adults with no religious affiliation, over time, according to different surveys and polls.

*Sources: General Social Survey (1972–2018; 2021) and others**

**GSS data taken from my own analysis of the original (weighted) datasets. Data from the other sources derived from the following sources:*

Pew (both): *Data tables available online at https://www.pewforum.org/wp-content/uplo ads/sites/7/2019/11/Detailed-tables-for-upload-11.11.19.pdf and https://www.pewforum. org/2021/12/14/about-three-in-ten-u-s-adults-are-now-religiously-unaffiliated/*

Gallup: *Data tables available online at https://news.gallup.com/poll/1690/religion.aspx*

Public Religion Research Institute (American Values Atlas): *Data available online at http://ava.prri.org/*

American Religious Identification Survey: *Barry A. Kosmin, A. Keysar, R. Cragun, and J. Navarro-Rivera, American Nones: The Profile of the No Religion Population: A Report Based on the American Religious Identification Survey 2008 (Hartford, CT: Institute for the Study of Secularism in Society, 2008), 20.*

Cooperative Congressional Election Study: *Data available online at https://cces.gov. harvard.edu/*

back, we can see how the two longest-running surveys, Gallup and the GSS, broadly concur in tracing this uptick to some point in the 1990s, though the latter picked up the signal a little sooner. In 2018, for example, we also have measurements from five separate surveys. The CCES, as usual, is way ahead of the pack with 31%. Meanwhile the GSS's 23% is smack-bang in the middle of what, were this the Tour de France, we might call the peloton of percentages, which ranges between Gallup's 20% and PRRI's 26%.

Eagle-eyed readers might have noticed Figure 3.1 also includes an additional datapoint from the GSS, separated off from the main 1972–2018 run: 2021's startlingly high figure of 30%. Why so much of this book is based on the 2018 data, instead of using 2021's newer, bigger numbers, requires a little explanation. Due to the pandemic, the planned 2020 wave didn't happen. Rather than miss out on surveying the American public at a critical period, however, the survey was run in 2021, but with "significant methodological changes."[14] The biggest of these was a shift from face-to-face interviews to online participation. All other things being equal, this in itself could feasibly produce in a higher-than-usual proportion of nones (as with the CCES's consistently high numbers, which are also the product of online polling). The trouble is, in 2021, "all other things" were far from equal. The pandemic itself has no doubt had some knock-on effects for religious identity and affiliation, but we don't yet know what they are, or how long-lasting they will be. Perhaps the huge jump in the GSS figures from 2018 to 2021 is not (only) due to the change in methodology: maybe traditional face-to-face interviewing would have found the same or similar.

The truth is, we simply don't know, and won't for some time. A good chunk of this book's argument relies on looking at how the proportion of nones in the US has *changed over time*, driven principally by nonversion. The 2021 figure is certainly suggestive, and to be fair, it is still well within the range of other surveys. Nevertheless, it is based on a very different kind of survey to those fielded between 1972 and 2018. Tempting though it might be to use bigger, bolder, brasher figures—which would make the whole phenomenon seem even more significant than it is already—it would simply be bad practice, a kind of academic bait-and-switch. And besides, the 2018 figures are plenty big enough for my purposes. Statistics such as "59 million nones" or "15 million ex-Catholic nonverts" are certainly estimates, but they cannot be accused of being exaggerations. I am actually being very cautious and conservative.

* * *

Who then are these millions of people? When were they born? What do they look like, think, believe?

When the questions are put like that, then it's easy to see that, well, they don't make all *that much* sense. What can it possibly mean to imagine some kind of "typical" none who somehow represents tens of millions of people, spread over a country of nearly four million square miles? And this is especially true given, as we have just seen, how very broad and encompassing this grouping actually is: all those people who, for whatever reason, tick "No religion" when asked what their religion is. Just think of the people in your own family or social circle, including online on Facebook, Twitter, Instagram, or wherever else. Now the odds are pretty strong that there's a good number of nonreligious among them. Some you may know would identify that way, but a lot of them, you won't. But even among those whom you either know, or would strongly guess, would describe themselves as having no religion: are they all alike? Demographically—that is, in terms of age, sex, education, class, ethnicity? In terms of religious background (if any), or even current spirituality or religiosity? (Not everyone who identifies as a none would count, on other types of measure, as being nonreligious.) In terms of politics? Movie preferences? Of course not.

Maybe, if you really thought about it, you could come up with several clusters of different types ("young adults raised by non-practicing Christian parents, living in urban centers or college towns," say; or "mostly white, middle-class, middle-aged liberals from either coast"). Maybe you could do that, though even so I'd expect that (a) there'd be a lot of difference even within those groupings; and (b) you'd still end up with a lot of exceptions or difficult-to-pigeonhole folks.

To a large extent that's what sociologists sometimes try to do at the national level as well. It *is* possible to corral people into loose "types," and these need not be without a certain interpretive value. If you think about it, we do that kind of thing all the time, most often with different age groups. We talk about millennials or Gen Xers or boomers in what are, at one level, ridiculously broad generalizations. After all, a baby boomer is simply someone who was born between 1946 and about 1964. That's a pretty broad group of people. That said, these kinds of stereotyping labels don't come from nowhere. As long as we don't take them too seriously, or mistake a highly impressionistic sketch of a whole group for something that tells us much about *specific individuals* within it, then these kinds of generalizations can often be quite helpful. The artist and poet William Blake once wrote that "To generalize is to be an idiot." On the one hand, that's a good principle to bear in mind. On the other, it is itself a generalization.

Anyway, a better and more helpful way of thinking about nones might be to think in terms of how, as a whole, they might "skew" in certain directions. This is worth explaining a little (don't worry if the specific examples mean nothing to you, it's the idea that counts).

It might be that, to give a silly example, *on average* the nonreligious *tend to* prefer soft-rock legend Chris Gaines to the country star Garth Brooks. Now the fact that, on average, they prefer Gaines over Brooks doesn't mean that, out of all 59 million of them, there aren't millions—even tens of millions—of die-hard Garth Brooks fans. It's simply that, as a whole, more of them prefer Gaines to Brooks, however slightly.

A further possibility: perhaps the nones *disproportionately* prefer Gaines to Brooks. Now what that means is simply that, on average, nones are more likely to favor Brooks than, on average, does the general population. In that case, we might say that the nonreligious "skew" toward Chris Gaines. But again, we're talking about big overall trends—statistical abstractions—representing tens of millions of real-life individuals.

With that caveat in place, let's look at the makeup of American nones *as a whole*.[15]

* * *

First up, age profile. Figure 3.2 shows what percentage of each of the five commonly designated "generations"[16] identified as nones in 2018. Also shown are the proportions of religious affiliates, divided between those attending religious services monthly or more, and those attending less frequently (including the many who attend never or practically never). While both of those attendance categories encompass a huge range of religious commitment, the "at least monthly" arguably captures a meaningful regularity of habit.

As is clear from the chart, millennials and Generation Z are disproportionate contributors to the none pool, with around a third of each cohort describing themselves this way. That said, the younger Gen Zers are somewhat less likely than millennials to be

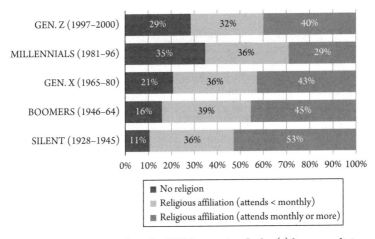

Figure 3.2. Proportion of standard US "generations" who (a) have no religion, (b) identify with a religion but don't practice regularly, and (c) identify with a religion and do practice regularly.
Source: General Social Survey (2018; weighted data)

nones, and moreover are almost as likely as their parents (Gen X) or even grandparents (boomers) to attend services regularly. That *might* augur the first stirrings of a generational religious rebound from the millennials' all-time low. Such things are certainly possible. However, the smarter sociological money would more likely be on Gen Zers, on average, *not yet* having had time to lose the religious identities and habits of their upbringing. After all, even the eldest of them were only twenty-one in 2018. Also note that since eighteen- to twenty-one-year-olds make up only a small proportion of the adult population, comparatively few of them show up in nationally representative samples, thus increasing likely margins of error. Even so, the youngest two generations are markedly more nonreligious than their forebears. Moreover, each of these prior generations has a higher percentage of nones than does the generation before it. Roughly one in ten silents and one in six boomers now identify as nones. Something else that's worthy of comment: the proportion of low or non-practicing religious folks holds fairly steady across the generations. That is to say, the rise of the nones cannot simply be the result of purely box-ticking Christians switching to no religion instead (an idea you often come across in more optimistic church circles). The proportion of committed religious people—committed enough to darken the door of a place of worship on a regularish basis, at any rate—in the US adult population is falling at the same time as the nones are rising. That *doesn't* mean that people are leaping directly from one to the other, though some may do just that. Much more important is generational replacement: as the members of older, typically more religious generations die off, they are gradually replaced by younger cohorts. These are both less likely to be (as) religious in the first place, and find it rather easier to shed any religious beliefs, behaviors, and/or belongings they might have.

But what of the age dynamics within the nones group? It's perhaps clearer to think about this in terms of age, rather than generations. Accordingly, Figure 3.3 shows two things. First, it shows their

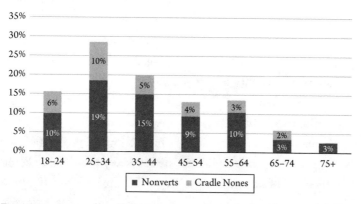

Figure 3.3. Age profile of US nones by age group, broken down by (non)religious upbringing.

overall age profile: note the particular spike—accounting for 29% of all nones—among the 25–34s (a cohort which includes all but the very oldest of millennials). All in all, two-thirds of nones are in one of the youngest three (spanning 18 to 44) categories. Since only half of American adults are similarly youthful, then that certainly means that the "typical none" of statistical imagination is rather younger than the US average. Still, let's not forget about the other third. The 45–64s account for one in every four nones. Note too that even though those aged 65+ only account for 8% of all nones, that still amounts to well over 4 million such people. Second, it shows the relative proportions of nonverts to cradle nones. As one might expect, given that they account for 70% of all nones, the former outnumber the latter across all age groups. Notice, however, that this is less the case among the youngest groups: a combination of greater numbers being brought up nonreligious in the first place, and a growing likelihood that those so raised will stay nonreligious into adulthood. All in all, these differences are not massive: the average age of cradle nones is 38, compared to nonverts' 41 (with the "typical none" averaging out at 40). Nevertheless, and as we will explore more fully in Chapter 7, the overwhelming likelihood that this trend will grow over time has significant implications for the future.

* * *

You sometimes come across the stereotype that the typical none is White—and that's true, so far as it goes. But in fact, according to the GSS's most basic racial categorizations, they essentially mirror the US adult population as whole. That is to say, 73% of nonreligious folks identify as White, and so too do precisely 73% of all American adults. The remaining 27% of nones are divided near-equally between Black and "Other," as also in the general population.

(Dividing the nones up between nonverts and cradles doesn't affect things much, though the latter are a percentage point or two whiter than the former.) So as a group, the religiously unaffiliated are as racially diverse as is the country as a whole. According to the GSS's more detailed self-classifications, the nonreligious include roughly 8 million African Americans, 3 million Hispanics, and a million each who identify as Chinese, Native American, and (South Asian) Indian. Japanese, Vietnamese, and Filipino nones together make up a further million.

You also sometimes hear that nones are mostly men. Is that the case? Well yes, though only just. The actual breakdown is something like 52% men to 48% women, which let's face it, is pretty much half and half. (And again, there's not much difference here between the cradle nones and nonverts.) A crowd of one hundred people mixed up in those proportions should look and feel evenly matched. Now this is a good example of something I mentioned earlier. As a statistical abstraction, "Most Religiously Unaffiliated Adults in America are Men" is, as it stands, completely true. But if you only think about those roughly 30 million men who identify as nones, you end up forgetting about the 28 or so million women who also do. So again, don't be misled by this broad generalization.

What about politics? Yet again, there's a general impression out there that nones are all socially progressive liberals. And while we can't really pinpoint ideology that way, we can say that a scant 9% of nones identify as Republicans. Still, that's more than five million voters.

A strikingly high proportion, over half of all nones, identify as political Independents—so they're politically as well as religiously unaffiliated. Interestingly, there is some evidence from the GSS that this is more true among nonverts than it is of cradle nones. At least in 2018—though a lot has happened politically since then, admittedly—cradle nones were slightly more likely than nonverts to identify as Democrats *or* Republicans. One tempting explanation for this is that the kind of free-spiritedness that might lead a person to cast off a given religious identity might also make them unwilling to outsource other aspects of their identity to party platforms. Whatever the reason, this independent streak can result in a fair degree of unpredictability in terms of actual voting. Analyzing data from Harvard's Cooperative Congressional Election Study, political scientist Ryan Burge shows that Joe Biden took 71% of the none vote in 2020, compared to Trump's 27%. This was, moreover, a significant improvement over Hillary Clinton's showing in 2016, when she lost a particularly significant slice of nonreligious Independents to Trump and third parties. Since Trump's vote share among both Christians and minority religious groups stayed reasonably stable between 2016 and 2020, the changing preferences of those whom Phil Zuckerman has dubbed "secular values voters"[17] plausibly played a significant role in the end result. Indeed, in Burge's assessment, "it's completely fair to say that these shifts generated a two percentage point swing for Biden nationwide."[18]

This is broadly in line with my own experience. On my travels I met a fair few nones who had felt torn between Trump and Sanders in 2016, with little interest in either party's "politics as usual," status-quo candidates. Sitting one evening with Chad and Bryan, two early-twenties Republican activists in the Pennsylvania Rust Belt, they tell me that Sanders and Trump "were the same people from different sides. A lot of Republicans felt they had more in common with Bernie than with Hillary. So obviously they're going to pick Trump, and they might have picked Bernie, but they never would have picked Hillary." Meanwhile our dining companion Sam, a 60-year-old ex-Marine, derides both main parties as "Communists." Nevertheless, despite having voted for Bill Clinton in the 90s, he too voted Trump. All three, incidentally, would fairly be described as strongly liberal on social and moral matters. They see no contradiction here. For Chad, a gay man himself, "Trump couldn't care less if you're gay." "Yeah, he doesn't give a shit about that," agrees Bryan, adding: "And that's the direction that the Republican Party has to go in or it will crumble eventually. Because that's just the direction, socially, that the world is moving in. You can't stop that." Sam, who is precisely nobody's idea of the vanguard of wokeness, is a good example of precisely this. While he personally cares little for "the transgender crap or the gay stuff," his basic philosophy is simply "don't tell me, I don't care, do what you want to do, I don't want to hear about it."

* * *

Finally, what about God? It's not going to come as a total surprise when I tell you that nones are markedly less likely to believe in God than is the US population as a whole. According to our trusty GSS, only 3% of Americans affirmed the statement "I don't believe in God" in 2018, compared to 13% of the unaffiliated. A further 5% of Americans opted for "I don't know whether there is a God and I don't believe there is a way of finding out," compared to 20% of nones. So while only about 8% of the US population counts as an atheist or agnostic according to these standard, rough-and-ready definitions, about 33% of the nonreligious are.[19]

Notice that *only* one in three American nones are straightforward atheists or agnostics. And get this: 21% of nones told the GSS, "I believe in God and I have no doubt about it." One in five: that's roughly 12.3 million people. A further 18% say either that "While I have doubts, I feel that I do believe in God" or that they believe in God some of the time, but not at others. And then there's the remaining 27% who say they don't believe in a personal God, but they *do* believe in a "Higher Power of Some Kind."

As it happens, this is one area where there are marked differences between cradle nones and nonverts. Figure 3.4 shows the overall distribution of God beliefs among all nones (circles), as well as the separate ratings from cradle nones (triangles) and nonverts (squares). This shows a number of things. First, cradle nones are notably more nonbelieving than are nonverts. Twenty percent of nonverts "know God really exists, and have no doubts about it," for example, compared to 14% of cradles. At the other end of the spectrum, 22% of born-and-raised nones opted for the most straightforwardly atheistic choice ("I don't believe in God"), whereas 15% of nonverts did. Second, nonverts are very much more likely to affirm a belief in a higher power of some kind, with over a third doing so (i.e., 35% to cradle nones' also relatively high 22%). Third, the nonverts are most closely aligned with the views of nones as a whole. This is, obviously, for the simple reason that most nones *are* nonverts, far more than are nones at birth.

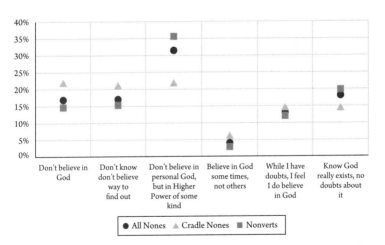

Figure 3.4. Distribution of beliefs about God among American adult nones, by (a) all, (b) just cradle nones, and (c) just nonverts.

Source: General Social Survey (2018; weighted data)

Obviously, how each person interprets the given answers, quite what they mean by opting for one answer over another, and the strength and significance of these beliefs is going to differ very, very widely. For example, what people mean by affirming a higher power is notoriously difficult to pin down, not just for researchers but for many such "higher powerists" themselves. As Christy, who identifies as a trans woman, told me in a New Orleans dive bar, "the idea of somebody out there to answer you, or even a force bigger than yourself who actually cares about you is, really, a powerful feeling." Trying to "tap into that sometimes" has helped "in my most painful moments," including after several suicide attempts. Meanwhile David, a Chinese American veteran also in New Orleans, credits experiments with hallucinogenic drugs after returning from Afghanistan with undermining his atheism.

> After one psychedelic experience I was like: "Alright, I cannot continue to be a fool and just believe that we magically showed up here, and then we're just going to end up being six foot in the ground one day. There has to be more, right?" Like, there just *has* to be more.
>
> Without turning this conversation into my psychedelic journeys . . . what I ultimately arrived at—and it's been rein-forced over the years—is that I believe that there is a Higher Creator and Final Judger. How that Higher Creator got where he got, it's either that humans aren't meant to understand it, or we don't have the capability to understand it. But, *something* put us here.
>
> That Final Judger—it's irrelevant if he or she is the same as the Creator; either they're one or not—all they care about is what you've done with the experience they've given you. The only thing that is relevant is how you spent your time in your

human experience, what good you did and what bad you did, including when you took inaction when you had a chance to do good.

Whatever kind of "ism" these are, it's a long way from factory-setting unbelief. Apparently the Dutch have a word for it: *ietsism*, which translates as "Something-ism."[20] It's the belief that there's a *Something* out there (often, as with Christy and David, a quietly benevolent Something), though not a Something that is felt to jive easily with any of the off-the-rack religious options. There is more than an echo of this when people express gratitude to "the Universe" for having helped bring about some favorable outcome—a new job, a clean bill of health, a romantic relationship—or when sending or soliciting "good vibes" in the hopes of one. As Christy puts it, "You're not necessarily praying to 'God' or, like, this idea, or figure, or anything. It's more of a wish, or a hope, or *something*. But I will send up a prayer every now and then. Most recently, I would say, the prayers I've sent were things like asking forgiveness." A quarter of nones say that they pray daily. That's low by American standards, sure. But it's markedly higher than, say, the 4% of British nones who do.[21] One is almost tempted to say that America puts the "religious" in "religious none."

This too, however, should not surprise us. America is demonstrably becoming less religious than it was—which is rather the point of this book. Nevertheless, the religious and spiritual climate is much hotter here than most elsewhere in the developed, democratic world. Furthermore, a very large proportion of even the country's *least* religious citizens were themselves brought up religiously. For some of our nonverts, this results in their going the spiritual equivalent of cold turkey: decidedly and determinedly not religious, and keen to expunge any trace of it, not just from their thinking but from their habits and heart to boot. This reaction is perhaps more common among those both brought up, and still living, in more deeply religious contexts. This makes sense when you think about it. Becoming nonreligious is far harder for such people. It takes more effort, more agency, more grit. It often also creates more problems, big and small, not least with family, neighbors, and co-workers. It is not unusual, therefore, to find the more convicted, thoroughgoingly atheistic nones in the more strongly religious areas of the country: the kinds of town where, as I saw on one of my southbound odysseys, even fast-food chain restaurants display the Ten Commandments on stone tablets. They are also more likely to feel a need to band together with like-minded compatriots, "behind enemy lines" so to speak.

But even so, such people make up only a minority *within* America's nonreligious minority. Many more nones either retain religious/spiritual beliefs and practices from their background, whether whole or in modified form, or else have acquired others somewhere along the way.[22] This is quite clear from Figure 3.5, for instance, which shows that good proportions of even (the more skeptical) cradle nones are quite comfortable believing in life after death, heaven, hell, religious miracles, or the supernatural powers of their forebears. Indeed, an eclectic, pick-and-mix approach to the supernatural is frequently a hallmark of the "spiritual but not religious." This is why automatic conflations of atheism, and especially its no-holds-barred New Atheist variant, with noneness-in-general are so misleading. Among my own interviewees, for example, there are plenty for whom Richard Dawkins' multimillion-selling *The God Delusion* (2006) is a fair representation of their own basic outlook. But there are just as many for whom, in the words of a woman not otherwise prone to such language, "I've seen a thing or two from Dawkins, but I haven't really gone into it. He seemed kind of a dick."

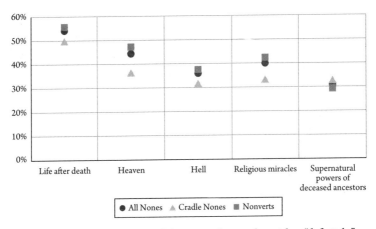

Figure 3.5. Proportions of US adult nones who say they either "definitely" or "probably" believe in selected religious/spiritual realities, by (a) all nones, (b) just cradle nones, and (c) just nonverts.

Source: General Social Survey (2018; weighted data)

Put another way, the vast majority of nones do not fit easily into the popular one-size-fits-all image of a rationalist and materialist Atheist-with-a-capital-A. Not only are the majority of nones not atheists at all—a consistent finding going back to at least the 1960s—but even many of those who actually are atheists are not *that kind* of atheist. Not believing in a God, gods, or even a kindly "Something" does not itself preclude believing in all kinds of other supernatural, spiritual, and/or paranormal phenomena. According to a 2019 study by my team, only a third of American atheists, and just one in ten American agnostics, "seem to have a wholly naturalistic Fworld view."[23] This coheres well with findings from other studies: levels of belief in one or more expressions of the paranormal—including ghosts, UFOs, astrology, and much else besides—are strikingly high throughout the whole US population, religious or not.

* * *

If this chapter has one lesson, it's that even at this big-picture level of statistical generalizations, the nones are not an easy group to pin down. At least not neatly, or with a single pin.

There may be lots of ways in which nones, as a group, diverge from the general population. Much more significant, not least for the future, are the ways in which the nonreligious mirror, more or less, the country. Truth be told, in many respects today's nones look much more like Americans-in-general than they did ten, twenty, or thirty years ago. This is so for two reasons. In the first place, they are now fully a quarter of Americans-in-general themselves. That is, whatever the "US average" is on any particular attitude or demographic, one-fourth of the ingredients making up that average *are* nones. And as nones make up a larger and larger share of the overall population, as they seem set to do for the foreseeable future, this effect will only grow. Nones are becoming more like the general population for the simple reason that they are becoming more *of* the general population.[24]

Parallel to this, another effect is in play. We might call this the mainstreaming of nonreligion. Not to put too fine a point on it, up until fairly recently to be a none was to be *weird*. In a culture where having a religion, even if a dormant one, is the norm, then it takes a certain willful self-confidence, if not outright bloody-mindedness, to insist on not having one. Human beings are social beings after all, and we have an inbuilt tendency toward conformity.[25] That's why peer pressure can have such powerful influence over us, for good or ill. It's also not as though simply *having* a religious affiliation is exactly arduous: being a non-practicing or lapsed Catholic or Methodist, or euphemistically being "between churches," has been a perfectly respectable cultural option for a long time. In such contexts, therefore, it is not surprising that self-identified nones would tend to differ sharply from the general population in significant ways: hence the timeworn image of nones being predominantly White, affluent, and well educated.

The relatively high number of college graduates, and indeed postgraduates, among the nonreligious has sometimes been used as proof for its inherent cleverness. It's easy to see why: if the better educated you are, the more likely it is that you are an "X," then that ought to be good evidence in support of Xism's superior intellectual bona fides. Such arguments get used all the time, not least in political discussions where the barely concealed inference is often "all those non-Xs" *who disagree with us* are stupid and ignorant; if they were smarter and more knowledgeable, *like our people*, they'd see we're obviously right." Trouble is, things are not quite so simple as all that.

In the first place, higher levels of education correlate with being all kinds of Xs. Membership in a New Religious Movement—a "cult" in popular parlance—has long been more common among the highly educated, for instance.[26] That's not to deny that many people become nonreligious for primarily intellectual reasons (though there's a lot of reading, thinking, and studying involved in joining Scientology, too). Rather, higher levels of education tend to go along with all sorts of other factors—higher income, leaving home during one's formative years (i.e., for college), social and geographical mobility, meeting and marrying people very different from one's hometown crowd, literate self-confidence—all of which might feasibly explain why such people are, on average, more willing and able to "go against the flow"—intellectually yes, but also in terms of outlook and lifestyle. It's not surprising that, in societies where the overwhelming majority of people see themselves as one from a set menu of respectable Christian options, the rebel few who end up becoming Zen Buddhists, Raëlians, techno-shamans, *or nones* might tend to hail from the ranks of the better-educated middle classes. Tellingly, in European countries such as Britain and Estonia, where having "no religion" is now the default setting for the population at large, ticking *Christian* on surveys now correlates with higher education.[27] The tide might have turned, but it takes the same sort of person to swim against it one way as the other.

Equally, there have long been certain "enclaves" where being nonreligious has been, at least by America's historically low standards, reasonably common. Portland, Oregon, for example, has a long reputation as the epicenter of a "none zone" encompassing much of the (urban) Pacific Northwest.[28] Indeed, a number of my nonverts consciously moved *to* Oregon for precisely this reason. But here too we see a clear minority effect at work, for Portland is proudly unconventional in other ways too—a fact brilliantly and affectionately satirized in the sketch show *Portlandia*. For instance, Oregon as a whole has provided fertile soil to all manner of minority religious groups, as of course Brandon discovered. Rajneeshpuram, star of the Netflix docuseries *Wild, Wild Country*, is surely now the most (in)famous example. But it is striking how often the histories of other outré religious groups—including Heaven's Gate, the Manson Family, the Children of God, the Moonies, and the sixties "Jesus Freaks"—include spells or outposts in the state.

Here's the thing: having no religion is no longer the preserve of nonconformists or self-consciously quirky enclaves like Portland or Austin ("the Portland of Texas," as an ex-evangelical Texan put it to me). With each passing year, being a none is rapidly becoming less socially and culturally odd. In many places, among many groups, nonreligiosity is now thoroughly normal. It is now a perfectly established and respectable "live" option for most people. That's not true of everywhere, of course. Yet like other erstwhile Portland specialties as craft beer, artisanal donuts, and veganism, it's gone mainstream.

Flatline Protestants

"I *was* Presbyterian."

"And now?"

"I'm nonreligious at this point. I think it has a lot to do with my age right now. I'm at that point where I'm 22, and my main focus is not making sure on Sunday I'm at church. Y'know what I mean? It's taken a back burner for me. I'm not saying I *won't* go back to being religious again. It's just a little like an inconvenience for me to be a practicing Presbyterian."

Bryan, whom we met in the last chapter talking Trump in a Rust Belt restaurant, wasn't always so lukewarm: "I did mission trips and was very involved. I was in the middle of the Amazon jungle, in Peru, working with indigenous tribes, providing humanitarian aid, all that stuff. But just right now I do not have time to be religious."

I ask him when all this changed.

"I think probably freshman year of college. I went from being super involved, going to church pretty much every Sunday, to— y'know—I go to church for Christmas with my grandma now. I don't have time for it."

"So it's not been a deep, existential, antagonistic thing?"

Bryan shrugs. "It's not like I hate it."

* * *

"It isn't love, it isn't hate. It's just indifference." Although this isn't a quotation from a former mainline Protestant—it's a line from a Taylor Swift song—it very easily could be. Bryan's transition from practicing Presbyterianism to nonvert, while swift, involved no great spiritual crisis or trauma. He just dropped it, as one might a gym membership, when he found other, more pressing things to be doing. Maybe Bryan will come back, maybe he won't. There was no fight or struggle, whether with God, his family, or himself. One gets the impression that he and Christianity have parted on good terms. It's as though both parties recognize church to be "a little like an inconvenience" for someone, *anyone*, with other things happening on a Sunday.

While Bryan's experience is not universal, it is remarkably prevalent. Sure, there are people brought up as middle-of-the-road Lutherans, Episcopalians, or Congregationalists whose ultimate nonversions are the result of profound spiritual, intellectual, emotional, and interpersonal struggles, and who now feel anything but "indifferently" about it all. We'll meet some of them. But in stark contrast to our Mormon, evangelical, and (less so, and differently) Catholic case studies elsewhere, most former mainliners' stories chime more or less in harmony with Bryan's: "It wasn't as much about religion and God, as it was about a community"; "we didn't really do too much prayer"; "bland."

It is a truth universally acknowledged that the Protestant mainline is in a state of serious, long-term decline. Eye-watering—literally so for its pastors and grandmas—stats are easy to come by. By one informed estimate, in the space of sixty-odd years, mainline affiliation has been hung, drawn, and more-than-quartered: from

52% of the US population in 1952, down to 12% by 2018. Only a further quarter of *them*, amounting to just 3% of the US population, say they attend church on a weekly basis.[1] Any such precise figures, of course, require a specific definition as to quite what and who "the mainline" actually consists of. Another truth universally acknowledged, however, is that it's no straightforward task, irrespective of how one goes about it—historically, sociologically, theologically. As we are about to find, the debate can become rather animated.

The basic idea of the "mainline" originates in a cluster of specific Protestant denominations, with long-standing roots and influence in and around the Northeast by the start of the twentieth century (the eponymous "main line" being the Pennsylvania Railroad, terminating in Philadelphia, site of the 1908 founding of the Federal Council of Churches). By the narrowest definition, the true mainline comprises a subset of historic churches within a host of historic Protestant denominations: Episcopalians, Congregationalists, Lutherans, Presbyterians, and northern branches of Baptists and Methodists.[2] Each was a significant and storied denomination in its own right: the Congregationalists are heirs to the *Mayflower* and founded both Harvard and Yale, for example.[3] Each had its own distinctive liturgical, aesthetic, organizational, and theological traditions and conventions; the Episcopal Church alone contains (or tries to) several of each. Nevertheless, all shared a basic common ground of moral and social outlook and, for the most part, a commitment to a certain set of basic (liberal) Protestant principles. All could, moreover, happily agree to disagree with both Catholics and fundamentalists. Uniting their powers like an ecumenical *Power Rangers*, the mainline churches were thus able to project an outsized vision and voice of "American Christianity," both to the country as a whole and to the wider world. They punched well above their weight.

Alongside the classic mainline churches may be placed a much larger group of fellow travelers, drawn mainly from the same denominational families though perhaps including others such as Quakers. Without ignoring the genuine differences both among and within them, these together established a sort of default setting for large swathes of the American populace, albeit with a fair degree of local and regional variation. Different flavors, certainly. But different flavors *of* the same basic product: namely, "ordinary, respectable, mainstream Christianity" as contradistinguished from "exotic" Catholics and Orthodox on the one side, and various sorts of rougher, wilder, and less "reasonable" Protestant cousins on the other. Viewed like this, the mainline becomes rather less the combined memberships of a defined set of heritage denominations and much more a religious and cultural style or mindset.

In this light, perhaps the clearest and keenest evocations of the mainline come not from historians or sociologists, but rather from popular culture. When movies or television want to explore either the supernatural or ethnically based crime cartels, the go-to religious idiom is the (largely lost) Catholic world of candles and confessionals, Latin and Holy Water, cassocked priests and habited nuns. But when they want to evoke the lives of "normal," American, middle-class suburbia, then—from *The Andy Griffith Show* to *The Fresh Prince of Bel-Air*—something generically "mainliney" normally gets the nod. Probably the best two examples of this come from long-running cartoons, *The Simpsons* (1989–) and *King of the Hill* (1997–2010). Churchgoing features regularly in both series. This allows them, in contrast to the one-off "church episode" coverage of many sitcoms, to build up a three-dimensional, mostly affectionate portrait of their respective places of worship.

In the case of *The Simpsons*, the First Church of Springfield's affiliation with the "Western Branch of American Reform

Presbylutheranism"—or "the one true faith," as Rev. Lovejoy describes it—is a satire on the mainline's signature blend of organizational hyperspecificity with a high degree of *de facto* interchangeability: the proliferation of distinctions without genuine differences. Nevertheless, with its traditionally "churchy" architecture, stained-glass windows, pipe organ, and exclusively male clergy, *The Simpsons'* church of choice is notably toward the "higher" (and when the plot demands, more morally conservative) end of the mainline spectrum. Meanwhile *King of the Hill* features a more consciously realistic depiction of sober, middle-of-the-road Christianity: Arlen First Methodist Church, pastored by the Rev. Karen Stroup. Arlen Methodist suits Hank Hill's penchant for serious, low-key dependability (this is a man who once titled an anniversary tribute to his wife "Twenty Years of Outstanding Service"). While both shows regularly feature more "exotic" examples of religiosity, both Christian and otherwise, these are normally the preserve either of side characters, or plot devices specific to a given episode (Homer founding his own religion; Bobby Hill as the possible reincarnation of a Laotian lama; family members joining a "cult" in both shows). Each family, and their shows with them, soon gravitate back to their "default setting," often with a renewed appreciation for the normalness and familiarity of their church home. Even converting to Buddhism, as Lisa does in season 13 of *The Simpsons,* presents no real obstacle.

> Lisa: I'm still Buddhist, but I can still worship with my family too.
> Marge: So you're just going to pay lip-service to our church?
> Lisa: Uh-huh.
> Homer: That's all I ever asked.[4]

After all, it's not like she hates it.

There is much more that could be said about the depiction of religion in both *The Simpsons* and *King of the Hill*,[5] but I think the necessary point here has been made. That is to say, the spirit and significance of the mainline is as much about a certain taken-for-granted ordinariness as it is about formal denominational lineages or a checklist of essential theological or liturgical characteristics. This was, for many decades, one of its great strengths: it was the religion you belonged to, unless you had a particular reason to belong to something else. This may sound dismissive, but it's not intended to be. It provided American Christianity with a good deal of its power, prestige, and persuasiveness. As Joseph Bottum has keenly observed, mainstream "Protestantism gave Americans code of manners. A state of mind. A mode of being. A political foundation. A national definition."[6] It set the cultural tone.

Not anymore. The mainline is no longer the culturally dominant expression even of American Protestantism, let alone American religion or indeed the nation itself. For Bottum, "the crumpling of the Mainline churches as central institutions in our national experience" is "the single most significant fact over the past few decades in America. . . . It is a collapse of numbers, certainly: a disappearance of parishioners at astonishing speed. Even more, however, it is a collapse of influence, the loss of religious institutions that had defined, supported, and challenged the nation for all its previous history."[7] Parts of this big-picture story, and its even bigger-picture ramifications, will feature in subsequent chapters. Here, though, we highlight the stories of individual nonverts behind the numbers.

* * *

"So my family were Chinese immigrants. It's a superstitious culture . . . a blend of Taoism, Buddhism, and Confucianism, sprinkled with different superstitions. And that's exactly what was carried over, in practice, in my family growing up. We have Buddhist/ Chinese cultural shrines at home—different ancestors, different gods." David, a thirty-something agnostic, speaks up so I can record his words over the noise of a New Orleans sidewalk café. "But interestingly, they stick me into a Lutheran Church when I'm five."

Though David's parents did not attend, and continued to uphold their own traditional practices, he was sent to church every week for the next seven years, first to Sunday school, and later graduating to a youth group. While their full reasoning is a little hard to reconstruct now—David's never asked directly—he ascribes it both to simple practicality ("in the sense of 'hey, you get to go somewhere free, you're out of my hair, and I got stuff to do'") and a conscious attempt at Americanization. Looking back, he sees this as part and parcel of the wider Asian American experience. The parallel he draws is to eating non-American food—a practice stigmatized among his second-generation friends: "It was like, 'Eww, you're still eating the motherland dumplings?'" Likewise, "not being a Christian in an Asian community with other Asian Americans, it was, "Ohh, you still believe in that stuff? How are you not a Christian?'"[8]

The week he was due to be baptized a Lutheran, at age twelve, David's mother abruptly pulled him out of the church, for good. Evidently mindful of the fine line between assimilation and full-on Americanization, she enrolled him instead in Chinese lessons and youth activities at the local Buddhist temple. While this switch was never fully explained, he went along with the parental flow, as children usually have to: "I still remember there were times I'd fight it, I'd be like, 'I want to go back to church, I have friends there.' I just got uprooted and left. But also at the same time I just kind of get deeper and deeper into these [new] activities. So I ended up thinking, 'sure,

I'm not going to fight you over this, this isn't a big deal.' And then that Lutheran church just kind of faded into memory..."

Fast-forward ten years, and having studied management and Asian studies at college, David decided to enlist in the Army—something else he sees as a textbook "part of my immigrant story: 'hey my family came here with nothing' ..." Filling out the paperwork, he had to specify his religion to be printed on his dog tags. Not having thought about religion for some years, he approached the question as the "jackass 22-year-old thinking he has the world figured out" that he then was. "Buddhist" meant little to him, beyond vague family associations, and he could think of no upside to actually identifying as such. Further narrowing his options, he ended up with a choice between "Muslim" or "Christian" on the basis that if either *was* true, then having officially associated himself with it, however nominally, might stand him in good stead should he be killed in action. (Meanwhile, if say Buddhism or Hinduism was true, then—as far as he understood their respective theologies—having been a Christian or Muslim wouldn't be held against him much in the afterlife.) Since he was likely to be deployed in Afghanistan, however, he further reasoned that "Muslim" might cause him problems in the Army itself. So, with the logic of a latter-day Pascal, he wagered on "Christian."

> Why did I have Christianity on my "final rites" tags? It was basically that, if it was my final barrier to a good afterlife, then if I get my Christian funeral and I show up at the Gates I get to say, "Hey, I'm an official Christian, I had my final rites, I did good my entire life, let me in!" I was still an atheist at that point, but the downside of writing "None" was the calculation that, if there *was* no religion, then I wouldn't lose anything if my tag said "Christian," right? I would end up six feet in the ground

and whatever happens next, happens next. There was no consequence. But in that 1% chance that Christianity was true, and
there's someone sitting in front of the Pearly Gates, then I'd be
this 22 year-old going, "Oh hey, it's imprinted on a metal plate—
you can't deny me entrance."

Viewed in a certain light, David's dog tag calculation, recounted
now with a good deal of gentle self-mockery, is not a million miles
away from his mother's earlier one. Although she wasn't prepared
for him to go "all in"—full-immersion style—she recognized the
various benefits that a familiarity with Christianity might bring to a
child growing up in America. Later on, during his pre-deployment
Army training, David recalls the series of imams and other experts
who were brought in to provide the soldiers with the necessary literacy regarding Islam and Afghani culture: "you never shake with
your left hand, you never show the bottom of your feet, you never
speak about Mohammed in bad terms, the Qur'an always needs to
be respected . . ." Without wishing to overstate the parallels, immigrant parents are likely all too conscious of the clear advantages of
being able to "fit in"—socially, culturally, professionally—in order
to thrive and get ahead. And one of the obvious places to help them
to do that, with the added bonus of being free, is of course the local
mainline church's children's and youth program. For this purpose,
Lutheran—as all followers of Garrison Keillor know—is a good,
solid, trustworthy brand.[9] And even though David's mother didn't
want him, as a tender pre-teen, to commit, he would always have the
choice of "owning" his Lutheran connection in later life (as he also
would his Chinese, Confucian/Buddhist one). You don't lose anything if your tag says "Lutheran," right?

This basic idea does not only apply to immigrant families.
Writing early last century, the German sociologist Max Weber cast

his own outsider's eye over America's religious dynamics. He noted, among much else, that "Membership of a church community 'of good repute' (according to American criteria) guarantees the good standing of the individual, not only socially, but also, and especially, in terms of business."[10] What Weber chiefly had in mind here was that, if one was known to be an in-good-standing member of a reputable denomination, then not only might this open doors among fellow members, but also signal to others that one could be trusted. He cites the anecdote of a doctor being assured by a new patient, prior to any mention of what was actually troubling him, that "I am a member of the Second Baptist Church, on X Street." Weber adds, with the waggishness for which German sociologists are renowned, the explanation: "This piece of information, of course, had no bearing on the etiology of his . . . condition, as the puzzled doctor realized. The real purpose of the statement was to convey something different, which was not without interest for the doctor, namely, 'Don't worry about your *fee!*'"[11]

While the salience of *this* kind of virtue-signaling has waned in the past hundred-odd years, it has not completely disappeared. (In one episode of the ever-keenly observed *King of the Hill*, our hero addresses a prayer with "God? It's Hank Hill here, Methodist.") The use of the *ichthus* (fish) symbol on billboard ads, signaling that the MD, real estate agent, or personal injury lawyer in question is a Christian (usually of the evangelical variety), is common in certain areas of the country. Studies published in both psychology and marketing journals suggest that these do have an effect on boosting potential consumers' trust, especially (though, fascinatingly, not exclusively) among committed Christians.[12] However, there is a trade-off here: some consumers react against such labeling, either from antipathy to evangelicals in general, or else toward the kinds of evangelicals who would "exploit" it in this way. The trick, as ever, is to know one's market. I'd guess that in parts of Utah, advertisers "subtly" hint at their LDS allegiance in other ways (as is suggested, while we're on the subject of religion on television, in an episode of *Big Love*).

Research by Christel Manning into nones' parenting practices, moreover, shows that they often make very similar calculations to David's parents, irrespective of their immigration status.[13] She notes how nonreligious parents are often keen to expose their children to religion, either for ethnic or family reasons (e.g., Jewish nonverts wanting their kids to have a sense of "who they are"), or to equip them with sufficient "cultural literacy" to get by in a country where having some kind of religious identity remains the norm. Naturally, the relevant cost-benefit calculation, explicit or implicit, differs depending on geography. For some none parents, especially those who retain a degree of religious believing, this involves the whole family becoming involved at a church or similar. A perhaps surprising number of others, however, are happy to "outsource": namely, sending the kids along to a church or church-related youth group, without practicing or otherwise reinforcing it themselves. As for David's parents, the mainline churches are undoubtedly an attractively safe option, offering the benefits of cultural socialization with a low risk of religious or moral radicalization. Even if the children do end up "going native"—the rhetoric of allowing one's children to *choose for themselves* is fundamental to many nonreligious parents' self-image—then their becoming an open-minded, socially liberal Methodist, Presbyterian, or Lutheran are among the better options. There may also be the hope that they'll be inoculated against religion altogether. Charles, an ex-zookeeper in his early sixties, relates why he and his fellow-nonvert wife sent their kids to an Episcopalian church in southern Georgia:

We thought that we'd go ahead and put them in the normative culture of the community. And a big part of me was thinking that I want them to have a good taste of religion before they encounter some cult person at an airport and I want them to be able to say, "I have had enough religion."

While we're on the subject of Episcopalians, Beth, a thirty-something Tennessean raised in the (Pentecostal) Church of God, explains her strategy in those situations when it would be socially or professionally helpful to pass as a Christian:

I don't lie about it, but it's good to blend in with the crowd. Most of the people I work with are religious, and though they're fairly open-minded I generally just avoid the issue. And when people ask I say that my parents were Episcopalian. Which is not *un*true—that's what my parents were raised—and it usually allows me not to have to discuss it with people that may or may not be influenced by it. I do feel like you have to be careful. People do get turned over for promotions in the South because they are nonreligious.

But why Episcopalian, rather than Church of God? For a remix of the same sorts of reasons we've already discussed:

The Church of God are very . . . they're almost as bad as the Baptists! Just kidding: maybe *worse*. I don't know, they're just very "churchy." So I don't want people to identify me with crazy people. But Episcopalians are a really very rational folk, they are pretty liberal. They are like "Catholic Lite," and Catholic is like "Christian Lite," so Episcopalianism is the whitest of white.

Nor is Beth alone in mentally situating the Episcopalians and their denominational fellow travelers at the extreme vanilla end of a Christian continuum. Al, a Chicagoan atheist and practicing Reform Jew in his mid-70s, remarks in passing: "somewhere I heard there's like 40,000 Christian sects—y'know, from totally loony to mainline."

* * *

The point here is *not* that mainline churches are composed only of people there for social and cultural benefits, still less that the mainline churches do not produce authentic, committed Christians. They are not, and they do. But American Christianity, like all religion everywhere, is always bound up with all sorts of wider social, cultural, economic, and political pushes and pulls. One need only read the New Testament, or other writings from the early Church, to recognize 'twas ever thus. The might of the mainline in generations past, as well as its newfound minority status, can only be fully understood against the wider—and changing—backdrop of American life.

"Nobody ever got fired for buying IBM" is an adage beloved of marketers. They mean that IBM is the standard option, the default, the "leading brand." If you buy IBM and it fails, that's their fault: anyone else would have done the same in your rationally risk-averse shoes. If you *don't* buy IBM, and what you get instead fails, then that's *your* fault. It's all on you for being a flying-too-close-to-the-sun IT systems purchasing maverick.[14] For the first two-thirds of the twentieth century (though its legacy—if in weakened form— extended long after), the mainline was the religious equivalent of an IBM. You knew what you were getting, and you didn't need to have a special reason, whether of ethnicity or religious conviction, for getting it. Nobody ever got passed over for a promotion for being a Presbyterian. The Oval Office, to give an obvious example, could justifiably have a "You don't have to be a mainline Protestant to work here . . . but it helps!" sign on the Resolute desk. Nixon as a Quaker jumps to mind a whole lot faster than Taft —Kennedy and Biden (Catholic), Carter and Clinton (Southern Baptist), Taft (Unitarian)—these are so memorable largely because they are just that, exceptions.

The mainline's power came from its close cultural, political, and moral fit with the *mores* of America. Of course there were differences—we're talking Baptists here, not the Borg—between and within denominations and individual congregations alike. But for the very most part such differences, whether on social or doctrinal questions, were positions held *within* a broad consensus of permitted possibilities.[15] The views of "conservatives" and "progressives" were, if one might put it like this, normally no more than a standard deviation away from the mean. The genius of the mainline, moreover, lay not just in finding a great deal of common ground among themselves, but in opening up an even wider civic religious language and space—"our shared Judeo-Christian heritage," "traditional American values"—that other major religious groups (Catholics, Jews) could tap into and benefit from, so long as they played nicely and treated their hosts with sufficient respect. Broadly speaking, this is the foundation of what Robert Bellah famously termed America's "Civil Religion": a set of "beliefs, symbols, and rituals," incorporating "certain common elements of religious orientation that the great majority of Americans share," and which "provide a religious dimension for the whole fabric of American life."[16]

Here's the trouble, though. Since the middle years of the twentieth century, a series of moral issues have come to the fore, disrupting the relatively comfortable, or at least awkwardly accommodating, fit between traditional Christian teachings and what many Americans regarded as being obviously good and right. Divorce, abortion, homosexuality, and women's equality (especially as it touched on religious ordination and leadership) all emerged as major bones of contention in the postwar decades. The 1960s and 1970s were a significant watershed here for several reasons: landmark legal and political developments (Stonewall riots, no-fault divorce, *Roe v. Wade*, wranglings over the Equal Rights Amendment); the baby boomers entering the workforce and electorate; and all occurring in the midst of a good deal of other change and upheaval (Cuban missile crisis, civil rights marches, assassinations, student protests, Vietnam, Apollo, Watergate). Whatever else one might think about the rights and wrongs of any one of these issues, or indeed of the myriad sub-issues that each throws up, they clearly opened up huge possibilities for deep disagreements. While America's mainline churches had done a remarkable job of downplaying or denying centuries of theological disputes in the name of ecumenism, these new, pressing moral matters could not be so easily ignored. Having carefully calibrated themselves to the American cultural, religious, and moral mainstream (and vice versa), these emerging rifts within the American mainstream naturally affected the mainline churches, too.

And how. Every church in America has been affected by these cultural riptides: to try to ignore them is itself a response, and probably not one that can last for very long. While they have played out differently in other traditions, the dominant trend in the mainline churches has been to reinterpret, "recover the original, deeper meanings in," "pastorally reimagine," or otherwise change long-held positions.[17] This is not without a certain rhetorical authenticity: progressive voices were not slow to note that the Reformation itself entailed a radical rethink of long-standing doctrinal and moral teaching in light of the signs of rapidly changing times.[18] Nevertheless, in practice it means that rather than being America's moral leaders—as at least segments of the mainline churches could justly claim to be in the past, from northern abolitionists to Social Gospelers[19]—they're now constantly left playing catch-up to the evolving cultural consensus. This has also often gone hand in hand with a steady erosion of other, hitherto-regarded-as-fundamental Christian "truth claims"—not at all excluding the Incarnation or, in some cases, even the existence of God (at least in any recognizable form). It is no surprise that even sympathetic observers now regard much of the mainline as no longer standing (still less kneeling) for anything much at all. As Margaret Bendroth writes in her fascinating history of US Congregationalism:

> Of all religious groups today, mainline Protestants seem the most deracinated, the least bound by historic Christianity . . . mainline churches seem to alter their ancient creeds, liturgies, and baptismal formulas at will, readily accommodating their beliefs and behaviors to modern sensibilities. Even in churches with centuries of denominational history, tradition has become fully negotiable.[20]

Maybe, just maybe, if the whole mainline had moved in step, and carried a good number of other churches along with them—as happened, for very different reasons, when changing their long-standing prohibitions of contraception a few decades earlier—then this strategy might have worked out more successfully (though I doubt it).[21] Instead, it left the mainline churches wide open to criticism, and thus competition, from outside (fueling the rise of evangelicalism, plus converts to Catholicism and Orthodoxy), and precipitated decades of rancorous arguments, often leading to painful schisms from within. Such severings of denominations, and often of individual congregations, are often likened to divorces, and with good reason: there's a lot of hurt on all sides, and battles over money and property can keep lawyers busy (and rich) for years. For Anne-Marie, another of my north Floridian interviewees, this parallel might feel a little on the nose. The breakdown of her own marriage, albeit for a range of long-built-up reasons, mirrored the breakup of their church community (also, adding to the irony, partly over marital troubles: gay marriage, in the church's case). She stayed behind in their original Episcopal church. Meanwhile her husband joined the conservative breakaway group that set up down the road, which, for curious reasons of Anglican geopolitics, formally became an outpost of the Church of Uganda.[22] They later divorced, and as if that parting of the ways wasn't dramatic enough, while she ended up leaving church altogether (having already lost faith in God many years before, while attending church for the sake of community and her family), he eventually became a priest and set up his own.

His and Anne-Marie's son, whom I also interviewed, is one of very few millennials brought up in the mainline who can claim to have spent "an exceptional amount of time" in church as a child (when staying with his dad). Yet despite, as he revealingly phrases it, "fulfill[ing] all my social expectations," he still "never really felt any personal resonance." Furthermore, his exposure to multiple churches growing up has had a relativizing impact on his now firmly nonreligious outlook:

> I've seen a lot of different kinds of church, and the evolution of lots of individuals *through* church. And I can see how the same setup can be good for one person, and terrible for another. Just like one person can hear a song and weep in sorrow, another can weep in anger, and another doesn't care at all. So I'm not one to think that there even could be some overarching truth that

would hit all people the same. I don't even think there's a statement you can really make that is always true.

* * *

"It was a sort of Christianity of convenience at times." Melissa, raised Episcopalian in Mississippi, is now in her late twenties. For her, and for many other cradle mainliners, there seemed to be very little actual "religion" in, well, their religion. True, they find little to criticize about it, which, when compared to the passion-verging-on-hatred of some former Catholics, evangelicals, and Mormons, might feel like a win. But this is a pyrrhic victory, mostly born from lukewarmness and indifference. This mirrors Dartmouth historian Randall Balmer's damning verdict on recent mainline theology—"so careful not to offend that its very blandness has become an affront"—and his observation that, "In the eyes of many Americans mainline Protestants have become so intent on blurring theological and denominational distinctiveness that they stand for nothing at all, aside from some vague (albeit noble) pieties like peace, justice, and inclusiveness."[23]

On a similar theme, note too that even the "mission trips," cited by Bryan at the start of this chapter as proof of his being a "very involved" Presbyterian, were described principally in terms of "providing humanitarian aid, all that stuff." This impression agrees with the memories of other ex-mainline interviewees. Cal, the Minnesotan atheist we met in the last chapter puzzling over his German/Hispanic/Native American ancestry, recalls his own mission trips to South Dakota and Mexico: "We went there, we fed them, we played with the kids, but we weren't handing out Bibles to them. So it was just helping people, helping a community that was suffering. . . . So there was spiritual moments, but it wasn't with, like, a higher power. It was with each other." Now, I've no desire to dismiss the value of humanitarian aid, or deny that it's something that Christians certainly *should* be concerning themselves with. But it is worth noting the very secularized sense in which "mission" is being used here, compared not only to the "mission trips" undertaken by young Mormons and evangelicals, but moreover to how mainline churches *used to* conceive of it. In the view of Rodney Stark, "The liberal denominations stopped sending missionaries [in the traditional sense] because they lost their faith in the validity of Christianity."[24]

It feels wrong to criticize mainline churches for devoting themselves—and roping in vast armies of bright young adults—to building wells and orphanages, running soup kitchens, providing basic healthcare, and educating the disadvantaged, both at home and at abroad. To repeat: these are activities that followers of Jesus certainly ought to be doing, and doing even more of than they do already (cf. Matthew 25.31–46). But churches, *qua* churches, cannot live on distributing bread alone. This, it's important to stress, is not simply a matter of bringing in new recruits, though mainline missionary groups were historically very good at that indeed.[25] Significantly here, it's critical for retaining the born-and-raiseds you already have. If a church doesn't inculcate in its members the feeling that what they have is something that's worth sharing with others—or at least trying to—then it sends the message that perhaps it's not so essential for *me* either. Conversely, actively trying to evangelize others cements the value of it for oneself. Not long ago, I took a couple of local LDS missionaries out to lunch; I paid for the food but, ace dealmaker that I am, I managed to haggle a free copy of the *Book of Mormon* out of them. Neither had yet succeeded in making a convert, and this fact clearly stung a little. Yet interestingly, from the perspective of the LDS Church, this doesn't mean that their mission trips have failed. The experience of spending two years trudging around rainy England, living in each other's (name-badged) pockets, and trying to strike up meaningful conversations with secular Brits is nothing if not character building. And while, as we've seen in Chapter 2, there's no guarantee, the odds of them returning home even more deeply committed to being upstanding lifelong Mormons, and raising their children to be likewise, will certainly have risen appreciably.[26]

These reasons, in collusion with another that we're about to explore, explain much of the mainline's precipitous decline. It's not just the kids of atheist zookeepers like Charles that they've been inoculating against religion.

Nothings Come from Nothing?

It didn't used to be like this. At the start of the twentieth century, "the private statistical sources" available to Max Weber suggested "well below one-tenth (about one-thirteenth) of the population as having no religion," which works out at roughly 7–8%.[1] While no more than an informed guesstimate, that might not have been so far from the truth, if perhaps a little on the high side. The statistical record then goes silent for the best part of fifty years, waiting first for George Gallup to invent modern opinion polling in the 1930s, and then for his organization to start regularly asking about religion. In 1948, Gallup found that 2% of the US population had no religion. Between then and 1967, two whole decades, the proportion of nones in Gallup's annual polling never shifted from 1% or 2% (Figure 5.1). In 1957 the US Census Bureau got in on the game—one of the very few times in its history that it has dared ask about religion—and came up with 2.5% of those aged fourteen and over. By the Bureau's own calculations, that amounted to 4.3 million people. That was not too far from its figure for the Jewish population at 5 million, though both paled in comparison to Catholicism's 44 million and the almost 112 million Protestants. Altogether, the Census Bureau's figures suggest around 93% of American over-14s identifying as Christians in the late 1950s.[2]

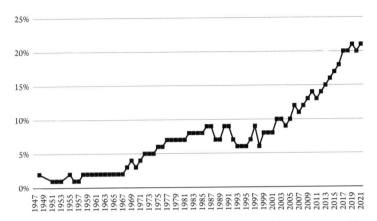

Figure 5.1. Proportion of US adults with "no religion" according to Gallup polls.

*Source: Gallup (1948–2020; no data for 1949, 1950, or 1954)**

All data taken from: Gallup, "Religion," available online: https://news.gallup.com/poll/ 1690/religion.aspx. The Gallup's question wording is: "What is your religious preference—are you Protestant, Roman Catholic, Mormon, Jewish, Muslim, another religion or no religion?"

Gallup's none needle began to move, fittingly for the first stirrings of a seismic cultural shift, in 1968. From 3% that year to 4% the next, the number of nones soon crept up to a new baseline of 6–9%. It didn't deviate from this narrow range between 1975 and 2001: a twenty-seven-year run. But then, over the last two decades, the rate of nones has more than doubled. Gallup's 2020 figure of 20% is moreover, as noted in Chapter 3, toward the lower end of serious polling organizations' estimates. The others, including our preferred GSS, date the start of the recent uptick several years earlier than do Gallup's figures. All suggest, however, that something significant happened sometime in the late nineties or early aughts. But *what*?

* * *

There's already several theories out there, in both scholarly books and journal articles and what academics like to look down on as more popular sources.[3] Rather than slavishly detail various theories already making the rounds, what I'd like to do here is present my own, considered take. This will be kind of a Grand Unified Theory of the rise of the nones, which builds on, modifies, and occasionally contradicts a number of competing explanations. Necessarily, my argument will touch and expand on many of the topics and themes appearing in other chapters; it would be worrying if it didn't. The individual stories told in this book tell us much: if you want to understand forests, you really do need to know your trees. But they don't tell us the whole story: there's a lot more to forestry than examining a succession of particular trees.

First off, let me state quite plainly that the *something* that happened was a real, consequential one. That is to say, the increase in American adults claiming no religious affiliation is no mere matter of appearances, leaving everything else untouched. Not everyone agrees about this. I mentioned in the Introduction the suggestion that the uptick in nones is mostly the result of purely nominal Christians now simply being more honest with pollsters (and themselves). Whereas in the past they'd tick "Methodist" or "generic Protestant" or whatever, now they just select "no religion." On this interpretation, the real religiousness of America hasn't changed at all—it's still doing just as peachily as ever, give or take—it's just being reported more accurately.[4] (A comparison sometimes drawn here is to, say, unemployment statistics: a different way of counting those out of work can dramatically change the figures up or down, but it makes no difference whatever to the actual health of the economy.)

Let's leave to one side the question of America's overall religiosity: Chapter 9 is its allotted time to shine. It is true enough that in the fifties, many of the most tenuously religious Americans would nevertheless have identified as some form of Christian. It is equally true that, today, a good chunk of their contemporary counterparts now identify as nones.[5] However, it does not at all follow that the only difference between then and now is an arbitrary switching of labels. The obvious question to ask is why, in the past, did much larger numbers of weakly believing and practicing folks still *feel* Christian enough to think of themselves in that way. One obvious possibility is that didn't really feel that way at all, they just felt pressured to say that they did for social reasons. Personally, I don't find that psychologically plausible: maybe some were "closet nones" in this sense, but I'm sure that the majority genuinely meant it. That is, they saw themselves *as* Methodists, Lutherans, Catholics, Presbyterians—even if, as they'd likely be the first to admit, not very "good" ones. And even *if* they were only pretending to be such to the nice man or lady from Gallup on the phone, then this obviously raises the bigger question as to why they felt they needed to, when today's nones clearly no longer do.

This is an important point, and one that goes right to the heart of what it means to think about "the making of ex-Christian *America*," over and above the individual "makings of ex-Christian *Americans*." Clearly, a world in which large numbers of people who neither believe nor practice Christianity nevertheless want to identify as Christians, and quite possibly see this as an important part of who they are, must be a very different world from one where roughly the same types of people certainly don't want to see themselves as religious at all. Perhaps in the former world, religion in general, and Christianity in particular, is held in high esteem: it is widely agreed to be a good thing, and its leaders and committed followers are regarded with respect and admiration. A high percentage of people you either want to be (high-prestige folks, from presidents and movie stars to the high school quarterback or cheer captain), or be with (one's peers: friends, family, co-workers, neighbors), or both, are actively supportive. More to the point, being religious/ Christian is, in all manner of explicit and implicit ways, bound up with the dominant shared understandings of "what's really impor- tant" to the other identities—family, ethnic group, country—one regards as being important to who *you* are.[6] Now, in such a world it is surely easy to see why large numbers of people might feel that, yes indeed, they too count as an "[insert socially acceptable brand of Christian here]." More to the point, they can point to plenty of justifications as to why this is really so: they were baptized as an X (and had their kids done, too) and were married in the local church, and they come from a long line of Xs, and they always give gener- ously at the Women's Auxiliary bake sale for the missions, and while they've not been to church for a *little* while there's just been so much going on what with one thing and another, and after all the "un- pleasantness" with the previous pastor . . . and besides, they're good, hardworking, patriotic citizens . . . which makes them a darned sight more "Christian" than some of those folks in the pews. . . .

The above is, of course, a fairly broad-brush caricature. But it ought to ring somewhat true. But now imagine a person with more or less the same theological views (i.e., not very many, and neither well nor often thought through), and more or less the same objec- tive connection to a church, as the one above. Suppose that he or she lives in a world where religion in general, and Christianity in partic- ular, is markedly less socially valued, is not widely practiced among one's own peers or the people one looks up to, and does not easily jive with the dominant morals and virtues of the other identities they take seriously—indeed, is often seen as being on "the wrong side" of whatever the cause-of-the-moment happens to be. In such a world, I suggest, they would be far less likely to see themselves as counting as a Christian. In fact, it's likely that even many who do identify as Christians are quick to offer some kind of qualification or disclaimer ("oh, but our church is super liberal"; "it's mainly just a family thing"; "well I guess I *am*, but I find myself really drawn to, like, Buddhism too . . .").

If I'm right about this, then it follows fairly straightforwardly that a rising level of nones in a population, even if it corresponds to little noticeable change in the individuals themselves (i.e., their religious views and practices, moral attitudes, political preferences, etc., remain unchanged), in fact signals something loud and clear about changes in the surrounding culture. The relevance of all this to thinking about the past half-century or so of American social, cultural, religious, and political history ought, I think, to be fairly plain. The trend is self-reinforcing: the more nones there are, the more acceptable it becomes to be a none, which breeds more of them. But consider this: the basic argument doesn't only apply historically. Imagine if a somewhat less starkly contrasting version of these two different "worlds" were separated not by sixty years but by a few thousand miles. The same person moving from the southern Bible Belt to the northwestern None Zone, or vice versa, might well find their religious affiliation "acclimatizing," probably unconsciously, to the prevailing religious weather, without any other obvious-to-pollsters differences occurring. In fact, given the fairly stable regionality of US religion, this, or something very like it, must happen a great deal.[7]

In the rest of this chapter, my basic argument will be a historical one, though regional differences will be important here too, since the same factors didn't necessarily affect everywhere equally or at the same time. In short, I'll try to explain why the proportion of nones in the USA has shot up, from a fairly negligible few percent of the population until well past the midway point of the twentieth century, up to the current level of around a quarter—and growing. While the full story is no doubt complex, I'll focus here on three or four of the biggest contributing *somethings*.

* * *

> *It is not generally known that there are Atheist Societies using the schools of the country as their battle-ground—attacking, through the Youth of the Nation, the beliefs that are sacred to most of the people.*
>
> *And no fanatics are so bitter as youthful fanatics.*

Though not quite as quotable as "A long time ago, in a galaxy far, far away," the above lines had a similar purpose. They come from the opening frames of Cecil B. DeMille's *The Godless Girl* (1928), the blockbuster director's final silent movie. DeMille, no stranger to a religious theme, was inspired by a spate of panicked press reports on student secular societies being formed—"Atheist Clubs Said to Be Active in State Schools," "Student Atheist Society Seen as Scopes Trial Echo," " 'Damned Souls' Society Is Formed at Rochester 'U' to Abolish Belief in God."[8]

The resulting movie is a strange mix of roistering slapstick caper, social commentary, romantic melodrama, and modern morality play. The plot centers on schoolgirl rebel Judy's attempt to found an atheist society, whose inductees are asked to "Swear that you don't believe on the Bible—the Church—or God!" with their hands placed solemnly on the head of "your cousin": that is, with a knowing nod to the then-recent Scopes Trial, a pet monkey.[9] Their inaugural meeting is, however, soon broken up by an equally zealous group of Christian students led by Bob, a suitably handsome, varsity-jerseyed young swain. Things take a much darker turn, however, when the ensuing riot results in the death of one of the atheists, plunging the opposing group leaders into a hellish reformatory on charges of manslaughter. Without wanting to ruin too much of an intricate plot, I'm not spoiling any great surprises in divulging that, out of this purgatory, Judy and Bob gradually, inevitably, come to find romantic common ground. Or that Judy, also equally inevitably, converts to Christianity. Although not a great commercial success in the United States, *The Godless Girl* was a smash hit in both Germany (with lead actress, Lina Basquette, receiving fan mail from an up-and-coming politician named Adolf) and, curiously enough, the Soviet Union. Surprised by this latter fact, DeMille discovered that the film had been shown in Russia without the final reel: "They simply played the picture as a document of American police brutality and the glorious spread of atheism among American youth."[10]

Such trickiness on the part of the Soviets would likely not have surprised a great many Americans, either then or for many decades later. Far more so than in other Western countries, the violent anti-religiousness of the 1918 Revolution was a leading theme in America's antipathy and anxiety. This has several deep-rooted causes, some no doubt leading back to Colonial times. More proximately, European travelers throughout the nineteenth and early twentieth centuries were struck by just how religious Americans were. The impressions of Germany's Weber have already been quoted in these pages. We might add here my own countryman Charles Dickens: "I am afraid to say, by the way, how many offers of pews and seats in church for that morning were made to us, by formal note of invitation, before we had half finished our first dinner in America . . . The number of creeds and forms of religion to which the pleasure of our company was requested, was in very fair proportion."[11] This religious enthusiasm had shown few signs of abating by the 1920s and 1930s. Note too that these years were the heyday of the mainline's ascendancy over the culture—before postwar cracks began appearing, and while "Catholic" and "Jew" had not yet elbowed their way beside "Protestant" in the civic pantheon.[12] It's not that there wasn't plenty else for Americans to decry in the Soviet experiment, but its very atheism was felt viscerally in the United States in a way it wasn't elsewhere.

This association of communism with atheism and nonreligiosity, and vice versa, reached its zenith after the Second World War. Senator Joseph McCarthy's momentous "Enemies from Within" speech, delivered in Wheeling, West Virginia, on February 9, 1950, was equal parts fruit and fertilizer of the zeitgeist in this regard. Though instantly famous for its charges of widespread governmental infiltration—or rather, "infestation" in McCarthy's own phraseology—we highlight here a different aspect of the speech.[13] McCarthy framed the stakes not, primarily, as the "US versus Russia," "communism versus capitalism," "liberty versus slavery," or "democracy versus dictatorship." Naturally, both he and the assembled ladies of the Republic Women's Club of Ohio County (the occasion being the "political boilerplate event" of their annual Lincoln Day memorial speech) thought it *was* all those things as well.[14] But the real, deeper opposition was nothing so prosaic. Rather, "Today we are engaged in a final, all-out battle between communistic atheism and Christianity.... Can there be anyone who fails to realize that the communist world has said, 'The time is now'—that this is the time for the showdown between the democratic Christian world and the communist atheistic world?" Even when discussing specific cases, McCarthy couched the subject in the language of spiritual warfare ("sold out the Christian world to the atheistic world"; "blasphemy was so great").

McCarthy's rhetoric was nothing terribly out of the ordinary; indeed, it was a fairly standard feature of stump-speech politicking at the time. In 1954, Democratic representative Louis C. Rabaut of Michigan duly informed Congress: "You may argue from dawn to dusk about differing political, economic, and social systems but the fundamental issue which is the unbridgeable gap between America and Communist Russia is a belief in almighty God."[15] Rabaut's remarks were made in debates urging the addition of "under God" to the Pledge of Allegiance. America's Catholics, of which Rabaut was one, had been campaigning for this measure for some years. Despite riding a wave of mainstream acceptability boosted in large measure by their church's unimpeachably anticommunist credentials—with the CIA going so far as to fund "Rosary Crusades" in Latin America, so simpatico were the missions of Church and State felt to be[16]—the initiative only gained sufficient traction when picked up by (who else?) mainliners, too. With President Eisenhower in the congregation of his downtown DC Presbyterian church in February 1954, the Reverend George Docherty seized his opportunity. Preaching that there was currently nothing in the Pledge that "little Muscovites" couldn't recite to "their hammer and sickle flag," he too urged that the Cold War was, above all else, a religious one: "It is Armageddon, a battle of the gods." And thus, "To omit the words 'under God' in the Pledge of Allegiance is to omit the definitive character of the American way of life."[17]

Notably, Docherty stresses that such a statement is not merely ecumenical, but avowedly interfaith: "one of the glories of this land is that it has opened its gates to all men of every religious faith." By contrast, "an American atheist is a contradiction in terms." While it's possible for such a person to be a good citizen and neighbor— "many have I known," he adds graciously—they are at root "spiritual parasites," living off the "accumulated spiritual capital of

Judeo-Christian civilization" such that their living out of "the ethics of this country" is an implicit affirmation of its status under the God whose ethics they are. Docherty's arguments evidently persuaded: within four months, the Pledge of Allegiance had two extra words. Two years later, Congress made "In God We Trust" the nation's official motto. Hopes in the next year, 1957, for a new constitutional amendment "to recognize specifically God Almighty and America's definite position as a great Christian nation"[18] were unsuccessful, however. Clearly Jews and Unitarians had better lobbyists than did the unbelievers.

But what does any of this have to do with the rise of those identifying as nonreligious some forty, fifty, or sixty years later? It's a good question, and has an important answer. The association of atheism with all things un-American was ceaselessly championed by Washington in the immediate postwar decades (i.e., those happy golden years before Americans had gotten quite so cynical about anything emanating from "The Swamp"). This was done most explicitly via the bipartisan House Un-American Activities Committee, which, even pre-McCarthy, was publishing 10-cent pamphlets such as *100 Things You Should Know about Communism and Religion* (e.g., "Here is the rule laid down by Lenin . . . 'Down with religion! Long live atheism! The spread of atheist views is our chief task!'").[19] The same views were echoed from press and pulpit. For those raised in this culture, such constant ingraining could have a long-lasting effect. When I asked Bernard, born in the mid-1940s, what he associated with the word "atheism," this gay atheist artist's kneejerk response went straight back to his fundamentalist Alabama upbringing:

> The church that I was brought up with always had to see themselves under attack, and some of my earliest memories were the

preacher preaching whole sermons about communism. And we were terrified because we viewed Russia as an atheist nation, and if Russia took us over then we would not be free to go to church and to worship. So that was my earliest thought, and it was a threat.

I have made the point several times, and will do so again, that identifying with "no religion" and being an atheist are not the same thing. Nevertheless, the two are, for understandable reasons, very frequently conflated. Besides, in a world where "being (Judeo-Christianly) religious" is so closely allied with ideas of Americanness, being "not religious," even if not an actual atheist, is no great point in one's social favor. This therefore meant that both being, *and being thought to be* (including by oneself!), a "none" was heavily stigmatized. There was no ban against it. There didn't need to be. Hence the near-negligible levels—1–2%—of nones throughout the late forties to the mid-sixties. Compare this to, say, Britain, which was very much more religious in this period than it is today. It was also one of the United States' most stalwart Cold War allies. (In fact, as I write this in my little Oxfordshire village, I'm just four miles from a decommissioned US Air Force base that housed nuclear weapons.) Still, the religious angle was never a feature of British Cold War rhetoric. Regular Gallup surveys from 1946 to 1963 here ranged between 4% and 11% with no religion[20]—still fairly low, especially by today's standards, but between two and six times the equivalent US figures. No doubt there were other reasons too, but I'm in no doubt that "godless communism," and all that was bound up with it, kept America's numbers lower than they might otherwise have been.

Let's not forget that the puzzle of "the rise of the nones" is, in large measure, a puzzle about why they never rose before. They did elsewhere, including in such obvious quasi-comparisons as Britain, Canada, or Australia.[21] But not in America—until, that is, they *did*. A large part of my argument here, therefore, is that the perceived un-Americanness of atheism directly, and hence of no-religion-ness by association, cast a long shadow. Nor was this due only to its connections, real and imagined, to communism.

Madalyn Murray O'Hair, founder of American Atheists and the public face of unbelief for many years, is a case in point here. Though she too had a communist past (she once tried to defect to the Soviet Union, but they refused her), this was never a big part of either her message or reception—mostly because she presented her critics with so much else to choose from. While Europe's famous unbelievers at this time tended to be men of letters (think Jean-Paul Sartre, Albert Camus, Bertrand Russell), America's was a divorced mother of two boys, both born out of wedlock and to different fathers. While such facts make her now sound like an underdog feminist hero—as to many she indeed is—at the time they helped make her a convenient shorthand for All That Is Wrong with Modern America. A 1963 feature written by the Associated Press' women's editor, and thus syndicated to local newspapers nationwide, thus carried the title, "What Kind of Woman is Madalyn— Militant Atheist Divorcee?" A 1964 *Los Angeles Times* article bore the headline "Blond Divorcee Sparks U.S. Movement."[22] I could cite no shortage of similar examples. She was best-known, and most hated, for a series of legal challenges. Some were successful (against school prayer in 1960), some weren't (against Apollo 8's astronauts, as government employees on the taxpayer's dime, reading Genesis 1).[23] All gained her a huge amount of publicity, little of it laudatory.

Nevertheless, she persisted, proudly dubbing herself "The Most Hated Woman in America"—a phrase which, especially when quoted as the title of a 1964 *LIFE* magazine profile, stuck.[24] (It later furnished the title for an excellent 2017 Netflix biopic.) O'Hair succeeded in nudging the public discourse about nonreligiosity. For one thing, she made it possible for the terms "atheist" and "nonreligious" to appear in print *without* being accompanied by "communist" or "Soviet." And soon, simply being an outspoken woman campaigner, or indeed a divorcee, was no longer seen as being so newsworthy or so negative. For many growing up in the sixties, media reports on O'Hair were likely the first time they came across the *idea* of not being religious, and proudly so, as a real thing that their fellow Americans did. (This was certainly true for Charles, our former zoo-keeper from the previous chapter: "In childhood there was a lot of social stigma with the words 'atheism' and 'atheist.'" I remember a woman who was head of the atheist group in the US, she was in *LIFE* magazine, and there was a big statement, 'I do not believe in God.' And I was kind of intrigued by this . . .") Unlike DeMille's original, however, this real-life *Godless Girl* reboot has no happy ending. Her eldest son became an evangelical, publicly repudiating her life and mission, in the early 1980s.[25] In 1995 O'Hair, along with her younger son and granddaughter, were kidnapped and murdered by a former American Atheists employee, who emptied hundreds of thousands of dollars from the organization's funds.

* * *

By the early 1960s, cracks were already beginning to show in "Christian America." For all the evidence of "a religious revival in America," pollsters were already warning in 1957 that "this spiritual renaissance has encountered a major roadblock in reaching the gen-eration now approaching adulthood." Or, as the headline writers put it: "Teen-agers Flunk Religion." In 1965, George Gallup him-self added to this doomsaying, pointing to declining rates of church attendance and the widespread view among college students that religion was losing its influence over American society, especially their own segment of it.[26] And the sixties most assuredly wreaked havoc on a good deal of established American religion, as we saw in the last chapter.

Elsewhere in the Western world, similar confluences of factors led to a significant mainstreaming of "no religion" from the 1960s onward.[27] For example, in Britain, by the start of the 1980s, between a quarter and a third of the adult population were describing themselves as such. America was not, as we have seen, wholly immune to these forces: hence the modest rise of the nones from 2% in the mid-60s up to the new normal of 8% or so from the mid-70s, though the bulk of this growth was probably focused in particular subcultural enclaves (liberal college towns, say). In most of the rest of the country, however, the normativity of being religious—and Protestantly so, by default—remained in force. Studies of the nones throughout this period tended to find that they were disproportionately middle-class, well educated, and affluent: precisely, that is, those people most likely to have the self-confidence, material security, and intellectual prepossession to swim against the cultural tide.

Thinking of oneself as a none, still less an atheist, was simply not a "live option" for most Americans in these years. It's not (as some scholars' imaginings seem to suppose) that their pen hovered over the "no religion" box on survey forms, but then they thought to themselves, "No ... I must keep on pretending; what if the neighbors were to find out?" before ticking Methodist or Baptist. It's that even if they were "unchurched"—a term which, having declined in usage throughout the fifties and sixties, suddenly shot up in popularity from the early seventies—and weren't sure what, if anything much, they still really believed from their Sunday school days, they still felt that they were Christians in some meaningful sense, even if only vicariously through being (good) Americans.[28]

If I'm right, then the psychological impossibility of being nonreligious for most people sheds interesting light on two more obvious trends in American religion during these years. The first is the rather colorful period of experimentation with different ways of being religious that sprang up in the sixties and seventies. This is most strongly associated with the cults and communes of the West Coast counterculture, though of course it went much wider than that, from New Age UFO groups to Native American vision questers, right down to Reiki and reflexology. Whatever its other causes, it certainly suggests a notable liberalization of the American religious market, and evidence of plenty of people dissatisfied with their "current provider" (even if, as many dabbling in various New Age practices certainly did and do, they still identified with it).[29] And indeed, it's striking how many of today's older nones arrived at where they are now only after an extended period of switching and seeking. One often gets the impression that, if having no religion had been more of "a thing" in their formative years, it might have spared them a lot of time, effort, and—since healing crystals and dreamcatchers don't always come cheap—expense in trying to find one they actually felt at home in. Today's young people dissatisfied with their (parents') church feel far freer to give up on religion altogether, rather than to go looking for a new one.

The second is the extent to which the churches themselves ended up adapting, with quite varying degrees of success, to a population that was less interested in going to church and yet still felt that maybe they *ought* to. It is surely remarkable how swiftly, in the sixties, seventies, and eighties, so many American churches started pretending that they were not churches after all. What I mean by that is the playing down of denominational "brands," worshiping in buildings that no longer looked like churches, rewriting prayers or liturgies to sound more like normal speech, replacing traditional church music with facsimiles of popular music, eschewing marble altars in favor of wooden tables, replacing ornate artworks with abstract shapes and primary colors, and modernizing furnishings, vestments, and other typically "churchy" markers. Some churches, especially those already less wedded to a "churchy" liturgical style, pulled this trick off in some style: the new megachurches, specifically designed to appeal to the growing ranks of the unchurched, largely succeeded in creating worship centers that neither looked, sounded, smelled, nor felt like "churches" but which nevertheless served up a robust dose of evangelical faith and practice. Most of the others, however, failed in this strategy of "dechurchification" while managing to turn off a good proportion of other people who *wanted* a church. Meanwhile, the proportion of people who still felt that they were Methodists or Presbyterians or Catholics, and would deign to visit "their" church every so often to get married or have their kids baptized, but had little interest in turning up at services not specifically dedicated to them or their family, continued to grow. Their own children, of course, would ultimately come no longer to have family, ethnic, or cultural attachments to church enough to feel even this weak sense of connection. Furthermore, by the time *they* came to tick boxes on surveys, the stigmas surrounding "no religion," which their boomer parents imbibed in childhood, had greatly weakened anyway. But for now—with "now" in this case being sometime in the seventies or eighties, as the boomers began settling down (typically further away from their more-religious parents than their parents had been from their own even-more-religious parents)—the rate of nones would just have to remain at a stubborn 6–9% for a decade or two longer.

* * *

As we saw in Chapter 3, by far the biggest bloc of America's nones
is made up of so-called millennials, those born between the years
1981 and 1996. There are three important things to note about
this group. First, as just noted, a sizable chunk of them have to look
back to their grandparents or beyond to find regularly practicing
Christians in their family tree. That is to say, their own parents,
while regarding themselves as Christians and going so far as to get
their children "brought up in it" to a certain extent, are likely not
faithful Sunday churchgoers. Many of these millennials, therefore,
don't have all *that* much of a Christian identity to lose in the first
place (although naturally this differs greatly from place to place, or
tradition to tradition).

Second, they have been raised in a cultural world where
the "right" stance on so many of the post-60s "culture war"
battlegrounds—women's equality, divorce, gay rights, abortion—
is, largely, taken for granted. And even if they aren't in their own
families or communities, they certainly *are* in—to channel Fox
News for a moment—the "liberal mainstream media": the TV
sitcoms, movies, and pop stars' Instagram posts punctuated with
hand-clap emojis they've grown up with. There's an impressive
body of sociological literature arguing that the rise of the nones is in
no small measure a reaction against the Religious Right: "Organized
religion gained influence by espousing a conservative social agenda
that led liberals and young people who already had weak attachment to organized religion to drop that identification."[30] On this
reading, conservative evangelicals and Catholics, and their political allies, succeeded in hitching Christianity in the popular mind
to narrow-mindedly reactionary right-wingery: millennials, seeing
through this cheap ploy, want nothing to do with it, and have hence

been put off religion forevermore. There's much truth to this line of reasoning—nones do indeed disproportionately hold the kinds of socially liberal values (although not, as noted earlier, uniformly) at odds with "traditional family values" politicking. But personally I think it's an unhelpfully ideological spinning of what has actually happened.

The standard narrative here depicts the *churches* as taking a conservative turn: abandoning the sane center ground in doomed pursuit of a morally conservative agenda. But of course, it was not so much that the churches lurched rightward on these issues as that significant sections of the wider culture have moved ever further away from the kinds of moral positions, not least on marriage and family issues, that it used to hold *in common with* the evangelicals, Catholics, and Mormons. In this view, the Religious Right is not saying all that much different from what, the day before yesterday, the religious center was saying about gay rights, divorce, sex education, and abortion. It just seems that way because the ones doing the judging have shifted so far to the left. Of course, once this process started, then it has taken on a zero-sum logic all of its own—with *both sides* becoming ever more polarized.[31] My point here is not to argue with the basic outcome of all this: I'm in complete agreement that there's a gaping "values gap" between many young adults and the views typically espoused by Catholic, evangelical, and LDS leaders, and that this is indeed a large contributory factor to the relative attractiveness of "no religion" for these people. But culture wars require two antagonists, not just one. It's not so much that these religious groups suddenly embraced a conservative agenda as that they were the only ones left holding it. It also doesn't follow, as is often also implied here, that had they only kept up with the wider culture on these issues, then the nones would never have risen. This is an idea one often hears, and to be fair, it has an intuitive plausibility.

Irrespective of doctrinal scruples, doesn't it make pastoral, evangelistic sense for churches to move (or "develop") with the times on moral questions? At the risk of seeming glib, I have only one response to this: *Remember the Mainline!*

Third, note that millennials and, even more so, Gen Z-ers (born 1997–) were brought up wholly or partly *after* the Cold War had ended, and thus a good generation or more after the peak of paranoia about "godless communism." Suspicion and prejudice toward atheists and the nonreligious still exist, as an entire cottage industry of sociological scholarship has now documented in detail and as many of my own interviewees are quick to stress (especially those from or living in the South).[32] But it's markedly less evident among these younger generations, even those living in the more religious areas. Evidently, talk of "a final, all-out battle between communistic atheism and Christianity" was much less a part of the cultural background for those brought up in the eighties onward than it had been for previous generations. Indeed, even for kids raised on such mid-eighties staples as *Red Dawn* and *Rocky IV*, the USSR was surely already less anxiety-inducing than it had been for those regularly drilled to duck and cover, even before what Reagan dubbed "the Evil Empire" collapsed so swiftly and spectacularly in the late eighties and early nineties.

More than this, very soon the most pressing geopolitical threat to baseball, Mom, and apple pie was not from those without religion but those with rather too much of the wrong kind of it. Religious extremism, in the form of radical Islamic terrorists, usurped the place in American nightmares that communist infiltrators used to occupy—and posed a clearer and more present danger to the domestic United States than their predecessors had, even if Al Qaeda never posed quite the existential threat to the nation that the Soviet Union did. It is no coincidence that the atrocities of 9/11 opened up the possibility for a full-throated presentation of Atheism-with-a-capital-A to gain a hearing (and vast book sales) in the early 2000s. Indeed, a brand of what one might call *patriotic atheism* was an explicit part of the New Atheism's pitch. Sam Harris, whose bestselling *The End of Faith* (2004) was the first blossom of this atheist spring, makes much in that book of how he started writing it on September 12. Richard Dawkins, promoting his multimillion-selling *The God Delusion* (2006), was not shy in pointing out that he had wanted the accompanying TV series to be advertised with an image of the New York skyline with a prominently intact Twin Towers, and the tagline "Imagine no religion . . ." Meanwhile the late Christopher Hitchens was welcomed onto CNN's *Lou Dobbs Tonight* on the evening of the 2006 National Day of Prayer (another anticommunist initiative, established in 1952), and had his recent US citizenship marked by the gift of a stars-and-stripes lapel badge:

> [W]hat if I had told you a year ago that one of America's favorite mainstream middle-class broadcasters, obviously relishing the coincidence of the National Day of Prayer, would give a slice of prime time on a major network to an author who is not only an atheist but an antitheist? And would round it off (having displayed one of my less reverent paragraphs on the screen) by deliberately associating atheism with patriotism? Most secularists of my acquaintance would have said it couldn't happen.[33]

Suddenly, an all-American atheism no longer seemed the obvious contradiction in terms (to use George Docherty's words) it once had to mainstream, middle-class America. And as the nation's atheists came increasingly to emerge from the closet—something that Madalyn Murray O'Hair had been explicitly urging them, to little avail, to do for years,[34] plain "no religion" had become all the more socially palatable. The reason for this is quite neat. America's newly emboldened activist atheist community pre-dated the New Atheism and helped push it to prominence,[35] while symbiotically gaining new vigor and cultural clout from it. Its no-holds-barred rhetoric, however, was far better at "energizing the base" than it was at winning hearts and minds among the public at large. A great many nones or near-nones, and indeed a good chunk of self-identifying atheists themselves, are thus quick to distance themselves from *those atheists*. Recall Mormon-to-cultist-to-atheist Brandon's comment, quoted at the start of Chapter 2, that he "doesn't like atheism." Later on, treating me to a fuller version of what he terms his "atheist rant," he specifically cited "a lot of arrogance and annoying aspects of Dawkins and Harris," and his particular hatred of outspokenly "ex-religious people"—"You can, like, smell them almost," he added, laughing. Cal, raised Lutheran but now a spiritual "probable agnostic," is also keen to distance himself.

> I don't know what the deal is with atheists. I mean, like online, those kinda troll people. I've had problems with those people. They kinda act fanatical, basically. Fanatically oppositional. I don't like extremists. I've hopped in conversations, you know, online, where they're just mean.

The existence of "extremist" atheists—not all of them; Cal admits to having an atheist friend who isn't like these online trolls—is used here to justify what he sees as his own more moderate, open-minded nonreligious view. This is a rhetorical tactic routinely used even by self-avowed atheists. A Google search for "I'm an atheist, but . . ." turns up all manner of book titles, blog posts, and *Washington Post* op-eds finishing the sentence with such things as "I had to walk away from the toxic side of online atheism," or "thank God I'm not a New Atheist." A 2015 *BuzzFeed* video, featuring a series of relatably millennial talking heads doing similar, accrued 1.7 million YouTube views, and almost fifty thousand Facebook "likes."[36] The phrase is used both to challenge prevailing stereotypes and to contrast the speaker's implicit reasonableness with *those other atheists*. Christians often do the same thing, of course ("I'm a Catholic, but . . . I'm pro-choice"; "I'm a Bible-believing Christian, but . . . I believe in evolution"), and for similar reasons. Think of it as being a little like a social version of how, say, advertisements differentiate their product from other leading brands ("Nine out of ten dogs pick BonzoBites over FidoFeed!"). Essentially, the growing willingness of American atheists to come out and speak up has opened up a bigger space behind them for "no religion" to establish itself as a more socially palatable, mainstream option. As we have seen, this is something that atheists themselves use to their advantage, too: "not religious" goes down much better in mixed company, or with one's churchgoing relatives, than "the A word."

This "atheist outrider" thesis for the opening up of "none" as a live identity option in the late nineties and early noughties builds upon two other factors we have highlighted in this chapter: the diminishing power of Cold War conditioning, and the generational weakening of religious attachment, both of which came to fruition with the millennial generation (and even more so with their Generation Z successors). These alone would satisfactorily account for *some* rise in the numbers of nones; one of similar magnitude, maybe, to the moderate uptick seen after the sixties. But for the kinds of figures we're now looking at—a quarter of all American adults, a third of those under thirty—requires something else, something big, in the explanatory mix. And frankly, there's only one serious contender.

* * *

"We're the generation where the internet came around while we were in elementary, or middle, or high school kind of thing. So the advent of the internet, for me, was early high school: between '96 and '98." Christy, sitting in a near-empty New Orleans roadhouse, tries to make me feel old. In among all the "pornography and trash like that," there were people out there who seemed to understand things that Christy, beset with doubt, shame, and confusion, was only dimly becoming aware of. Reaching out to one of them, asking questions, "I got at the time what I felt was a really harsh reply that, you know, 'Don't talk to me. You can't talk to me. You can't ask me about these things. Go talk to your parents.' And, in retrospect, you see that, you know, they're only like answering in the best way they can which is that 'I can't play a therapist for you. You have to go actually talk to people about it.'"

As it so happens, Christy's nascent online awakening wasn't about religion, or at least not yet. It was about being transgender. I highlight it here, though, since it parallels so many of the accounts I heard about be(com)ing nonreligious, including several of the ex-Mormon testimonies already quoted, the one difference being, of course, that there were plenty of people *only too willing* to encourage others in exploring their religious doubts.

One of the most striking features of the internet, especially following the explosion of the first generation of "social media"— ListServs, forums, chatrooms, MySpace, and GeoCities fansites for those coming of digital age in the late nineties; Facebook, Twitter, TikTok, Parler, Instagram, and all manner of other household names now—is the endless possibilities it throws up to find a "tribe," no matter how esoteric one's interests are.[37] Normally described in terms of "echo chambers" or "filter bubbles," where they are used to explain (perceived) pathologies in the body politic, these digital dynamics are built upon standard features of social psychology. Simply put: beliefs, attitudes, identities, worldviews of all kinds are easier to acquire and maintain when they're shared.

Suppose that you're a grown man who's caught a few episodes of the children's TV show *My Little Pony*, and rather enjoyed them. Now, that's probably not the kind of thing that you bring up at the auto plant water cooler the next day. As such, beyond watching the odd episode with your daughters, it's unlikely ever to become a big part of your life. You could even spend your life living down the block from another grown-up man who enjoys the show, but the likelihood of your ever discovering this shared interest is basically nil. Unlike your little girls, you're not exactly going to find fellow Rainbow Dash fans by wearing T-shirts advertising the fact.[38]

Now suppose that, suddenly, you acquire this newfangled thing called the internet. And sitting idly one day, you ask Jeeves (remember him?) about adult MLP fans. Then *WOW*: not only do you realize that you're not alone, but you discover there's a whole grown-up world of commentary, history, exegesis, collectibles, and fan fiction out there. Obviously, these guys are a bit much (and a few of them . . . well, let's just say you soon learn from traumatizing experience what the letters "nsfw" stand for). But there's no harm in just checking in every so often, and maybe some time you could float that theory you have about how the economy of Equestria wouldn't work. Needless to say, the next thing you know, some of your best friends are fellow "Bronies" (including the guy down the block), you're an integral part of the community, and you're thinking up cosplay ideas for next year's convention.[39]

I've never been a Brony myself, despite what my students insinuate whenever I wheel out the above extended analogy. But I have been part of similar tribes at different times, and well know the power of them for sustaining several of my even-nicher-than-being-a-Brony interests. These range from various music fandoms in my teens (my first email address was the long-defunct "steve@chrisgaines.zzn.com"—representing an even more *outré* subculture in the UK than it was in the US) to, in paunchy middle-age, a support group for parents of kids with a rare medical condition. Writing over two decades ago, Robert Putnam prophesied that "social networks based on computer-mediated communication . . . organized by shared interests rather than by shared space" could become a significant countertrend to his decline-of-social-capital thesis, as famously typified by the trend of Americans bowling alone, rather than in organized leagues:

> Thousands of far-flung, functionally defined networks [have] sprung up, linking like-minded people as disparate as BMW fanciers, bird-watchers, and white supremacists. [Some theorists] have speculated about millions of "virtual neighborhoods" based on shared avocations rather than shared space. Certainly cyberspace already hosts thousands of hobby and special interest groups, and if participation in such groups becomes widespread and durable, then perhaps the prediction may be right.[40]

Now rather than an adult fan of pastel-hued equines, suppose instead that you are a small-town teen with religious doubts and dissatisfactions. Everyone you know, in your family, at school, and at the suite of church youth programs you're involved with, is some kind of believing Christian. Maybe there *are* others you know who feel like you do. But how would you know? Sure, those weird Goth kids at school talk the talk about Marilyn Manson and Cradle of Filth—but aren't they, like, *Satanists* or something? And besides, those kids are just posers; your mom knows their moms, and you know for a fact that they dress up nice for church and when Grandma comes to visit. In any case, it's not like you've worked out what you believe, or don't—there's just a lot of things you're not quite sure about. The apologetics books your youth pastor recommended (you told him you had a cousin who's stopped going to church, and you wanted to bring them back) didn't help; in some ways, they made things worse. But it's not like there's anyone you can talk to about it. And that one time you raised the subject with your dad, he shut you down pretty quick.

I suspect the above scenario will feel fairly plausible to a good few nonverts of a certain vintage, raised throughout vast swathes of America. Think of it as a less extreme, mass-market analogue of the experiences of those raised in the Mormon-majority towns of Idaho and Utah. For them, the advent of the internet was "the game-changer, right? Because before, where would you go to find that? It was never out there, it was never publicly really available." Mark, our now "ethnically Mormon" New York dentist, tells me over pizza how a close relative who had moved out of state, sensing in him a kindred spirit, started emailing links to all manner of LDS history websites. Pretty soon he discovered whole online communities of peers, raised just like he had been, who were now mutually encouraging each other in their nascent post-Mormon identities. Remember too how, for Keira Knightley fan Elizabeth, her own stereotypical Mormon wife life "easily unraveled," and so swiftly, "due to the wonderful thing called the internet." But this was by no means only an LDS phenomenon. The internet brought unabashedly nonreligious texts, ideas, and—most importantly—acquaintances and friends into millions of Christian homes. Some people, naturally, went looking for this stuff: precisely the kinds of teens, as sketched earlier, with prior reasons to go in search. And, thanks to there already being a vibrant atheist activist presence online since well *before* AOL brought dial-up internet to the mainstream, there was no shortage of websites, message boards, and new friends out there to be found.[41] For many others, however, it's likely that "something they saw on the internet"—something, that is, they *wouldn't* have seen had it not been for the internet—ended up sparking, or otherwise contributing to, a gradual path of nonversion. Rhett, whom we'll meet properly very soon, has this tongue-in-cheek advice for the kinds of Texan evangelical churches he and his wife grew up in: "don't let people access the internet."

> If I was in Texas in the nineties and I sought out an atheist in real life, I would be very much a pariah. People would *know* and I would have no social group left. However, I'm starting to get on the internet a little bit more and starting to read some things and seeing some alternative views . . .

* * *

Naturally, the kinds of online social dynamics we're dealing with *can* work both ways. If it's possible to find one's tribe via Usenet's "alt. atheism," Reddit's "r/exmormon," or Twitter's "#EmptyThePews," one can equally do so via one of the internet's endless variety of pro-religious websites, groups, and YouTube channels. But here's the thing. Prior to the internet, while Americans had a limitless supply of the latter's offline equivalents, the vast majority of them had almost none of the former's. Sure, they existed alright— campus secular alliances, humanist chapters in major cities—but just think how many more, and better funded, religious competitors there were. So the growth of home internet suddenly brought new nonreligious possibilities where there had been few or none before. Remember, too, that this most affected a generation with markedly less resistance to the idea of nonreligion than their Cold Warrior parents and grandparents had.

The impact of the internet is not, we might add, *only* evident in those who ended up falling in with the none crowd. There are vastly more nonreligious millennials and Generation Zs than could possibly have been deeply involved in one or other of these groups, no matter how prevalent they are. Obviously then, they weren't all nonverted in this way. However, there are reasons for thinking that the internet, and social media especially, might be having a subtler but much more widespread secularizing effect on American society. For all the attention given to online "echo chambers" deepening participants' commitment to a shared view and collectively pushing them to ever great extremes, I suspect for most users social media has a net relativizing effect. In general, worldviews are strongest when they present themselves as "givens" and can thus be taken for granted.[42] It's easier to be an evangelical if everyone you know, or at least everyone whose opinions you care about, are evangelicals, too.[43] But a person's Facebook or Twitter feed likely includes many "friends," or people one chooses to follow, with a whole range of positions on all manner of topics. It's possible to police one's network very carefully to prevent this from happening, but I'm not sure very many people are sufficiently committed to ideological purity to bother. In the past, our social circles were much smaller (though likely deeper), and focused largely on where we lived and worked, plus a very select few people we actively kept in touch with at further distances. These were chiefly relatives, though perhaps with a couple of old school friends or college roommates in the mix too. Now it's common to be aware, on a daily basis, of the doings and thinkings of a diverse collection of far-flung relatives, people you barely spoke to even when you were in the same room at school together, colleagues you met once at a conference, and all manner of others, many of whom you've never met once in person. You probably know a good deal more about what's going on in the lives of many of them than you do about your own next-door neighbors or co-workers (unless they're *also* Facebook friends).

Given how much more willing people are to talk about religion and politics online than they are in person, you're therefore probably exposed to all manner of different viewpoints. Sometimes, maybe one of these makes you think differently about a political policy or religious doctrine—or even if not, it makes you a little less sure about it than you used to be. Given the sheer amount of time many people tend to spend on social media platforms, it's not hard to imagine that the cumulative effect of all this might well be to chip away at lots of hitherto unexamined convictions. And that this, combined with some of the other factors we've been exploring in this chapter, might help nudge a good number further along the path away from religion—and to shove a few of them down one or another shortcut to Advance Directly to Go(dlessness). While there's much more research to be done on this topic, the early evidence is certainly suggestive. Paul McClure's rigorous examination of survey data on internet usage and religiosity found that "Internet use is associated with increases in being religiously unaffiliated and decreases in religious exclusivism." He further writes that, holding other relevant variables statistically constant, "the more time one spends on the Internet, the greater the odds are that an individual can be predicted to be religiously unaffiliated." McClure's work supports earlier research using GSS data, also showing that "Internet use is associated with decreased probability of religious affiliation" and speculating that this factor alone "In the 2020 U.S. population . . . could account for 5.1 million people with no religious affiliation."[44]

* * *

This chapter has covered an immense amount of cultural ground in a relatively short space. So let's briefly recap. The basic puzzle to be solved is why, at some point around the late nineties or early aughts, the proportion of American adults identifying as nones suddenly started to rise, having remained steady for two or three decades. That in itself, however, raises a prior puzzle; at least it does to someone who, like me, is looking at the situation from the outside. This puzzle essentially flips the first one on its head: why hadn't the numbers of American nones already risen *before* the late nineties? Even accounting for the higher religious temperature in the United States compared to, say, Canada or Britain, its levels of nones were still remarkably low in the forties and fifties. Furthermore, even the "perfect storm" of factors coalescing in the sixties, despite having all manner of other disruptive and destabilizing effects on American culture, society, politics, and religion, only nudged the numbers of nones up to a slightly higher decades-long plateau.

Seeing the rise of the nones as comprising two puzzles, and not just one, has been the guiding theme of this chapter-long solution. Yes, new somethings happened in the final years of the twentieth century and the first years of the twenty-first: and these helped drive the uptick of nones. But these happened at the same time as the long-lasting, none-depressant effects of a much earlier *something* had more or less worn off, especially among the emerging generations most affected by the new somethings. It is this combination of factors—akin to pulling one foot off the brake as you slam the other down on the accelerator—that explains quite why the nones rose so suddenly and (seemingly) out of nowhere.

In short, the argument is this:

1. Cold War oppositions between "godless communism" and "Christian America" engendered a Pavlovian association

between being un-religious and being un-American. While atheism bore the brunt of this, it more generally ruled out associated ideas and identities—including thinking of oneself as having "no religion"—as live options for the great majority of Americans.

2. This meant that even though, as in other countries, much of mainstream American Christianity—especially the Mainline, but also Catholicism—emerged from the sixties and seventies rather battered and bruised, Americans were odds-on to keep thinking of themselves as some kind of Christians even if they no longer believed in classic Christian doctrines or moral teachings (something that various "progressive" streams within American Christianity were happy to encourage them in), or else to consciously seek out—and be sought out by—religious or spiritual options that either *weren't* churches (New Age, Eastern religions), or those that *were*, but were doing their damnedest not to look or feel like it.

3. Meanwhile, the cultural fault lines that begin obviously opening up in the late sixties—gender equality, sexual liberation—kept on widening, with new generations socialized into ever more liberal baselines. This created a growing values gap between traditional Christian views and the wider mainstream culture, on topics that were very personal to, and thus felt very deeply by, people on all sides. This meant that, while churches tended to be most visible on the "conservative side" of various battlegrounds, they were also often deeply riven by internal versions of the same debates. This further weakened many churches' attractiveness to any one side of the debate: religious progressives denounced their own traditions as bigoted and outdated, religious conservatives spent their time decrying how those same churches were now

infiltrated by woke liberals who had sold out their Christ-mandated birthright.

4. The Cold War thawed, and secular Soviets were replaced by religious extremists in America's anxieties. While old prejudices die hard, Americans brought up in the eighties and after were exposed to vastly lower doses of anti-atheist antipathy (and thus suspicion toward nonreligiosity in general).

5. While these various factors would, presumably, have resulted in gradual increases in people regarding themselves as nonreligious anyway, a communications revolution hit in the mid- to late nineties. This acted as an accelerant for all sorts of social identities, suddenly bringing together all manner of people who had hitherto "thought they were the only one" into new, supportive, and mutually encouraging groups. That was as true for gender-questioning Louisiana high schoolers as it was for Britain's Garth Brooks alter-ego aficionados. It empowered autistic people to celebrate their and others' neurodiversity.[45] And—I would guess—introduced foot fetishists to a whole new world of fellow toe bros. It also, of critical importance here, created spaces for those from close-knit religious subcultures to share information, perspectives, horror stories, and in-jokes. Add to that the overall relativizing effect, identified by researchers, of social media usage and its knock-on effects for disaffiliation.

6. Finally, once the rate of nones did start rising and began attracting notice in the press, the ensuing headlines further helped to advertise being a "none." Not only was being nonreligious a thing that lots of people already were, it was *growing*, signaling to others that it's worth their while to join in too. Note that this doesn't only affect those in the younger generations, even if they were the early adopters. Lots of older

Americans, who had been unthinkingly ticking the "Catholic" or "Presbyterian" box for decades, were suddenly introduced to a new religious-identity brand on the market, allowing them psychologically to shed the one they'd inherited from their parents and been dissatisfied with for so long.

And so there we have it. That's the bigger picture, at least as it seems to me, shaping the individual stories at the heart of this book. If this book were a sitcom, then this chapter would likely be titled "How the Gang Got Together" and feature the main characters sporting comically retro clothing and hairstyles. Mercifully, it isn't.

With that out of the way, it's high time we talked about proselytizing puppets, beefcakes shredding phonebooks for Jesus, and some interesting uses for funeral caskets.

Exvangelicals

"Oh my God, you don't know what the Power Team is?"

I'm stumped. "Power . . . *Rangers*?" I venture, lamely.

"Dude, you need to look up the Power Team."

For someone who prides himself on his knowledge of obscure Americana—I once got into a Facebook fight over Cawker City, Kansas, and Darwin, Minnesota's competing claims to have the World's Largest Ball of Twine[1]—I take this as a personal failing. I hang my head, defeated.

"So, imagine a world where you can't watch wrestling, but there is a wrestling shaped hole in your heart. Then *these dudes* come along, and they break stacks of cement blocks . . . FOR JAYYYSUS."

"They get filled with the Spirit. Boom!"

"I think I got saved at a Power Team show like three times . . ."

"Because if you got saved, you got to meet them."

"They could tear a phone book in half. They could bend a crowbar with their arms . . ."

"Oh my God, I had completely forgotten! I had a yellow Power Team T-shirt that I was so proud of. Oh. My. God. I thought I was pretty hot stuff."

"I'm still not as cool, and never will be as cool, as they were."

Melissa glances over at her husband of over a decade, then shakes her head ruefully. "Until you can rip a phone book in half, I don't even want to talk to you again."

Now in their late thirties, she and Rhett are making the most of a rare night away from the kids, reminiscing about the pop culture of their youth while someone else buys the drinks. And there's plenty to reminisce about. Rhett was brought up in a small town north of Austin; the more urbane Melissa, in an outer suburb of Houston. After both attending colleges in Texas, they met in one of the state's major cities. She had a job at the same church where he was volunteering as what he now describes as a "failed Bible study leader . . . ironically, my small group is all atheist now. So, I was the best fucking leader ever."

On the face of it, their religious upbringings might seem rather different. In Rhett's town, religious diversity meant you could be any kind of Baptist, so long as it's Southern. Melissa's family started out Methodist, but they later joined a nondenominational Pentecostal church: "dancing, speaking in tongues, raising hands—no snakes." Melissa recalls this switch, when she was about seven years old, as marking "a really stark change":

> I had this life as a kid where I had Michael Jackson posters up on my wall and I had Michael Jackson albums—just your normal kid living in pop eighties world. And all of a sudden, I had to get rid of all of it. I had to get rid of my Darth Vader play figurine because he represented evil. And I remember the first Christmas after all of that, we had to throw away all of our Christmas decorations. I was devastated; it was just really harsh. We couldn't put anything on the Christmas tree except for these

home-made paper ornaments that had Bible verses written inside them, and these "Jesus is the reason for the season" stickers
on the front.

Denominational differences aside, their religious upbringings
were very similar. Both attended church multiple times a week:
Sundays (twice) and Wednesdays were "kind of a thing," with
Monday and Thursday Bible studies and youth groups later on top.
Both were pulled out of public school before third grade, because
"that's when they start teaching you evolution, and *evil*-ution is not
something my parents want me to learn—because, well, it's evil,
it's in the name." Rhett adds, "Home-schooling, when we started,
wasn't as cool as it is for kids today. They have legitimate, actual
teachers home-schooling them, people with actual teaching degrees
in co-ops. But we really just had: if mom didn't know it, then it didn't
matter." Furthermore, both possess a vast shared store of pop culture shibboleths, trivia, and in-jokes, all emanating *not* from mainstream 80s/90s America, but from the separate-but-parallel world
of American evangelicalism. These United States of Evangelica
came replete with their own-brand, Christian versions not only of
WWF wrestling, but of rap, rock, and pop music, kids' cartoons
and drive-time radio, self-help gurus, bestselling novels, and much
else besides. Not even cutesy kitsch escaped this treatment: Melissa
goes into a reverie recalling the much-loved *Precious Moments* Bible
she received to mark her getting "saved."[2]

Pinning down precisely what, or who, *counts* as an evangelical
is no straightforward task.[3] For our purposes, I'm comfortable in
framing it more broadly than a matter of affirming a discrete set of
doctrines, or being an in-good-standing member of a specific ecclesiastical lineage. I say this for two main reasons. The first is that
evangelicalism is manifestly a trans-denominational phenomenon,

exhibiting a significant degree of internal diversity, and lacks sharply defined boundaries. Of course, there are classic examples, which serve to define the genre: the megachurches which began springing up in the seventies and eighties, capturing a significant segment of the Protestant churchgoing market, being the most obvious.[4] But *megachurch* is primarily an indicator of size: there's a vast ecosystem of smaller, equally-as-evangelical churches offering much or all of the same "ethos and aesthetic."[5] In my time, I've attended unimpeachably evangelical services at a sprawling, manicured campus in the Houston suburbs, the function room of a Nashville motel, and the front room of a Kansas farmhouse: all left me filled with free coffee, baked goods, and a heady dose of Jesus. A number of mainline denominations are copying a winning formula by adopting evangelical-esque music, preaching, and/or branding.[6] The same is true to a lesser extent in parts of the Catholic Church, especially those influenced by the Charismatic Renewal—a Catholic analogue to the various Pentecostalist strands within the evangelical big tent.[7] Less explicitly, and influenced in part by a number of prominent ex-Protestant converts, a large number of US Catholics now feel perfectly at home with such traditional evangelical hallmarks as talk of being "born again" or having "a personal relationship with Jesus," extempore prayer, contemporary worship music (mostly outside of liturgical settings), and *really knowing* their Bibles. While this kind of "evangelical Catholicism"[8] goes beyond even the broad scope of evangelical as I'm defining it for this chapter, it serves to highlight the wide appeal and draw of the wider evangelical subculture, and its gravitational influence far beyond the borders of its traditional home grounds of Baptists, "non-denoms," Pentecostals, certain (non-mainline) brands of Methodists and Lutherans (especially those in the South, and in predominantly Black congregations), and a panoply of assorted others.

My second main reason for framing evangelicalism in a cultural way is that this places me very firmly in good scholarly company. While not denying the importance of doctrines and church polity, much of the best work in recent decades has focused on American evangelicalism as constituting a distinctive subcultural world: a "sacred umbrella" in Christian Smith's phrase, providing a shared identity, language, and worldview—along with prescribed norms and practices, as exemplified by its own communion of saints and martyrs—for the many millions sheltering underneath.[9,10]

A central element of this subculture's success has been its transposition of much of mainstream, middle-class consumerism into an unabashedly Christian key. This was, in the early days, a deliberate marketing tool: early megachurch builders copied the aesthetics and production values of upscale malls, corporate HQs, and Disneyland to ensure a seamless "culture fit" between church and modern living. Likewise, Christian rock flowed out of 60s' and 70s' experiments at fusing Christianity with popular (counter)culture; Christian-themed clothing and consumer goods—think WWJD bracelets, Jesus-fish bumper stickers, silver purity rings—emerged out of the technicolor pins and T-shirts of the "hippies for Christ" Jesus People.[11] Very soon, however, this subculture took on a life of its own: by the end of the seventies, Christian rock musicians were no longer just copying Bob Dylan; Bob Dylan was converting to Christianity.[12] Furthermore, from the 1970s right up until the present, the bestselling evangelical books have often enough been the bestselling books, period.[13] This in itself is proof enough that, as subcultures go, evangelicalism has long held a high degree of commercial and cultural power. The same is, if less than it has been, amply true of moral and political clout, too.

For all their treasures, stored up in heaven or elsewhere, America's evangelicals are suffering a bad, though not terminal, case of nonversion. For proof, one only need browse the shelves of the Christian bookstores that have traditionally been among its main cultural carriers—assuming that Covid hasn't killed the last ones off. The past decade has seen a slew of books devoted to evangelical "prodigals": those who have left and who, the intended reader is hoping, will eventually return. Even a small selection of their titles conveys a sense of scale and depth of the problem, and the heartache it's causing to those still within the fold: *Reaching Your Prodigal, Generation Ex-Christian, Praying Prodigals Home, You Lost Me, Engaging Today's Prodigals, Church Refugees, Help! I Have a Prodigal, Hope for the Prodigal, When You Love a Prodigal, Praying for Your Prodigal*. From the other side of the equation, there has likewise been no shortage of memoirs published, narrating the process of leaving evangelical churches. Evidently, these too are finding a ready readership who find these accounts of hard-won liberation intensely relatable. Anyone who doubts that this applies to a large and diverse number of those brought up in the evangelical subculture need only follow the popular Twitter hashtag #exvangelical, which serves as a digital bat signal for the rapidly growing movement.[14]

* * *

"So it was a Wednesday, just a normal day. We ate at the fast-food restaurant before church, chatting, like always. And then we get to the big Fellowship Hall, and the double doors are blacked out. We walked in, and immediately knew something was wrong. All the leaders were really somber—very quiet, y'know?—just saying, 'Keep your voices down, just find a seat. We're doing something different tonight.'"

Like Melissa in eighties Texas, Alison in nineties Iowa was initially brought up moderately Methodist: "It wasn't a huge part of my life. It didn't impact me." Her parents also then converted to Pentecostal evangelicalism while she was still in elementary school. "I feel like they drank the Kool-Aid. Everything we did was tied back to the church. So as I grew up, that was my whole social circle. None of my best friends went to my school: they were all at my church. Same with my parents. It's just who we hung out with." Fortunately, Alison got the opportunity to hang out with church friends *a lot*. By the time she was a teenager, "undisputedly every night we were at church." Sundays typically meant three hours in the morning, back at one for the service in Spanish (which she was learning in school), then normally back with her parents again in the evening. But the highlight for Alison was the midweek Youth Service—"typical teenagers away from their parents: flirt with the boys and be with your friends, but with a God component to all that too"—a common fixture in evangelical churches (which, as does the LDS, devote much effort and resources to youth and young adult ministry).[15] Hence this particular night, when Alison was fifteen, was quite the change of pace.

"So you go and sit down, and there's this beautiful, big, pearl coffin sitting up on the stage. The pastor's looking somber, and then he says, 'We're here to celebrate the life of Hannah. Y'all know Hannah. . . . Well, Hannah's no longer with us.' And the implication was that she had committed suicide. They played 'her favorite song,' which was that 'I wish you would step back from the ledge, my friend . . .' one [i.e., "Jumper"] by Third Eye Blind. It's a song about suicide, and they were basically like, 'this is what she was listening to in her final moments.' And then we had a slideshow about her."

Hannah, two years Alison's senior, was known within the youth group—"we all knew each other's business, because y'know, you just *knew*"—for not having always lived up to their collective purity norms: "She'd done some sinful things in her past"—Alison imitates her younger self with mock-primness. This was alluded to in the pastor's sermon, which was along the lines of "we *all know* Hannah's life—but let's try to honor her memory by living for God."

Then, ninety minutes into the service, the coffin pops open. Hannah sits up and says, "hi." Right on cue, the pastor announces: "Hannah has died to her old self. She has now been reborn." Whereupon, "She got up and gave her testimony, more or less about how 'I'm not going to engage in premarital sex. I am a born-again virgin. I'm going to live for God. I've shed my old self, my old self is in this coffin.' And then that was the end of the service. Everyone laughs, a little shell-shockedly, and heads for home."

Looking back on all this, Alison shakes her head in wide-eyed astonishment: "I'm like, Where did you get the coffin? Like, did you rent that? Can you rent coffins? I don't even know . . . What the hell did you just put all these kids through?" Bear in mind that, at fifteen, Alison was by no means one of the youngest there: the youth group was for those aged thirteen to eighteen. Even at the time, something felt rather off about the whole performance, a little bit what-the-hell-just-happened. One of her friends, Donna, never went back to church again. However, Alison and the rest of her friend group ultimately blamed Donna herself for this waywardness: "we totally missed the part where she was saying, 'this is fucked up.'" In any case, Alison's own initial discomfort was soon subsumed into a wider, socially shared narrative:

It initially felt weird—but then *hey, look at that, I guess Hannah's on the right path now, and good for her, and what a dirty non-virgin* . . . There was a huge emphasis on sex, absolutely. Promise rings, purity rings. We would make vows, and have this "daddy–daughter date night" when your dad would give you the ring. I also recall distinctly there being sermons when they would break up the boys and the girls, and as girls we were told, "it's on you to dress appropriately, so you don't hurt the boys or tempt the boys. It's on you, and they can't help themselves."

* * *

Among the many memorable aspects of growing up in the evangelical subculture, almost all of my thirty- or forty-something interviewees emphasized so-called purity culture, with many citing it as a major factor in their permanent prodigality. This is most keenly felt among the women. While Melissa and Rhett both "totally had a purity ring," he still thinks he has his at the back of a drawer somewhere. She, tellingly, "threw mine away."

As previously discussed, one result of the sexual revolution of the 1960s—which, fifty years on, feels rather more of a "permanent revolution" (*pace* Mao[16]) than a one-off event—has been a growing gap, now a gulf, between the wider culture's sexual mores and practices and those of traditional Christianity.[17] In fact, given the numbers, cultural traction, and political sway of evangelicals (with Catholics and Mormons as welcome fellow-travelers; the culture wars have done more for ecumenism than is often realized), this has proceeded much less rapidly in the USA than elsewhere. The fact of the matter, however, is that with each passing decade the baseline conviction of "no sex before, or outside of, heterosexual, 'til-death-us-do-part" marriage has been increasingly at odds with the prevailing culture. Hence inculcating it into each new cohort of teens and young adults is becoming a steeper and steeper uphill struggle.

As others have noticed, the evangelical ideal is one even the most committed young Christians can find difficult to live up to—despite the best efforts of a whole industry of parachurch programs, ministries, and publications dedicated to helping them.

This, in itself, should come as no surprise: nobody ever said the path of virtue would be a smooth one. Falling short, however, inevitably brings with it a great deal of guilt, shame, and often despair. No doubt this nudges some toward unbelief, or at least belief in a Something who is a little more free and easy about such matters: this means of alleviating both guilt and cognitive dissonance makes both psychological sense and is supported by a decent amount of evidence.[18] The overall effect does, however, seem to be a limited one. This too makes sense. Presumably those likeliest to feel intense guilt at violating God's rules are those with the strongest prior reasons to believe in God and his rules to begin with.

At least for my own informants, the real stumbling block came not from the baseline ideal itself, nor directly from their own honestly admitted struggles in fully living up to it. Melissa confides in me, while Rhett's gone to the bathroom: "So, I was working at the church and we started dating, and we started sleeping together, which was a very conflicting thing for me—a very turmoil-filled thing for me, for both of us. And so we talked about it and decided, "Right we've got to stop." And we did, and then we got engaged a few months after that, and got married three months after we got engaged." Problem solved. Rather, the real sticking point came from two adjacent factors: the overarching way in which chastity—*especially* girls' and young women's—was framed within the wider purity culture, and the hypocrisy of some of those promoting it.[19]

Now it is not true that young men get a free pass in all this. Quite the opposite, in fact. Much is expected of them, and many fight valiantly against their baser urges to be "worthy" of their future wife. As Rhett comments ruefully, while pointedly ignoring Melissa's skeptical eye-rolls, "I turned down a lot of sex in college." More seriously, Tom, an ex-Pentecostal atheist in his mid-thirties, relates how he spent his early teens "in turmoil, just hating myself

. . . To find someone attractive—'to lust after them'—was absolutely a sin. So every thought you have after you hit puberty is a lustful thought. Everything like that was just super taboo." Though he too manages a joke: "Pious was definitely the word. I had never even experimented with myself, much less anybody else." Still the focus, and thus most of the pressure, of purity culture is placed on girls. For example, I've no idea how representative the Hannah-as-sexual-Lazarus ploy actually is within evangelical churches, though the scripted theatricality of the whole thing makes me suspect it was borrowed from some youth ministry playbook or other. But I'd bet a fair bit of cash that it's more commonly used with a girl than it is with a boy. The whole world of "born again virginity" (incidentally, the subject of an episode of *King of the Hill*) is, moreover, a very heavily female one—mirroring, of course, the wider societal double standards around male virginity (bad, loserish, mocked) and female virginity (prized, alluring, a "gift" for one's husband). Do teenaged boys attend "mommy–son dances" to receive jewelry for pledging to safeguard their virginity until they make Miss Right into Mrs. Right? On this score, perhaps evangelicals aren't nearly countercultural *enough*.

For Melissa, all this is just one feature of a much bigger problem. One of the things that attracted her to worship and work at the church where she and Rhett met was that it *seemed* to be different from the "very legalistic, women-controlling type of environment" she'd grown up in. "My dad had wanted me to go to a Christian college where they have separate sidewalks for men and woman there, and I was like: *No*. That was what I liked about this church: I felt like it was not *that*. It was like, you can just be who you are—and you can be with God." But it wasn't all that long before she became disillusioned.

For example, I was in this women's small group, and there was this issue that came up about whether girls should wear bikinis: "It leads men astray, blah, blah, blah." And I was just like, "This is a load of bullshit, I'm sorry. I am not responsible for men's thoughts." Basically, the leader of this small group was trying to say, "You shouldn't wear a bikini." So, it started shifting into this legalism. To me, it felt it was just very *déjà vu-y*. And I was like, No. I can't. I can't do this anymore.

What's more, working in HR she was party to the inside story on a lot of things. "There was a lot of stuff going on around women specifically, sinning in various ways—usually, in sexual ways—losing their jobs, or being punished and reprimanded. *But there was never a man.* I'm like, 'What the . . . ?'" When asked to fire a colleague whom it'd been discovered was sleeping with her fiancé, Melissa pleaded with the church management to let the woman stay: "I was like, 'I understand if you want her to sit down for a meeting or whatever, that makes sense. But I don't think she should lose her job.' But they fired her anyway." At this point, Rhett chimes in to correct the record. "They didn't just *fire* her. They fucking humiliated her." Melissa continues: "They made her go before the entire staff, and confess her sin. Most of these people she didn't even know. Some of them had just started like two weeks before. It was awful, horrific."

Finally, after being blackmailed by her assigned "accountability partner"—that is, "one random person from work, who you need to divulge your innermost thoughts, fears, concerns, et cetera to"— to whom Melissa had confessed that she and Rhett had slept together before getting married, she was forced to confess her own sin in front of a panel of (all male) colleagues. They didn't fire her: an act of clemency due to her honesty, and the fact that all this was now several years in the past, and with the man who was now her husband. Instead, they put her "on a Restoration Plan, to make me whole with Christ" and "dictated that I see a therapist who was affiliated with the church, and that I had to allow her to disclose my sessions to them. And I would say that was my breaking point. That was when I was like, This is a load of shit. You are going to decide when I am restored to Christ? I'm sorry, can we just take a step back and just take in the hubris here?" Now "broken and losing my faith," she was desperate to get out. But since "this is 2009 and the economy is tanking, so we're going to take the work we can get," she had no choice but to go along with it. Then completely out of the blue, "literally the week after I got this Restoration Plan from them," a recruiter she'd interviewed with the previous year got back in touch. A new company was opening up in town, and she'd be perfect for a certain role. "This is one of those things that make it hard for me to believe that there isn't some kind of Higher Power directing things. I ended up getting the job and it was my salvation. And so it was like, 'I don't fucking believe that there is a God who would put me through this. But how can't I? This just feels like divine intervention here.' It was very bizarre."

Faith in God intact, at least for the time being. But church? "I didn't ever want to walk through the doors of a church again. We were like, 'We're done. It's not this church. It's *all* of them.'" Despite everything, this was uttered more in sorrow than in anger. For Rhett: "Neither of us would even have thought of leaving if we hadn't run into legalistic systems, and the general shaming of others. We probably wouldn't ever . . . There is still so much we miss. We really miss the culture, we miss the idea that you can just go somewhere and have people pretend to love you." And for Melissa: "I do miss the support system. I miss that you could have a group of people where somebody just, when you have a baby or whatever, spontaneously brings a meal. I miss that community a lot, you know? But I don't miss the judgment. I don't miss feeling that I have to live my life in a certain way because somebody else might tattle on me to someone."

* * *

This feeds into a related issue, one I like to think of as the "Harper Valley Effect." In truth, the idea came to me when brooding on Catholic scandals, but the basic point applies amply here too.

The Parent–Teacher Association of Harper Valley Junior High, as I'm sure you recall, is the eponymous villain of Jeanie C. Riley's— or for my money, Dolly Parton's—classic broadside against small-town hypocrisy. It is a smug, self-congratulatory clique of drunks, adulterers, liars, and predators, who nevertheless have the temerity to upbraid others on their moral standards and propriety.

The song is very clever in this regard. Careful listeners may think the PTA's missive to Mrs. Johnson is not, in objective terms, wholly unreasonable. "Drinkin' and runnin' round with men and goin' wild," impolitic though it is to say so, mightn't be the optimal way to be raising her "little girl." Nevertheless, it's hard not to end the song very firmly cheering on this "Harper Valley widowed wife." How dare the PTA criticize in others, and from an assumed position of power and respectability, what they themselves are practicing be-hind closed doors (if not, in widow Jones' case, shuttered windows)?

The fact is, it simply doesn't matter whether the PTA's (official) moral stance is right or not. It also doesn't matter if there are many other morally upstanding members of the same committee. (Mrs. Johnson only calls out five or six of them; I presume PTAs are typi-cally larger than that.) The rest of the PTA, even if personally blame-less in a narrow sense, certainly seems to tolerate or turn a blind eye to their colleagues' misdemeanors. Their sins seem, after all, to be an open secret. In this sense, Mrs. Johnson's certainly in the right: "You're *all* Harper Valley hypocrites."

What does any of this have to do with contemporary nonversion? In all likelihood, rather a lot. There is a good deal of evidence that human beings are evolutionarily hardwired with a keen "hypocrisy detector."[20] We're biased toward believing things people tell us, when their own actions align with the implications—especially costly ones—of those beliefs. Martyrdom is the extreme example here: being willing to die for a belief is a good indicator that you really believe it's true. But it applies in all kinds of other areas, too. The time and effort you take to brush your teeth morning and night is, for instance, a decent indicator that you think it has a causal role in preventing tooth decay. Contrarily, if you constantly lecture your kids about oral hygiene but never brush your own teeth, they'll have a hard time believing that you're actually serious. (By the way, the same is true of telling children how important it is to go to church: if you only bother to go yourself when your own parents are in town for the holidays, your children are highly likely to take that as proof that it isn't important—either to you, or as a general rule—at all.) Talk is cheap. Actually practicing what you preach is often costly, whether in terms of one's time, effort, health, prestige, or cash. What's more, conspicuously failing to "walk the walk" reflects badly not only on the talker but on the truth of the talk.

This is most true, furthermore, when the claims being made are already regarded as dubious or at least up for debate. In the recent pandemic, for example, anti-lockdown pundits made much of politicians failing to abide by the rules they so tenaciously imposed on others: Fox News viewers will know exactly what I mean by the phrases "Nancy Pelosi's haircut" or "Gavin Newsom's birthday party." Likewise, the spectacle of environmental campaigners riding private jets to chi-chi resorts for "climate crisis summits" is taken as signaling that, perhaps, slashing carbon emissions might not be so urgent after all. The oft-quoted phrase "I'll believe it's a crisis when people who tell me it's a crisis start acting like it's a crisis" captures this perfectly.[21] (Contrariwise, one of the reasons Greta Thunberg has become such an icon of the climate-change movement is precisely her single-minded consistency: her two-week voyage on a zero-carbon yacht to attend a 2019 UN climate conference in New York was a classic example of the medium being the message.) Meanwhile, Democrats indict Republicans for claiming to be pro-life while not supporting welfare and healthcare measures that would help more mothers to keep their babies, or not being more willing to adopt, or being anti-life in other ways (e.g., supporting capital punishment, opposing gun reform). My point in giving these examples is not to adjudicate which "side" is right or wrong, it is simply to emphasize that the hypocrisy card is a powerful rhetorical tool.

It's no surprise, therefore, that exvangelicals should so easily recall times when their own spokespeople for "sexual purity" failed to practice what they so earnestly preached. Several had stories of youth ministers' lapses with members of their flock. Alison recalls one pastor of her youth group, keen to encourage girls to aspire to being a "Proverbs 31 Woman," who was especially keen to point out any minor lapse, such as a visible bra strap.[22] "Then coincidentally, that pastor ended up having a sexual relationship with a sixteen-year-old in the youth group. Wow. And coincidentally, further, she was one of three girls that was with me in India . . ."—that is, on a church mission trip where they trekked to remote villages to show them videos about Jesus—"and he was also in India. And that's where it started." Her ironic, repeated use of "coincidentally" here is revealing. The subtext is that the pastor's predation on young girls is anything *but* coincidental to his championing of purity culture and

Christian missionary activity. That is to say, his actions reflect badly not only on him but on the very principles that he claimed to stand for. This is the Harper Valley Effect in full force.

The downfalls of Jim Bakker, Jimmy Swaggart, Ted Haggard, Carl Lentz, or Ravi Zacharias are the same thing, only magnified and amplified.[23] In an era when "traditional family values" are viewed as unrealistic, if not outright oppressive, the conspicuous failures of some of their most vocal spokespeople—namely, evangelical pastors with a national platform—are naturally taken as "proof if proof were needed" of their moral and intellectual bankruptcy: if not even the people who *pretend* to believe in them actually do, how can anyone else take them seriously? Logically, of course, this doesn't necessarily follow: failing to practice what one preaches is not, in fact, proof that one doesn't really believe it. (An alcoholic may truly believe in, and know from bitter experience, the harmfulness of excessive drinking, and be zealous in warning others against it. But he or she may, nevertheless, still sometimes succumb: "The spirit indeed is willing, but the flesh is weak.") Furthermore, there are plenty of *other* spokespeople who do manage to live up to the ideals they profess, no matter how hard it may be. But the *psychologic* of these public falls from grace, especially on those already skeptical of the precise conception of "grace" being fallen from, is far more powerful than the logic alone requires.[24] Since powerful, high-profile figures tend to have others—often including the senior staff or board of directors of the organization of which they're the boss and star attraction—enabling, turning a blind eye to, or actively trying to cover up their misdeeds, when these do eventually come to light, there are often swathes of others who are, or are suspected of being, complicit. This further gives the impression that it's the whole system, and not just one or two renegades, that's the problem. "*All* Harper Valley hypocrites" indeed.

As a final note: that all this is fueling the growing numbers of prodigals leaving evangelicalism for "the distant country" of mainstream America has not escaped those who miss them and pray for their return. Writing in response to revelations of sexual abuse by the late apologist Ravi Zacharias, Russell Moore, the respected theologian and sometime public policy czar for the Southern Baptist Convention, commented in February 2021:

> The church is bleeding out the next generation, not because "the culture" is so opposed to the church's fidelity to the truth, but just the reverse. The culture often does not reject us because they don't believe the church's doctrinal and moral teachings, but because they have evidence that the *church* doesn't believe its own doctrinal and moral teachings. They suspect that Jesus is just a means to an end—to some political agenda, to a market for selling merchandise, or for the predatory appetites of some maniacal narcissist.... Anger is not the ultimate answer. But it's a start.[25]

* * *

Since we're quoting prominent evangelical scholars, here's Baylor history professor Thomas Kidd commenting on another controversy: "The 2016 election [was] the most shattering experience for evangelicals since the Scopes Trial."[26] Now, it's certainly fair to say that not all evangelicals share Kidd's view here. A fair proportion of them were downright jubilant in the small hours of November 7 that year, and little of what happened during the next four years did much to change their initial assessment. In a certain sense, however, this is precisely what Kidd is getting at.

The ongoing adventure of Donald Trump and the evangelicals—which, not all that long ago, would have sounded like a straight-to-VHS comedy rather than one of the most momentous religious and political stories of recent years—is fittingly "yuge": well worthy of a book of its own.[27] While the full complexities are not our direct concern here, we'll dig into a couple of specifics in the following paragraphs. Suffice it to say that the full story is rather more nuanced than it's often presented.

From the perspective of *ex*-vangelicalism, however, the link with Trump might seem straightforward. It is no coincidence that the exvangelical movement has gained traction since 2016. Many of its leading voices highlight the Trump presidency, and many of their erstwhile evangelical confreres' support for it, as the major catalyst.[28] The movement's power builds on a rejection of much of evangelicalism's moral and social agenda (e.g., on abortion, LGBTQ rights), which was already widespread among many of those raised evangelical—including many still within the fold. But it adds to this the potent charge of hypocrisy for evangelicals' enthusiastic rallying around Donald Trump, *of all people*, as the means of furthering it. The sociologist Philip Gorski has expressed this lack of obvious "values fit" between Trump and American evangelicalism well:

> Why did so many evangelical Christians vote for Donald Trump? Why did they vote for a man who has six [*sic.*] children by three wives? A man who bragged about "grabbing" women? And who nonetheless claimed that he's never done anything he needed to be forgiven for? A man who hadn't darkened a church door in decades? Why, in short, did they rally behind someone who seems the very antithesis of most everything they have ever claimed to stand for: family values, piety, humility, and mercy?[29]

For many exvangelicals, the answer to all these questions, in short, is that there is—and long has been—something rotten at the core of evangelicalism. Trump is not the cause of it, he's the logical and inevitable outcome of what was there all along. As Rhett puts it, with his customary dad-jokery, "Wasn't Galatians 2.16 '. . . and grab them by the pussy'? I learned that in Bible drill at high school." More expansively, he and Melissa both now view their erstwhile "Christian bubble" as stuck in a toxically codependent relationship with the GOP.

> Republicanism *is* the religion, and they've been fighting for that for at least twenty-five years—just to turn it into a religion. So, that it doesn't matter what they do—and let's be honest, Trump is probably one of the worst humans in the whole universe—my dad will never be able to do anything other than be on this "religion team" because he's told that it's *his* religion team. And all they have to do is play their religion card and it's like, "Religion team says this," and he gets to turn his whole brain off and do everything against what he says.

As noted in the previous chapter, the closeness between the GOP and evangelicalism—"the Religious Right"—is a long-term fact of political life, normally traced back to the 1970s with the emergence of groups such as Jerry Falwell's Moral Majority.[30] And it has long, and plausibly, been cited as a driver of younger generations' disaffiliation.[31] (Although as also noted, it takes two to tango: evangelicals' rightward drift *toward* the Republican Party can likewise be viewed as the Democrats' leftward shift *away* from a number of core matters of concern for Christians.) Given the steady, generation-by-generation liberalization of Americans' views on many moral issues, this will no doubt continue. And indeed, we saw similar dynamics at work among young Mormons in Chapter 2.

One element of the Trump-and-the-evangelicals narrative that often goes unnoticed, however, perhaps reveals something significant about the bigger picture. While committed White evangelicals certainly did support Trump in large numbers, he was not their first choice: Ted Cruz was the favorite among the more religiously practicing. The same was true in 2012, where despite rallying round the party's nominee in the general election, it was fellow-evangelical Mike Huckabee, rather than Mormon Mitt Romney, whom they would have preferred.[32] What one might call the "committed Christian caucus" in the GOP is not, that is to say, as all-powerful as it might once have been. The same is even more true in America as a whole. As conservative commentators from across the Christian spectrum—including such #NeverTrump stalwarts as Ross Douthat (Catholic), Rod Dreher (Orthodox), and the aforementioned Russell Moore (evangelical)—have been arguing for a long time, Christianity's sway over mainstream American mores is waning rapidly.[33] Viewed in this light, evangelical support for Trump comes partly from a place of cultural weakness and quasi-desperation. (Incidentally, this is a key aspect of the "Trump as King Cyrus" trope, popular in some religious circles, that is sometimes missed.) To put it bluntly, when a fried chicken restaurant and a crafting superstore are among your most important cultural carriers, you're not exactly at the vanguard of contemporary society.

Then again, feeling "embattled" has been a major part of American evangelicalism's self-understanding for a long time. Paradoxically, it has also been a major source of its strength: perceived tension with the mainstream culture and values is an effective way of shoring up one's subcultural defenses (hence the willingness of many evangelical parents either to home-school or pay for private Christian schools rather than risk the corrupting influences of public education; also the flourishing of robustly Christian colleges and universities).[34] Just because you're paranoid doesn't mean that the wider culture isn't out to get (away from) you.

Here, we might end on rather a tempering note. While it is undoubtedly true that Trump has damaged the evangelical brand in the eyes of many, this ought not to be overstated. In the first place, the effect is surely strongest among those for whom the brand was already tarnished. Evangelicals' unholy alliance (as they see it) with Trump is further confirmation for them, but isn't what caused it. Meanwhile, it is worth stressing the fact that Trump is actually rather popular among large swathes of the US population. He did, lest we forget, win the 2016 election. Even in the one he subsequently lost, a good 74 million people voted for him, *despite* both an impeachment (the second one would come later) and hundreds of thousands dead from a pandemic in his final year in office. That is to say, the evangelical brand might not be so tainted by association as many in the media and academia assume.[35] The Trump years might well have been the trigger for a fair few Democratic and Independent evangelicals to finally stop identifying as such—and there is some survey data that would support this. But religious and political identifying is a two-way street. Trump's continuing popularity with the GOP base might well also keep some Republican voters to still think of themselves as evangelicals ("*our* religion team"), who otherwise would drift away.[36] What is more, there is intriguing evidence to suggest that Trump support is a factor in attracting people to evangelicalism in the first place. A recent Pew study shows that between 2016 and 2020, among White non-evangelicals expressing warm feelings toward Trump, around one in six *began* identifying as "born again" or "evangelical" (compared to just one in a hundred of White non-evangelicals with cold or neutral feelings toward Trump). All told, to quote the title of Pew's own summary of these findings, "More White Americans adopted than shed evangelical label during Trump presidency." And even among non-Whites, as many began identifying as evangelicals during the Trump presidency as stopped doing so—7% in both cases.[37]

* * *

"I remember in college I was still in the puppet team. I got really into the puppets." Lightning Jones—I explained to her that interviewees would be assigned a pseudonym to preserve their anonymity; "Lightning" picked her own—is a mid-twenties Michigan émigrée now living in Oregon. Though we meet over a late-afternoon coffee, and she's been up since the early hours for her job, she visibly perks up at the mention of puppets. It's clear she expects me to as well.

"Err, we don't . . . umm . . . puppet teams aren't really a thing in England." I try to cover my lack of immediate excitement.

"Oh. How sad."

"These are, like, *Christian* puppets?"

"Like the Muppets, but for preaching. It didn't really matter what you say to kids with the puppet—they love it because it's a puppet. I went to Costa Rica with the puppet team too: we'd call ourselves an 'International Traveling Puppet Team.' We would set up in town squares on this big stage, and everyone would just be like, 'What are all these white people doing? Let's go and find out!' And then we'd pull out puppets—and *everyone* in the world loves puppets, you know. We did shows in Spanish about the love of Jesus and prayer. But we were also pretty silly, kind of goofball writers. So we wrote some pretty wacky skits, and we'd get into really weird in-jokes. . . . Oh, it was so much fun, it was great! And there's a point where I definitely was like, I don't think I even believe in God anymore, but I was still doing these puppets because they're awesome." She laughs at the happy memories of it all. "It was just all about the puppets—I had to hold it together for the puppetry. I think I did it for, like, six years. There was a while where I only went to that building because of puppets, and I was like 'I haven't been to a service here in forever.'"

I hope you know me well enough by now to guess how thoroughly intrigued I was by all this. "And were you the only Christian puppet team in the world?" I ask, dimly recalling a *King of the Hill* subplot involving a puppet ministry called "The Manger Babies," which I'd always assumed was pure, over-the-top invention. "Or is it competitive?"

"Oh, I wish it *was* competitive: we'd have smoked 'em! We went to these Christian puppetry conventions, and they were terrifying, absolutely terrifying. But we always liked going, because we felt way cooler than all these teams with cheesy names like "Hands for Jesus"—whereas we were, like, real hard operators. And there was a company called One Way, who held the monopoly on the Christian puppetry industry. So we were always trying to 'take down' One Way. So yeah, it's a whole big thing. *Real* deep into American Protestantism."

In the hands of a better—or maybe more cynical—writer, this story about evangelicals and puppets would be doing some serious metaphorical work. But I really don't mean it to. I include it here because I find it charming, lighthearted, and fun, much like Lightning herself. There's no big reveal coming about how the Christian puppet world was rocked by a drugs and high-finance scandal in the late nineties, or how recent conventions have turned into pitched and bloody battles between QAnon and Antifa. For once, it's really what it purports to be: the happy, half-ironic reminiscences of a young woman, from deep inside the evangelical subculture, who was kept within the Christian fold for longer than she otherwise might have been because she found it a fun, supportive, creative home in her wacky, goofball teenage years. "Church was wonderful in that way, you know."

For all the recent focus on exvangelicals and prodigals, the fact remains that evangelicals, like the Mormons, are doing a much better job at keeping people in the fold than many other religious groups—as we'll see in more detail in the next chapter. America's religious market is shrinking fast, and evangelicalism, after several decades of impressive growth, certainly looks like it's starting to stall. Here's Kidd again:

> By the mid-2010s it became clear that the [Southern Baptist Convention] also had entered a pattern of dwindling baptisms and membership, though not a decline as severe as the mainline churches experienced. From its high mark of 16.3 million reported members in 2003, the SBC dropped to 15.2 million in 2016. It remains to be seen whether a flurry of new SBC church plants will counter that trend.[38]

Even so, while more long-term—and thus more speculative—prophecies as to the future place of evangelicalism within an ever more *post*-Christian America will have to wait for the final chapter, rumors of its demise have been greatly exaggerated.

7

The Ex Effect

Back in the Introduction, I flagged up the idea that people's past roles, relationships, and experiences frequently exert a powerful influence on the present: hence, as noted there, the continuing salience of being an ex-spouse or a recovering—note the present tense—alcoholic. And that this applies to all manner of areas of people's life. Consider, for example, the significance that being a military veteran often has for a person's own self-image, as well as how others (ought to) regard and treat them. This is true in a generic sense, applying to any and all who used to serve in the military but now no longer do. But it also admits of any number of particular sub-identities. To be an ex-Marine or an ex-SEAL, or the vet of a specific campaign, often expresses something particular, not least to oneself and one's fellow ex-somethings, though often to others, too. While this is not an exclusive-to-the-military thing, it doesn't apply universally. I spent several years of my youth working in libraries, but I don't think of myself as an ex–library assistant, and I don't suppose it colors my present life in appreciable ways. But had I spent the same number of years as high school cheer captain, a child movie star, in prison, or as a police cadet, I might feel differently. At the other end of life, studies of retirees show that certain sorts of lingering professional identities—ex-cop, or former doctor, say—play important roles in well-being and mental health.[1] "The past is never dead. It's not even past," as William Faulkner famously put it.[2]

* * *

The very concept of a nonvert is, of course, a claim about the ongoing relevance of people's previous *religious* identities. All nonverts are members of the generic category of nones, insofar as they now regard themselves as having no religious affiliation. But in the same way that being a Catholic *convert* specifies something more than does simply being a Catholic, so too does *nonvert* convey something beyond simple noneness. Catholic converts are an apt comparison since they do differ, on average, from other Catholics. They tend to practice their faith more regularly, be more orthodox in their beliefs, and give more money to the Church. They also—or so cradle Catholics tell me—have a tendency to be more annoying and (over)zealous.[3] Fans of Amazon Prime's *The Marvelous Mrs. Maisel* may also recall the running joke about the devout Jewishness of Midge's convert sister-in-law Astrid. All of this makes perfect sense. Those who actively choose to join a religion as an adult will naturally have higher-than-average levels of commitment and conviction, when compared to the typical born-and-raised adherent. It is a classic case of selection bias at work. This is true not just of those who convert for straightforwardly religious reasons but also those who, like Astrid, marry into the faith. Since social networks and relationships have a strong influence on people's beliefs and identities, such incomers very often prove the adage "no zealot like a convert"—a phenomenon that religious leaders have long known about and encouraged (cf. 1 Corinthians 7.12–16). In any case, the main point I'm trying to make here is this: in all these cases of *conversion*, the "before" continues to affect the nature, color, and texture of the "after" state. So too, come to think of it, does the precise means of, and reasons for, moving from the former to the latter.

This book is, therefore, premised on the idea that *both* "the rise of the nones" *and* "what it means for America" can be elucidated by gaining a better understanding of nonverts and nonversion. After having addressed it a bit in the Introduction, this argument has mostly been implicit in the intervening chapters. It's high time we focused on it in a more head-on manner.

In the first place, our nonvert's-eye view of religious change is fundamentally a causal one. Religious groupings wax and wane due to various combinations of factors, including birth rate, retention, and migration flows. The single biggest fueler of the rapid growth in those claiming no religious affiliation, however, is nonversion: that is, the propensity of people brought up with a religious affiliation to lose it and, having done so, to feel little need to acquire another. As shown in previous chapters, the proportion of nones in the US adult population has risen from single figures until some point in the mid-nineties, up to somewhere between a fifth and a third by the late 2010s and early 2020s, depending on which survey one chooses to go by. We have tended to favor the General Social Survey herein, for various reasons of practicality, longevity, and methodological rigor. Conveniently, the GSS comes out with an estimate of the none population roughly in the middle of the polling pack: a little under a quarter, as of 2018. The significance of nonversion is made abundantly clear in Figure 7.1. Each of the five graph "bars" combines data from consecutive iterations of the GSS (five annual waves in the case of 1974–8 and 1984–8, and three of the bigger biennial waves for 1994–8, 2004–8, and 2014–18). Combining consecutive years in this way enables us to increase the sample size we're analyzing, which is helpful when dealing with fine sub-slices of data, such as distinctions *within* the small number of nones in the early years of

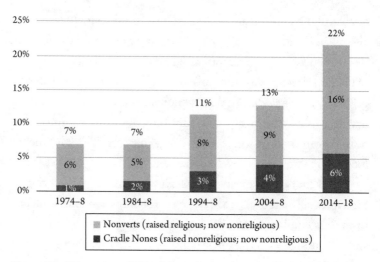

Figure 7.1. Proportion of US adults with no religious affiliation, divided into those brought up with a religious affiliation ("nonverts") and those brought up with no religious affiliation ("cradle nones") over time.

Source: General Social Survey 1972–2018 (pooled N for the entire sample ranges from 7,521 in 1974–8 to 9,290 in 2004–8)

the GSS. It also helps us to concentrate on discerning the major "signals" over time—using decadal intervals in this case—without the distracting "noise" arising from year-to-year fluctuations.

Quite evidently, the bulk of nones throughout the whole four-decade span covered by the graph are nonverts. Of the 7% of US adults identifying as nones in 1974–8, nonverts outnumbered cradles by six to one. Forty years on, in 2014–18, the nones category as a whole had increased over threefold. Nonverts now make up 16% of the US population, with cradle nones adding a further 6%, for a combined total of 22%.[4] Hence nonversion accounts for somewhere between two-thirds and three-quarters of all US nones. Explaining "the rise of the nones" is therefore largely a case of explaining how it is that, mostly within the last thirty years or so, about one in six Americans opted out of religion. Furthermore, since the *vast* majority of US nonverts—fully fifteen out of every sixteen of them—say that they were brought up as Christians, this is overwhelmingly a story of people leaving Christianity.

The second reason for foregrounding nonverts follows from the observations made above, about the lingering importance of "ex-" identities. As should have come through loud and clear in the "deep dive" case-study chapters of this book, nones turn out differently depending on what they were raised as. Nones raised as Mormons differ from those raised as evangelicals. Both differ, perhaps even more than from each other, from those raised in Mainline churches. And all differ, in different ways, from the kinds of ex-Catholic nonverts we'll be meeting in the next chapter. Of course, each one of these groups also exhibits significant internal diversity too: there's no one "ex-Mormon mold" just as there's no one "ex-anything-else mold." Nevertheless, there *are* broad traits and tendencies that are more or less prevalent in one group over the other. This can and has been demonstrated in large-scale, nationally representative surveys. In Britain, for instance, ex-Catholic nones and ex-Anglican nones tended to vote differently on Brexit—both differently from each other and differently from cradle nones. The overall effect, though small, was a real one, even when other potentially relevant factors, such as the demographic makeup of each group, were held statistically constant.[5] More generally, one recent cross-national study, which included US data, found that "Formerly religious individuals (i.e., religious 'dones') differed from never religious and currently religious individuals in cognitive, emotional, and behavioral processes."[6] The authors of another 2021 study, meanwhile, argue that "the psychological repercussions of religious commitment can persist after people cease identifying as religious. . . . This religion residue effect may contribute to differences in values between those who were once religious but no longer identify as religious and those who never identified as religious."[7]

This is certainly something many of my own interviewees would easily recognize. For instance, people with similar "ex-" religious backgrounds sometimes mention picking up on subtle clues and vibes. As reluctant atheist Brandon put it to me:

> I can always recognize ex-religious people. I remember I was having beers with a group of people, and there was this one guy and I was like "You grew up religious, didn't you?" Because there's certain characteristics that I notice with incredibly religious people who have left.

Note that this isn't a general observation about all nonreligious people. It's specifically about nonverts. Such people are viewed here, by one of their own, as a distinct group, set apart both from the religious and from nones-in-general.

At least for certain kinds of formerly religious folks, this sense of distinctiveness is both personally keenly felt, and actively—or even "desperately," as one hitherto-fundamentalist atheist living in the Deep South put it to me—sought out in others. For example, here's Utah-raised lawyer Abigail talking about the ex-Mormon community she's found online.

> I sort of migrated onto the Reddit board, which as I tell people is really just free therapy. I enjoy it because it's a chance to talk to people who know the ins and outs of some of these weird things that you've been saddled with. And there's a lot of shorthand there, because people just *understand*. I can complain about my parents doing something and, you know, the whole group of them know what you're talking about, and they can sympathize

with you or they can offer strategies to help. Like "oh this is what's helped me get along better with my parents" or "this is what I would do in your scenario" and stuff. So, I both reach out for help and try to [help others].

The mutual support and camaraderie among group members is built upon their common Mormon-specific backstories, creating a shared store of in-jokes and pop (sub)culture references: "r/exmormon," the Reddit forum that justifiably brands itself as "The Best ExMormon Site on the Internet!" plays host to much clever and creative meme-making along these lines. But as is clear from Abigail's testimony, it's equally a source of *present* advice, consolation, and encouragement for members, not least as they navigate awkward issues around family and relationships. It has also helped her to understand and relate to her own still-Mormon relatives, by getting to know others who stayed in the church longer than she did.

Weirdly enough, now I understand my parents' motivations more, my parents and my brother more. Because I left church before I was really an adult, I was never immersed in the adult side of it, which is its own thing. It's interesting to hear, to understand more of the background, because it really helps me put it more in context—in that sense it really is like a therapy thing. It's like "Oh I understand now more about why all this stuff happened as a teenager, I understand more of my parents' motivations, I understand more about my sister-in-law's fear of me." I mean it helps, you know. I think it helps me sort of understand. In a way, even though I think that most of the active Mormons would say a place like Reddit is a really hateful place, I think in a way the steam gets blown off there, and what's left is people are probably more understanding and tolerant of the devout community than they were before.

Even when not in need of "free therapy," it's well known that people often tend to seek out, and feel more relaxed around, people like themselves. There's a technical term for this—*homophily*—but it's effectively summed up in folksy phrases like "birds of a feather flock together." For example, interviewees often mentioned close friendships or romances with analogously ex-religious people. No doubt part of this is simply "the luck of the draw": certain age groups, in certain places of the country, will naturally have a large pool of such people. But over and above that, it gives people something significant in common. Even if two people aren't from the same religious background, this can still work, especially if they are from ones of similar "intensities." Here's Abigail again:

> It was probably funny that the one relationship I had that lasted a long time was with someone who had a very similar background to me. Even though it was a different church, I used to love to listen to him talk about it. But he had such pride in his religion, he used to tell me stuff and I'd say "Oh, the Mormons do that too." *[laughing]* It would like break his heart. He was brought up, like a lot of those faiths, he was brought up to know how to discredit Mormons, right? They'll have classes and stuff on why the Mormons are wrong, and I used to tease him about that. I was like "You guys didn't even tick our radar! No one taught me how to argue against the Seventh-day Adventists because nobody *cared.*"

As noted earlier, the salience of these kinds of connections also varies based on local context. Those living in the more religious parts of the country, for example, often especially valued having a "safe space" of fellow nonverts. This could range from a select number of trusted friends to a quasi-formal Meetup group. I spoke to several members of one such group, catering particularly to women, in the Florida panhandle—someplace where if "there's anybody who has a problem to talk about, no one's going to go, 'oh, let's pray about it.' I mean, we're not going to get the platitudes because that just makes us all want to choke someone."

* * *

Our two main reasons for focusing so intently on nonverts, specifically, will not apply forever. Even as the nones continue to grow for a while yet, the *proportion* of nonverts among them will almost certainly fall. This follows for several reasons. In the first place, there are now simply more children being brought up by nonreligious parents. Recall that around a third of America's eighteen- to thirty-year-olds already see themselves as having no religion. Some will end up raising their kids religiously, either because they rediscovered their religious conviction (in the case of "revert" prodigals) or for more prosaic reasons, perhaps relating to family or school choice. The majority, though, including most of those whose own "religious upbringing" was fairly low-key, will not. Second, as being nonreligious becomes more and more the norm in large parts of American society, it will become easier and easier for the growing ranks of "cradle nones" to retain this identity into adulthood.[8] This all applies on the opposite side of the coin as well: the fewer people being raised religious, the smaller the pool of potential nonverts.

This is already happening, in fact. Around 55% of cradle nones born from the fifties through the eighties still identified as nones when the GSS asked them between 2010 and 2018. For those born in the eighties and nineties, the rates were 71% and 77%, respectively. Those retention rates were higher than for those raised Protestant or Catholic. We might think of what's happening here as the gravitational attraction of "no religion" growing as the category gains mass, meaning it both keeps a greater number of those brought up within its orbit and pulls increasing numbers of those brought up elsewhere in America's religious universe. In previous decades, the odds were good that a significant proportion of those brought up without a religious affiliation would end up acquiring one in later life. This was effectively a socio-religious version of "regression to the mean." (As I have mentioned before, much the same thing often happens when people move across country, too. Relocating from Seattle to Shreveport is, on average, likely to boost one's own religiousness, and vice versa.) But this trend looks like it's beginning to flip. Soon there will be a greater likelihood that a person brought up *with* a religion will end up *without* one than someone brought up without a religion will acquire one. Already among under-thirties in the 2018 GSS, for instance, those brought up as nones now claim a religious affiliation at roughly the same rate (27%) as do those brought up with a religion who now claim to be nones (26%). This is a combined effect of nonreligious retention strengthening while religious retention weakens. Since, however, more of the GSS's under-thirties were brought up religiously than not, this parity of retention in fact results in a significant net gain for the nones. For every *one* cradle none in the dataset who now has a religious affiliation, there are *five* who were brought up religiously who now identify as nones. That's five nonverts for every convert.

What all this means is that American religion is currently going through one of its periodic resets. Right now is a watershed, as the *status quo* is shifting. Quite what that new normal might end up looking like is the subject of this book's final chapter. Here, though, I want to keep our focus firmly on the present. For the reasons outlined above and in earlier chapters (especially Chapter 5), today's bumper crop of nonverts is both symptom and side-effect of this transitional moment. Cradle nones, brought up with little or no direct connection with religion, are indeed growing as a proportion of the overall pool of nones. But for the time being, over two-thirds of America's nones *used to be* religious. And it's not surprising if they carry with them all the hang-ups and baggage, knowledge and understanding, anger and hurt, memories and affections of exes everywhere. I suspect that this bears significantly on how nonverts think about and interact with religion. This can and does take many forms, and we have seen a very wide spectrum of possibilities in these pages. Here, though, it might be useful to abstract from individual cases and think how all this might "average out" as part of the bigger picture.

Writing these words in late 2021, and even viewing it all from across an ocean—thanks to the pandemic, this is probably the longest period I've gone without visiting a Cracker Barrel since my late teens—it's fair to say that America is going through rather a turbulent period in its history. The past eighteen months alone have seen roughly three-quarters of a million deaths from contagion, a tanking economy, serious civil unrest around multiple issues dear to various shades of "left" and "right," a bitterly contested election followed by a not precisely peaceful transfer of power, a migrant crisis at the southern border, mushrooming conspiracy theories, bitter debates around "cancel culture," growing anxiety about the power of tech giants, and much else besides. The frequently fretted-over "polarization" of American culture and politics is something one can watch in real time, simply by channel-hopping among the various networks' evening comment, chat, and comedy shows.[9]

Obviously, noting a certain febrility in contemporary American society, culture, and politics isn't the most original of observations.

And there's no shortage of diagnoses on offer for what ails the nation.[10] I don't want to add to them in great detail here, except to point out that the "making of ex-Christian America" certainly plays a serious, if complex, role in all of this—sometimes the cause, sometimes a catalyst, sometimes the effect. To be perfectly honest, it would be altogether strange if it didn't. After all, religion is bound up with all sorts of things, including politics, family, morality, identity (both personal and group), sex, marriage, childrearing, race, ethnicity, and community participation. It would be curious if all these were to shake and shift, and in different directions, *without* there being knock-on effects to religion. And likewise, it would be odd if, in the space of a couple of decades, a single segment of the US religious market should suddenly expand its share from less than a tenth to a quarter or more without it playing havoc with areas of American life that religion has for so long been intimately connected with. In reality, and as often happens in complex systems, we're probably looking at a tangled web of pushes and pulls coming from all directions, reacting and interacting with each other in endless feedback loops. More thunderbird effects than butterfly effects, you might say.

One striking way in which ex-Christians differ from simple non-Christians is that they have, to steal a phrase from a dear Kentuckian colleague, "a dog in the fight" when it comes America's churches. For understandable reasons, nonverts often feel a hard-won entitlement, and perhaps even a duty, to criticize or call out things they disagree with, especially if it relates to their own (former) denomination. Furthermore, they are more likely to be listened to precisely *because* of their perceived insider knowledge. (This is a general principle of social psychology. We are more likely to take seriously an ex-addict's arguments against drug-taking than we are someone who's never partaken. It's also why the testimonies of "whistleblowers" can be so damaging to organizations.) I'd be very surprised if former Catholics were not disproportionately represented among the Church's most strident critics. The same goes for many other groups. The most prominent opponents of Scientology are usually themselves ex-Scientologists, which is no doubt part of why the organization goes to such extreme lengths to dissuade current adherents from associating with former ones.[11] At the other extreme, while few people have strong negative feelings about Episcopalians, I've heard some *very* arch comments about them from their former co-religionists.

This is surely a factor in the emergence of a significant activist strand within American atheism, incubated online but also evidenced through a growth in campus secular societies and an increasingly vocal public presence from long-standing secular campaigning organizations. The remarkable explosion of the New Atheists onto primetime TV and bestseller lists in the mid-aughts would have been impossible without a decent segment of the US public ready and willing to see religion in general, and Christianity in particular, mercilessly attacked and lampooned. Around the same time, recall also the runaway success of *The Da Vinci Code*, a book whose plot—albeit with a very different MO to Sam Harris or Richard Dawkins—also revolves around both the stop-at-nothing corruption of the contemporary Church and the falsity of Christianity's origin story as a whole. Now, *The Da Vinci Code* is a very different sort of book to *The God Delusion*, aimed at a very different readership. But the thematic commonalities between them ought not to be dismissed lightly. It is no great stretch to suppose that millions of ex-Christians, with decidedly mixed feelings about their religion-of-upbringing and their own connection to it, were a well-primed market for such themes, if presented in an entertaining way. In fact, *The God*

Delusion is deliberately pitched at just such people, announcing on the very first page:

> I suspect—well, I am sure—that there are lots of people out there who have been brought up in some religion or other, are unhappy in it, don't believe it, or are worried about the evils that are done in its name; people who feel vague yearnings to leave their parents' religion and wish they could, but just don't realize that leaving is an option. If you are one of them, this book is for you.[12]

Of course, that's not to say that every one of either Dawkins' or Dan Brown's readers would have believed or agreed with them—although significant numbers no doubt did and do. One needn't be completely convinced by a book in order for a good deal of its central message—even if more in the issues it's addressing than in the conclusions it draws—to resonate in significant ways.

This "Ex Effect" shows up in other areas. Rarely a week seems to pass, for example, without reports of some new controversy over the place of religious symbols or actions in American public life. These typically relate to the presence of a cross on government land, displaying the Ten Commandments at courthouses, religious invocations made before public meetings, and so on.[13] Some such things have been in place for many decades, attracting little controversy over the years. Now, however, they are frequently challenged on the grounds that the First Amendment—"Congress shall make no law respecting an establishment of religion, or prohibiting the free exercise thereof"—renders them unconstitutional. In 2019, for instance, the Supreme Court ruled on whether a 40-foot-tall cross memorializing those who died in the First World War should be allowed to remain standing on public land in Bladensburg,

Maryland. The Peace Cross, paid for by private donors, has stood there since 1925. Commenting before the Court heard the case, an article on the American Civil Liberties Union's website argued:

> On the surface, the case appears to be about one religious monument located at one busy intersection in one town but the stakes are, in fact, much higher. A Supreme Court decision upholding the Bladensburg cross could upend nearly 50 years of First Amendment law and risk further marginalizing religious minorities who are already facing growing bigotry, discrimination, and violence.[14]

The Court ultimately came down 7–2 in favor of the "cross-shaped monument," primarily on the grounds that although "the cross originated as a Christian symbol and retains that meaning in many contexts," nevertheless "the symbol took on an added secular meaning when used in World War I memorials." Furthermore, "The Cross has also acquired historical importance with the passage of time" and "has thus become part of the community."[15] However, the specificity of its rationale is unlikely to close down future challenges to other such monuments.[16]

The Bladensburg case attracted special attention since it reached the Supreme Court, but all manner of smaller state-, county-, and township-level controversies have been springing up all over. It is perhaps tempting to see these as an outgrowth of American religious diversity, with the growth in America's non-Christian religious groups meaning that they now have the numbers, resources, and confidence to challenge the de facto Christianity baked into various aspects of American civic life. And indeed, the ACLU's mention of "religious minorities who are already facing bigotry, discrimination, and violence"—the article elsewhere ties this point explicitly to Trump's infamous "Muslim ban"—would seem to confirm this. But the case itself was brought by the American Humanist Association, one of the country's oldest atheist organizations. Other such cases tend to be brought by groups motivated by secularist concerns, with the Freedom From Religion Foundation, founded in 1976, also a major lobbyist and litigator in this sphere.[17] Perhaps the most notable, and noticed, player in recent years, however, is The Satanic Temple, which is perhaps best thought of as a kind of "performance art" collective dedicated to advancing "an atheistic philosophical framework that views 'Satan' as a metaphorical construct by which we contextualize our works."[18] Rather than directly challenge the public, governmental promotion of Christian symbols, its usual tactic is to request that its own symbols receive equal billing. The ploy itself is not new: American Atheists, the organization founded by Madalyn Murray O'Hair, funded the erection of an "atheist bench" festooned with quotations extolling church–state separation, outside a Florida county courthouse in 2013. This was part of a brokered quid pro quo arrangement following protests concerning a Christian group's paying for a nearby monument to the Ten Commandments: rather than remove the latter, the county declared the patch of land a "free speech zone" permitting multiple (non)religious groups to put up their own statuary. Instead of granite benches quoting Tom Paine, The Satanic Temple's aesthetic leans more toward 3000-pound bronze statues of Baphomet, which it also seeks to have displayed alongside Christian monuments on public land. This and many similar media-savvy ruses are explicitly intended to act as a "poison pill" in the Church/State debate.[19] The idea being, of course, that schools, county courthouses, and state legislatures will end up blanketly avoiding all religious invocations rather than admit Satanic idols, prayers, afterschool clubs, and other intentional provocations to the ecumenical and interfaith pantheon.

Needless to say, these organizations do not "speak for" all atheists—or even all Satanists, for that matter.[20] Still less are they necessarily representative of nones, or nonverts, as a whole. But they evidently *do* represent a certain committed segment of America's unbelievers—and, for reasons discussed earlier, these will certainly include a high proportion of nonverts. Furthermore, neither litigation nor public monuments come cheap. All therefore rely on large networks of members and donors. Given how frequent these First Amendment challenges have become, it is clear that such activities are supported and encouraged by each organization's grassroots: they wouldn't pursue them if they alienated their supporters. The sheer number of them in recent years suggests the opposite: that they help to fire up the base (and open up their wallets). Again, I strongly suspect that there's an Ex Effect lurking behind much of this. This is most clear, I think, in the work of The Satanic Temple. Many former evangelicals especially were raised in a world of Satanic panics and parental bans of *Dungeons and Dragons, Buffy, Harry Potter,* and *Twilight*. Rhett and Melissa, whom we met earlier, said their dads were both avid readers of Frank Peretti's millions-selling novels: "the whole series relies on this idea that everybody who is not a Christ follower has a demon that is attached to their soul and is feeding them thoughts." This notion of there being a "secret demon world" is one they took to heart. Melissa recalls, for example, "my dad came to me one time when my brother was a newborn baby. I remember I got up one morning and my dad shared with me that he had seen a demon in the house that looked like our dog and that was trying to kill my brother." She also remembers a car trip with a friend's family, and their dad gravely informing the two girls that the hum of the tires on a particular stretch of highway was "the demons singing." "And he was not kidding. He was like, 'We're driving through a really demonic part of town right now.'" As such, it is not hard to imagine exvangelicals finding a mischievous, transgressive frisson in kicking in a few dollars to a GoFundMe campaign to build a monument to Satan outside the Oklahoma State Capitol. It's precisely the same impulse that Lil Nas X, the gay rapper raised in Black evangelical churches in Tennessee, targeted so astutely with his 2021 "Satan sneakers" and Easter-released music video for "MONTERO (Call Me By Your Name)"—which, if my Facebook and Twitter feeds were anything to go by, thoroughly delighted many exvangelical millennials. Nor should we underestimate the role of the media in all this. The Satanic Temple's provocations have attracted no shortage of cheerleading coverage from outlets such as *Vice* and *BuzzFeed*: they know what attracts their vast readerships, too.

* * *

If I am right in these speculations, then it seems likely that America's growing pool of nonverts means that we can expect many more of these controversies both in the courts and in the wider culture. And of course, we can also expect a good deal of pushback from the other side too. What one side sees as a long-overdue rebalancing of entrenched Christian privilege, the other side views as an all-out assault on religious freedom, morality, and general decency. These disputes are all the more intense, furthermore, because they're intensely personal to all involved. Divorce litigation is often reputed to be the fiercest, bitterest kind. I don't suppose corporate legal wranglings are exactly an episode of *The Get Along Gang* either, but the parties involved presumably have fewer feelings of hurt and betrayal, and less desire for scorched-earth vengeance. America's current religious wranglings—and here we can add in battles over various issues around gay marriage, abortion, and contraception coverage in healthcare provision, next to which the kinds of issues we've been discussing above are mere (if revealing) skirmishes—are so heated because they aren't only a civil war but, in a literal sense, a family feud writ large.

Naturally, that's not the whole story. For exes don't only relate to their pasts with feelings of anger and contempt. There's very often nostalgia, affection, love, goodwill, and gratitude in abundance, too. We've seen this from our own nonverts. Several of them genuinely miss much of what they've left behind. Others speak sorrowfully of the wounds that leaving their religion has left on them and their family members, their mothers especially. Even black sheep remain and feel part of the family flock. And for all the eye-rolling that might go on about the religiosity of siblings or siblings-in-law (no doubt fully reciprocated), there's no shortage of undying care and affection there either. One can "hate the church, but love the church member," to retool a phrase. This side of things, I'm sure, is also part of the nonvert phenomenon, which to some extent tempers its more fiery impulses. Unlike in much else of the Western world, religion isn't something alien or unfamiliar to most Americans. In most places, most people know a good number of actively religious folks, whether as relatives, neighbors, friends, or co-workers. That's simply not the case in somewhere like, say, Britain.[21] That's perhaps partly why, despite there being vastly more "entrenched Christian privilege" on display—including state funding for religious schools and chaplaincies, a legally mandated daily "act of worship" in all state-funded schools whether religious or not, a "religious test" on the highest office (well, throne) in the land, and twenty-six bishops from the Church of England sitting in our rough equivalent of the Senate—nobody really cares all that much. Allergic reactions to religion in the public square are not an automatic feature of nonreligious cultures. But they make perfect sense in newly nonverted ones.

This is why the changing makeup of the nones over time is important. At the moment, there's a particularly large crop of nonverts in the mix. Hence, as we have seen, there is a striking empowerment and quasi-radicalization of nonreligious activism. But as the other main nonreligious "denomination"—that is, those born and raised nonreligiously—continues to grow due to strong retention and a shrinking pool of potential nonverts, this will surely wane. By then, even though there will be a good many more nonreligious people, they'll feel less investment in fighting them. This will partly be because a good number of battles, of symbol and substance, will already have been won, but mostly because if you were never religious, you have no ex to badmouth.

Recovering Catholics

"I would be upset if, for some reason my daughter—not that she would—went to the Church. I mean, she could end up Buddhist or Hindu, it won't bother me."

"But if she became Catholic? If she were to rediscover . . . ?"

"That *would* bother me."

I met Luisa for dinner at her upscale, West Coast private members' club. It's her treat, thankfully—she had me at "best whiskey list in the State"—and a welcome change of scene from my usual fieldwork sites of cafes and dive bars. In her early forties and leading the leisured life of the upper-middle-classes—"I love my life. I'm completely spoiled. I play tennis all day, come here, eat good dinners, drink these drinks . . . "—she is, on the face of it, an alumna of whom the Los Angeles Catholic school board can rightly be proud. A third-generation Mexican American, raised by parents who were active in their local parish, Luisa grew up in neighborhoods where "everybody" was Catholic. She graduated from Catholic schools with an impressive GPA, and returned from college to marry another Latino Catholic in her home parish. Luisa's own daughter was baptized Catholic, she's the godmother to one of her nieces, and, thanks to her husband's business successes, is well-off enough to send regular donations to support the retired Irish nuns—an odd mix of traditionally habited Sr. Mary Athanasiuses and skirt-and-sweater-sporting Sr. Sharons; American Catholic religious orders having been on a quest to "find themselves" from the late 1960s onward—who taught her: "They did everything. If it wasn't for them, everything would have just fallen apart. But at the same time, they weren't respected." Sure, she may not make it to Mass very often these days: other than for baptisms, weddings, and funerals, she normally only attends at Easter, when her extended family congregates back "home" in Mexico. (When they do the same each Christmas, Luisa nobly volunteers to stay at home with the children to let everyone else attend Midnight Mass.) But, as Catholic authorities have been trying to convince themselves and each other for several decades, that's just the way of many "devout Catholics" these days.[1] Being "a good Catholic"—an outdated, pharisaical, and exclusionary term—is *far much more* than merely going to church.

Luisa's antipathy toward the Church, and toward the idea of her daughter ever embracing the religion into which Luisa herself had her baptized, is nonetheless deep-seated.

> I never felt a connection. Never. Not even as a little child, when you're supposed to. In eighth grade, when they say "You're blessed now, you're old enough, you've learned enough to accept the Sacrament. And when you accept it, you pray, and you'll feel special." And I never—ever—ever [she bangs the table for emphasis on each *ever*]—did. I expected to, and then didn't. I never felt it.

A self-described "good girl" throughout her school days, she dutifully attended church with her family each Saturday evening (which has officially counted as Sunday for American Catholics since the early 1970s). As in many parishes, the Mass in this time slot was specifically engineered—"contemporary, more light-hearted, involving 'the people,' folk music"—to engage young people like her. It didn't work. "It was the longest hour of my life every week." Her main abiding memory of it testifies to how badly in her case it failed at "ensur[ing] that the faithful take part fully aware of what they are doing, actively engaged in the rite, and enriched by its effects" (to quote the Church's own liturgical Key Performance Indicators).[2] Channeling her former self-conscious teenage self, she recalls: "I was relentlessly teased for having sweaty palms, because you have to hold hands during the Our Father, and nobody wanted to hold my hand. And everyone was like, 'No boy's gonna wanna marry you.'" She also recalls noticing how few of her own Catholic peers, or their families, ever turned up. "We went to church every week, but I didn't see much of anybody else there. Any of those classmates. They wouldn't come every week, but we had to be there."

Rather than make a big deal of it at home or school, Luisa instead "just suffered in secret, just rolled with it. I took religion classes. The nuns make you feel that if you're more quiet, more pious, and you're listening, you're *better*. So I just gave them what they wanted." Learning about Greek mythology, with its "pagan" shrines and goddesses, further cemented her skepticism and undermined her personal allegiance to Mary—the one Catholic thing she found "harder" to give up, given her family's own ethnic brand of religiosity with Our Lady of Guadalupe front and center.

> That made me stop and think. And I'm like, "That's funny. That's what *we're* taught to worship." Because being Mexican, our parents had taken us to Mexico City to go see the Shrine, and we've been brought up with this. And then you read the history later, and they needed to convert all these Indians: "They

love their goddess. . . . Let's give them a goddess!" And that's the Virgin Mary.

To cut a long story—interrupted only to check on the Dodgers' progress in the World Series ("I'm an LA girl") on the silent screen behind the club's swanky cocktail bar—short, having attended church every week of her life up until that point, the moment Luisa left home to go to college, "I was free. I don't have to go to church every week. I don't have to stop my life every week to do this thing that I don't believe in." And except for special occasions, she's never been back since. Furthermore, both her distance from, and disdain for, the Church seem only to have increased with each passing year. The priest who married Luisa and her husband soon left the Church to get married himself. Her cherished nun teachers were, as she sees it, left to "rot in their retirement" in some "crumbling, crumbling" old people's home (hence the regular checks). Her sister came out as gay, married a woman, and had kids of her own. And when, of course, "all the scandals came out, about the Church. That solidified everything." She pauses. "Yeah. I *really* dislike the Church."

* * *

American Catholicism is, to use a language it doesn't use much it-self any more, *sui generis*—that is, a class of its own. It doesn't slot neatly into Protestant-calibrated scales of "liberal to moderate to conservative" or "mainline to evangelical to fundamentalism." Nor, for that matter, into common binaries such as rich or poor, old or new, homegrown or immigrant.

This ought not to surprise us. Catholics not only have a long history in America—a continent named, lest we forget, after the Italian Catholic navigator Amerigo Vespucci—they have a much longer one than do Protestants. French and Spanish Catholics had successfully colonized a good chunk of the present United States long before the English settled in Jamestown (and, as recent archaeological discoveries have shown, there were Catholics there, too).[3] But American Catholicism has continued to *also* be an immigrant religion ever since. Wave after wave of new arrivals have come in from every corner of the globe: Venezuelans and Vietnamese, Irish and Indians, Ugandans and Ukrainians, Poles and Pinoys. This fact is proudly celebrated at the National Catholic Shrine in Washington DC, where dozens upon dozens of national groups have their own chapels devoted to each homeland's favored "Our Lady of . . ." sumptuously decorated in the devotional aesthetics of their great-grandparents' home.

Another key Catholic distinctive is the sheer diversity it encompasses, not just ethnically and racially (though certainly that), but socially, culturally, and ideologically too. This might sound a strange comment, given the seemingly monolithic—doctrinally constrained, canonically regulated—nature of *official* Catholic theology, practice, and pastoral life. And that is true, *if* one compares Catholics to, say, "all Protestants" or "all other Christians." But it is manifestly false if one, more sensibly in this context, considers US Catholicism alongside either (i) individual denominational organizations (e.g., United Methodist Church, North American Lutheran Church, Southern Baptist Convention); (ii) denominational families made up of multiple (and sometimes very different) church organizations such as "Baptists" or "Methodists" or even, given the recent fracturings mentioned in Chapter 4, "Episcopalians"; or (iii) even the kinds of Big Catch-All Christian Genres so beloved of pollsters and sociologists (me included), like "mainline" and "evangelical." *Some* of these might, perhaps, admit of further extremes than the Catholic Church on one or more dimension: Methodists as a whole run the gamut on, say, hot-button moral matters; evangelicals are far more racially mixed than outsiders might expect.[4]

But viewed in three dimensions, the Catholic Church is in practice a very broad church indeed. This is the case even on core theological or moral principles, which in theory are the most carefully defined and policed of all church matters. Official red lines often admit, in practice, of a great latitude of interpretation and "pastoral application," and it is very rare indeed for a bishop, priest, or theologian to be silenced or excommunicated—and any who are can almost always find a very welcoming and affirming home in some other corner of the US Catholic Church, whether in a different diocese, a different religious order, or at a different university.[5] Compare this to the kind of "heresy trials" routinely carried out in conservative Protestant churches and colleges.[6] Or indeed, to the fissiparous nature of American Protestantism as a whole. With only few and numerically marginal exceptions,[7] the schisms of both "left" and "right" that have beset so many US denominations—as discussed in Chapter 4 regarding Episcopalians—have been almost wholly avoided by the Catholic Church, which has preferred to keep its culture wars civil (in the 1861 sense). It is notable, for example, that the Catholicism of the United States' forty-sixth president has been chiefly controversial *among other Catholics.*[8]

For these and other reasons of "Catholic exceptionalism," the ex-Catholicism of someone like Luisa doesn't translate easily onto other brands of American ex-religiousness. For one thing, in the terms of Catholic sacramental theology and canon law, Luisa isn't, *and never can be,* such a thing as a former Catholic. They don't exist. For many Protestant denominations you stop being "a member" when you stop turning up (or cancel your direct debit). Mormons, orderly people that they are, have a proper administrative process for leaving. Jehovah's Witnesses, pioneers of cancel culture before it was cool, disfellowship you if you choose no longer to live by their ways.[9] But Luisa, and the millions like her, will always be Catholic—howsoever "irregularly" or "imperfectly" they live up to this irrevocable, sacramentally sanctioned fact.

Given this theological underpinning, it is perhaps no surprise that Catholicism has traditionally had an expansive understanding of continuing membership. "Once a Catholic, always a Catholic," as an old adage goes. Even the lapsed-est of lapsed Catholics, as many Catholic writers have explored,[10] is but a good confession away from being restored to the premium membership plan: no countersigned paperwork necessary. What's more, the multiple ways in which Catholicness is bound up with notions of family, culture, ethnicity, and nationality further muddy the waters of identity (or rather greens them, in the case of the Chicago River on St. Patrick's Day). While such issues are not exclusively a Catholic phenomenon—Norwegian Lutheranism in Minnesota is one example; a good deal of American Jewishness is an even better one—it is particularly pronounced here. Hence, for example, Luisa's otherwise puzzling engagement with a Catholic Church she intensely dislikes and misses very little about, up to including having her daughter baptized and enrolled in Catholic school—the very daughter for whom it would "bother" Luisa if she were really to *become* Catholic.

Luisa's understanding of her and her daughter's relationship with Catholicism, then, differs markedly from the Church's own official understanding. Luisa definitely doesn't see herself as a Catholic, and hasn't for a long time. And as we've seen, she is a very long way from being alone in today's America. Sacramental theology notwithstanding, over a third of all cradle Catholics now no longer see themselves as such. And over half of *those*, amounting to almost one in five out of everyone who says they were raised Catholic, now say they are nones. They've mentally and psychologically "checked out" of the Church, and don't much care if its official policy is "you can never leave." This sociological fact is, moreover, not lost on the Church itself. There is now a growing number of Catholic books, ministries, and programs focused on understanding and/or reaching the Catholic equivalent of "prodigals."[11] Curiously, despite nonversion being a far bigger and more long-standing phenomenon in the Catholic Church, it still doesn't receive nearly the same attention or worry as it does in the evangelical world. *Why* that is, I'm not so sure. But I suspect a combination of (i) relative differences in "zeal for souls," which applies as much to attracting new ones as to keeping those one has already; (ii) plenty of new, keener-than-average Catholic immigrants (and converts) streaming in the front door, distracting attention from those quietly slipping out the back; and (iii) the fuzzier boundaries of Catholic belonging, making it much easier to imagine that many more of the lapsed are still "there," even if temporarily mislaid, and that *their* baptized-and-schooled children will grow up to be there too.[12] Regarding the latter point, it's true that a few people like Luisa's daughter will indeed end up as believing and practicing Catholics, and will thus be taken as confirming the wisdom of what one might call "the long game of cultural Catholicism." But the vast majority won't. And since *they* won't have been brought up in the kinds of rich, practicing Catholic subcultures their parents had, or indeed with a need to "keep happy" parents who valued the importance of Mass-going and church weddings, then *their* own children won't even count as Catholics by the Church's own definition.

* * *

An ex-Catholic and an ex-Jehovah's Witness walk into a bar . . . so I order them each a beer and ask them, in the manner of Oprah to Meghan and Harry, to tell me their "truths."

"He likes to talk *a lot* about the Jesuits," Stef, the disfellowshipped JW, remarks of her partner.

"Did you go to a Jesuit school?" I ask Daniel, since so many US Catholics, ex and otherwise, have done. He didn't, though.

"Because of my own criticism of Catholicism, I started reading more about history. I enjoy it. It's a—what, over a billion people?—massive, rich organization I was forced to be a part of. I have much to say about organizations I was forced to be a part of . . . where was I?"

"Your love of Jesuits."

"*My love of Jesuits.* Right. There's this one book, I think called *The Jesuits,* where some bishop or whatever was criticizing the Jesuits as being heathen, anti-pope. And I'm just like, 'That's *awesome*.' The Jesuits have done a lot of evil themselves, but as the ones who apparently as an Order were meant to be free-thinking and started schools to teach people to be free-thinking, I'm like *that's awesome.* And then in grad school, I met a Jesuit, and he tried to recruit me. And I think I accidently helped him lose his faith. So: Me one, Jesuits zero." He laughs. "But despite being part of the Catholic Church, I like that they were critical. Like I think organizationally they're not part of the hierarchy of the church. It goes: the pope, the Jesuits on the side, and then everybody else. So they give them kind of a privileged place to be able to reflect on the church and be critical and do whatever. So I guess I like that they're almost 'underdoggy' in that way."

"And the pope's a Jesuit. . . . "

"I don't know how the Catholic Church has let that happen. He's going to undermine so much of their power and so much of their oppressive dogma. How did you let that happen? Good for you, Pope!" Laughing again—I'm not sure he ever stopped, come to think of it—Daniel suddenly remembers his forebears' fatherland. "Though as a Polish person, we cannot recognize anyone other than

John Paul. *John Paul was the last and only pope.* But Francis . . . he's, personally speaking, a better one—more liberal—but as a Polish person he's second."

Now there's a lot to unpack here. Daniel is, it's worth stressing, "currently a pretty hardcore atheist." He's a psychotherapist, and a significant minority of his clientele are "either nones or people struggling with their religion—one Muslim, two Scientologists, a bunch of Jehovah's Witnesses." He's also worked a lot with "Native Americans and their spirituality, though their experience is very different." While his patients' problems are quite varied, religion in one form or another is often "where a lot of the suffering comes from." Since this perhaps helps to explain the struggles and anxieties of some of the other people we've met in this book (several of whom mentioned their own visits to therapists), Daniel's professional assessment is worth quoting here at some length.

> It's usually, to some degree, some struggle against the beliefs they were raised with. Either "I individually struggle with it" or "I'm still in this culture and I can't live the life that I want." And they may be aware of that, they may not, but that's the message I'm getting. And they may not identify it as that, but in getting their history of what happened: "Oh, I experienced this abuse, and I had to go to these meetings where people told me that my . . ." or "The fact that I was gay is against the . . ." So they got all these messages that there was something wrong with you. And they may not see it as the religion per se, but as "I'm trying to live a life that's authentic to me but my parents have a problem with it" or "I feel this incredible amount of anxiety whenever I go to Mass or to church and I don't know why, and what I want to do is not feel anxious but still go to church." And to me I see that as, "Hey, the anxiety is probably not the separate thing that you're doing

that's preventing you from going to church. The anxiety's probably tied into that religion or some part of you going 'something's not right but I can't really see what that is because that's too scary for me.'"

It's Daniel's own case history that is my main interest, though. Raised by Polish parents, first in Canada then later in the United States, Catholicism was naturally entwined with the Polish culture of his upbringing.[13] Culture is, however, perhaps the operative word here: his mother would send him and his brother to Mass every week, yet never went herself. Then, when his brother stopped, Daniel declared that he didn't believe, and so he would stop too. His parents were fine with this, admitting that they didn't actually believe in Christianity, and explaining, "'We sent you to church to inoculate you against something worse. We sent you to church so you would learn all these beliefs, and at some point you would be like, "well that's bullshit," and then resist it if other religions came along.' It was a vaccine against religion—and to be fair, that actually worked."

In contrast to the other, mainline childhood-churchgoing-as-inoculation stories we encountered in Chapter 4, in Daniel's case *something* stuck. Not faith, certainly, but instead a kind of Catholic love/hate fascination.

> I see myself as an atheist, but I also think of myself as a recovering Catholic. I like the term as a tongue-in-cheek idea, but I think it speaks to this difference—for some Polish Catholics— between "Catholic faith" and "Catholic culture." And when I say recovering Catholic I guess I mean that I don't believe any of the dogma, and I don't go to Mass, but I'm still culturally Catholic— and some of that has infected my thinking. Some of it I'm aware of, and some of it I'm not.

At this point in the conversation, Stef jumps back in. "It's interesting with him, because having known him for nearly five years now and listening to him speak a lot about religion, he *is* an atheist, I'd even say a militant atheist. But when Catholicism comes up he has what I would call a soft spot." (A soft spot that *she* doesn't have for the Jehovah's Witnesses.) "He's both defensive of Catholicism and appreciates Catholicism in a way that he wouldn't appreciate other belief systems."

"It's true," he agrees. "The schools I went to were very liberal, but they had Mass and religion class. Being a little bit of a shit-stirrer myself, I always struggled against that. And I always struggled against the things I was raised to be as a Catholic—I wanted to carve out my own thinking. But now, I'm pretty comfortable with my worldview. So then it becomes a sort of reintegration of those elements of Catholicism, or Polish/Catholic upbringing, that are useful, or at least I have a soft spot for."

He adds that however "extremely conservative: anti-sex, anti-condoms, anti-women" the Catholic Church might be—"and it *is* those things"—meeting and working with (former) Mormons, Witnesses, or evangelicals has made him appreciate just how much worse an upbringing can be. "I go, Wow, it could be so much more conservative, it could be so much more oppressive! In comparison I look at the Catholic Church and be like: 'Not doing such a bad job . . .' They're doing a lot of terrible things, but y'know, they have a chief astronomer, and the current pope talks about climate change. They're fairly accepting of science, which some religions aren't."

* * *

Daniel's complicated, ongoing relationship with Catholicism is in many ways the flipside of Luisa's. Both remain oddly tangled up with a religion neither believes in nor supports. Luisa possesses zero affection or appreciation for it, and keeps a strict "don't ask, don't tell" policy with even close friends and family members (one that even the practicing Catholics among them seem to sense and respect). Nevertheless, she continues to "perform" Catholicism in concrete ways, through Easter Mass attendance, rites of passage, and her daughter's schooling. Paradoxically, these things help her to enforce her "don't ask, don't tell" stance, since by doing the bare minimum of what's expected, she can avoid any painful reckonings with her relatives or heritage. Meanwhile, Daniel has few concrete entanglements with the Church, and needn't even attend church for form's sake when visiting his parents. And yet, he has an abiding fascination with, and grudging respect for, Catholicism. This is partly professional, since his day job forces him to think and talk about religion on a regular basis. But it is personal, too. He's obsessed with Jesuits, has a "soft spot" for Catholicism, and is a fan of the (Jesuit) pope. Daniel and Luisa are thus opposing sides of the same, culturally Catholic coin.

The ongoing salience of a Catholic upbringing, even long after one has fundamentally rejected it, was mentioned by several people I spoke to. Thus Charles, the ex-zookeeper who sent his kids to the Episcopalians to get inoculated against religion (just as Daniel's mother sent him to liberal Canadian Catholics), remarks: "Sometimes I tell people that I was raised Catholic. It's funny because a lot of the friends I have now were raised Catholic. And you kind of connect a little because that's a club that you were once a member of." That's the kind of comment we've also seen in these pages from ex-Mormons, such as the "ethnically Mormon basically" Mark. Recall, too, Daniel's being a Jesuit history buff. In the same way, and I suspect for precisely the same psychological reasons, the ex-Mormon world includes many experts, amateurs and academics alike, on aspects of LDS history. (We've met one already, in fact. The "stone-cold atheist" Norah, briefly quoted in Chapter 2, peppered our conversation with lines such as this one: "So, anyway, Philo T. Farnsworth was my kids' great-great-great-great-great-uncle. His son was also named Philo T. Farnsworth and he is one of the three or four people who invented the TV at the same time."[14]) One senses something similar among those brought up deep within the evangelical subculture, with a shared store of pop-culture in-jokes about the Power Team, puppetry, Precious Moments, or cringe-worthy purity presentations. In both cases, this all often sits alongside genuine feelings of loss or nostalgia and/or the types of still-raw wounds of trauma and anxiety which help to pay Daniel's bills. Either way, it's a long way from the "it's not like I hate it," take-it-or-leave-it indifference that characterizes former mainliners.

That said, and returning now to the Catholic context, it's no coincidence that Luisa and Daniel were raised in immigrant subcultures, whereas Charles was brought up in Virginia in the 1950s and 1960s. Here we see the above-discussed *capaciousness* of American Catholicism come back to the fore. Importantly, among Catholic nonverts one also finds plenty who sound much like ex-mainliners in terms of how little impression their religious upbringings made upon them, then or since. "Even as a kid I remember going [to Mass], and we were just checking off a box, you know"; "I was baptized in a Catholic church for family reasons, but that was it. My parents just never even brought up it"; "I wouldn't count being brought up as Catholic as [making me a Catholic now] because I'm not kidding when I say it really didn't come up much." Something else that comes up a lot in Catholic interviews, but almost never in, say, Mormon or evangelical ones, is that even in families that went to church weekly there came a point in the early-to mid-teens when church attendance was optional. In some cases, this was made explicit: "about thirteen or so, my mom said, 'You can decide if you want to go or not.'" In others, it was more tacit: "we probably started sliding away from going to church every week after Confirmation"—that is, after all the Church's, and often *school's*, sacramental boxes had been ticked. Tellingly, this would sometimes also become the trigger for the parents to stop going regularly, too. (Assuming that both parents had attended before, that is; there are plenty of stay-at-home dads when it comes to Mass-going. And as we saw in Daniel's case, some stay-at-home moms too.)[15]

In these mainline-esque cases, a definite generational pattern is often apparent: genuinely devout grandparents; parents who are noticeably less personally committed but who promote Catholic participation to varying degrees, ranging from getting the kids baptized and going to Mass only when the grandparents are in town, up to weekly Mass and grace before meals; and then our own nonvert interviewees, who were raised with a significantly weaker dose of childhood Catholicism than their parents had been and who feel little connection to, or affection for, the Church. This broad generational pattern has many and complex contributing factors, as I have explored in much more detail in a previous book.[16] Some of these are wider social changes over the past half-decade and more, such as we have already charted in Chapters 4 and 5. Others, however, are Catholic-specific: a good deal of liturgical, pastoral, devotional, and moral turbulence in the wake of the 1960s; a conscious project of disenchantment, or perhaps better *de-weirding* or *vanilla-ing* of traditional teaching and practice, that is nicely summed up by the term "beige Catholicism." However causes are to be assigned—and it would be fair to say that expert opinions differ—the overall effects are clear enough in the harvest of nones that the Church is reaping, largely grown from seeds sown decades before. Across all US cradle Catholics born since 1970, a

"Catholic upbringing" has produced twice as many nones as it has weekly Mass-going Catholics.[17]

The impact of this "mainlining" within the US Catholic Church is evident to different degrees in different places. This is partly due to geography, reflecting both general variation in religious climate (e.g., North/South, urban/rural) as well as a significant, long-standing regionality within American Catholic culture(s).[18] But it is also due to parish-level differences in demography and, to a lesser extent, "style." A downtown parish in what *used to be* a heavily Irish or Italian enclave but is now a gentrifying neighborhood of young professionals will have a very different composition from one just a few miles away, near a major hospital that employs a significant number of doctors and nurses from southern India and the Philippines. Likewise, a hitherto-failing parish that has now been entrusted with a niche ministry—whether to traditional Latin Mass devotees, Korean speakers, or ex-Episcopalians[19]—and which draws its congregation from a wide catchment area of people committed enough to travel to it, will be very different from the next-door parish with a mission to all comers who have been coming in progressively fewer numbers for the past forty years. As noted above, the diverse makeup of the American Church—a diversity reflected as much *within* individual congregations as at the diocesan or national level—means that most churches in most places will have a genuinely mixed congregation, both demographically (ages, ethnicities, immigrant statuses, class, life-stages) and in terms of religious belief and commitment. Many will also now have a significantly larger "shadow congregation" comprising all those living within the parochial boundary who were baptized as Catholics—and who, according to Catholic canon law, are therefore parishioners—but who have rarely or never darkened the church doors nor have any desire to. And even if they read books about the Jesuits, the likelihood that *their* children will is very slim indeed.

* * *

Even if there was nothing more to add to this story, the Catholic Church would have a serious problem with nonversion. Cultural Catholicism, when not packaged up with personally owned belief and practice, only passes on for a generation or two: the children who were baptized only to please their Polish, Mexican, or Bostonian grandmothers will not grow up needing to placate their own mother when it comes to their offspring. And that's when the going is good—when, broadly speaking, a Catholic family background, especially entwined as it so often is with a proud ethnic identity, is something to take pride in. Even for those who no longer believe, and only attend church for baptisms or funerals, what's not to like about drinking Guinness on St. Patrick's Day or eating *zeppole* on the Feast of San Giuseppe?

However, these often now aren't the first things that leap to mind when people think about the Catholic Church. Instead, it's the sexual abuse of minors by hundreds of priests over many decades, with church authorities often ignoring, denying, enabling, covering up, and, as a last resort, reaching for the checkbook and a nondisclosure agreement. It's the former cardinal "Ted" McCarrick, who rose to the very top of the US Church despite being a serial abuser of young men and boys and whose influence and cash gifts leveraged a shocking degree of "benefit of the doubt" for decades.[20] It's the fact that, for approaching *forty years* now, there's been a constant stream of horrifying revelations followed by grave assurances of "lessons learned," "zero tolerance," and "never again," followed by further horrifying revelations. It's all these things and much more, both in the national news, and in people's own parishes, communities, and families.

While none of my interviewees divulged direct involvement in these vile matters, they nevertheless took their toll on any lingering attachment to a personal Catholic identity. Sam, the straight-talking, sixty-something Pittsburgher whom we last met in Chapter 3, was "raised Catholic—the whole nine yards, catechism, and all that; I did the church thing." He recalls how in "the early 1980s, after I got out of the Marine Corps, I'm sitting at home, and the Catholic Church comes on the TV. It started a $10 million super-fund, to fund legal fees for pedophiles. . . . And that shocked me, that shocked me." From the timing, it's likely that this was connected to the then-emerging allegations against Fr. Gilbert Gauthe, a priest of the Diocese of Lafayette in Louisiana who was at the center of the first such scandal to gain widespread media attention.[21] Louisiana's own Reverend Judy, whom I dare say you'll remember from this book's opening pages, also remembers the case all too well. It was right around the time when she was still "devout, devoutly Christian and was very, very devoutly Catholic and was very serious about what I thought was a vocation" to the Catholic nuns who had taught her. Even though the events were already very close to her Cajun Catholic home, she particularly recollects the impact that the national media, which otherwise never deigned to mention local happenings, had on pressing home the gravity of the situation.

The eighties is when a lot of the sex scandals came out of priests abusing children. And when *the* news is carrying it, it's a big, big deal. It's not just making the nightly news on the local stations. You know, *60 Minutes* is talking about it, and that's national.

Suddenly the Catholic Church no longer seemed quite the spiritual safe haven she had been hoping for.

> When you grow up abused and you grow up mistreated and you grow up believing you have all these situations. When the organization you have trusted your faith into and—y'know, "God is the answer," right?—is also perpetrating abuses on people like me, that can really break something that is almost irreparable. So, to escape from one, I had to escape it all.

It was this, around the age of sixteen, that made her realize that women's religious life, at least as the Catholic Church conceived it, wasn't for her. Nor, actually, was the Church more broadly: "I stopped participating in the outward trappings of the church. I notified the Mother Superior at the convent here that I was no longer interested in pursuing a vocation. I stopped doing youth group, I stopped doing Sunday school, I stopped doing Mass except on High Holy Days." This was the beginning of the end of her feeling, or even wanting to feel, like a Catholic. "By my early twenties, I was definitely, if you'd asked me I would have said I was, a lapsed Catholic." Though she hadn't yet given up her belief in God (that would come later), her belief in the Church which claimed to represent Him was shattered beyond recovery.

> In my twenties, I would have said that while I have doubts, I feel like I believe in God. My step away from religion was really only the first step. Moving myself away from religion did not change the way I viewed my spirituality, my faith. *God* wasn't abusing those kids. In my head, God wasn't abusing those kids, and he wasn't telling those priests to abuse those kids. It wasn't God who was stepping away from the priesthood for carnal love and carnal

desires. Those priests were doing those things, that was their lack of faith. It was a brokenness in them, not in God. That's how I would have thought about that, and did think about it then.

Speaking to other, mostly younger ex-Catholics, these kinds of faith-shattering stories are markedly less forthcoming. They certainly weren't unaware of priests' and bishops' crimes and cover-ups: in fact, a good number of my interviews were conducted in August 2018 when, due to soon-to-be-former-cardinal McCarrick and the Pennsylvania Grand Jury report, these subjects were rarely out of the headlines.[22] Ex-Catholics often brought them up in our conversations: "They're coming out of the woodwork—people who were supposed to have a connection to God, and they're doing highly inappropriate things and going to great lengths to hide it"; "it's not like there's a bunch of bad apples, it's fairly systemic"; "all of the negativity within the Catholic church, it's big in the news in the US right now. I mean, this isn't a new thing, it's really a tip of an iceberg"; "there are so many things that the Church up until this point has tried to lie about or sweep under the rug, like the molestations . . ." But critically, these observations were not being cited as having *triggered* their disenchantment with the Church. Rather, they're offered as, at most, supporting evidence for why, being already long done with the Church, or else—despite being notionally "raised Catholic"—never having felt like a Catholic in the first place, was naturally the moral, rational, and right option. None of them, least of all those in their twenties or thirties, express the kind of shock that Sam, thirty or forty years their senior, recounts. Much less do they exhibit the visceral feelings of disappointment and betrayal that Judy did and does. This too, I feel quite confident in suggesting here, is a product of the decades-long generational waning of Catholic commitment across large swathes of the American Church. It's not that they're not horrified by the abuse crisis—of course they are. But it's the detached horror of outsiders looking in. It isn't the shame and revulsion of people who feel that the Church's failings hit *them*, and their own sense of identity, personally.

* * *

Millennials and Generation Z-ers have grown up familiar with news reports, movies, documentary series, and any amount of jokes from primetime hosts and shows such as *South Park* and *Family Guy*,[23] all reinforcing the link between the Catholic Church, child sexual abuse, and "conspiracy to cover up." Even the oldest of millennials, who were born around the time of the Lafayette scandals, would only have been college-age when the *Boston Globe*'s Pulitzer-winning "Spotlight" reports began appearing in early 2002.[24] In Chapter 6, I argued that scandals in evangelical churches undermine faith not only in the preachers themselves but in what they are preaching. This is compounded when a good part of what they are preaching is a sexual ethic that is already a hard sell in the eyes of the wider culture. This argument applies all the more powerfully to the Catholic Church, and for three reasons. First, because official Catholic teaching is, in certain respects, even more countercultural: many of the most conservative of Protestants count as "you do you" libertines when it comes to artificial contraception.[25] Second, because the sex scandals most associated in the public mind with the Catholic Church (i.e., involving children) are more heinous than the ones that most readily leap to mind with evangelicals.[26] And third, because however autonomous different Catholic dioceses or religious orders are in practice, they are all understood as divisions or branches of a single organization: corruption in one part of it necessarily taints the rest by association. This is also true in the evangelical world, but surely less so, where even some big denominational "brands" operate more like a voluntary federation of likeminded affiliates rather than as the headquarters of a franchise business. It is accordingly easier to ascribe problems in one church or group of churches to pathologies peculiar to it, rather than to the overarching body as a whole.

Given all this, it is all the more remarkable that, in a group of interviewees generally critical of all religious leaders (occasional mention of the Dalai Lama being "amazing" notwithstanding), one who *was* often spontaneously praised is the leader of this Church: Pope Francis. Daniel's approval of him as a Jesuit fifth column was quoted above. Juanita, whose "very Catholic" 1980s upbringing included churchgoing "actually only on Easter and Christmas," and for whom "Buddhism is closest to my personal outlook on the world, but I always say 'none' or 'not applicable' when people ask me my religion," nevertheless waxes lyrical when it comes to Francis: "the new pope is the best, he really is, he's such a wonderful person. . . . He obviously has the connection to animals because he chose the name Francis. He has, so many times, gone out of his way to admit the wrongdoings of the Church in the past, and try to make up for it, and that is so commendable." This popularity was even more striking among those *not* brought up Catholic. For Melissa and Rhett, whose journey out of evangelicalism we followed two chapters ago, "In the current pope you do see a little bit of the love, a little bit of 'let people live and just love them for who they are.' He seems nice, and if these Christians were all nice, we wouldn't fight them." According to David, whose Chinese parents outsourced his Americanization to Lutherans: "His papacy is a representation of what I believe shaping religion in a positive way [would look like]." Shirley, a New Orleans costumier in her early fifties, who was raised generically and non-practicingly Protestant in Maryland ("I guess we just went the American way"), is more effusive still: "I think there's issues in the Catholic Church that needs to be addressed and he's addressing them. Will he resolve them? I don't know. The Catholic Church is pretty slow on doing stuff, so I don't think we can expect a lot. But I love that he doesn't live above his means. I love that little car that he drives in. He just seems like a wonderful man that really wants to do good and honestly is trying."

In one sense, this should not be altogether surprising. Francis is, after all, a very popular world figure, much admired by most Catholics and non-Catholics alike.[27] Since his very first evening in office, he has received warm, and often rapturous, coverage from the media: "The narrative was established. Francis the reformer. Francis the media sensation. Francis the people's pope. Francis, the great liberal Catholic hope."[28] The media, and thus popular, narrative of Pope Francis draws much of its power in contrast to an opposing narrative, or perhaps better here "construction" of what the Catholic Church itself is taken to stand for and represent. Most obviously, Francis is depicted as an *Untouchables*-esque crusader against sexual abuse and related corruption. This is certainly a part of my nonverts' conception of Francis and their reasons for liking him so much. But it goes much further than that. Dorothy, an early-fifties Mississippian whose religious upbringing was divided between Pentecostals and Southern Baptists—neither of whom are renowned for their papal appreciation—neatly sums up a number of themes evoked by others.

He seems to represent Christianity the way I would want it to be. So he's tolerant, and he's accepting, and he's given people some personal agency to be who they are and make the mistakes that they're going to make, but still be accepted by God or Christ. So, he's not condemning gay people. He's not condemning people that have—I'm not really sure, now that I say, where he stands on birth control and all that—but I think he's more lenient than others, but not outright saying it's OK. Him saying that evolution is a possibility was huge. I mean, just an acceptance that there might be information out there we haven't considered, and we need to start considering the new information. That has been amazing for me.

A more accepting, tolerant approach to people from all walks of life was cited by several of my conversation partners. Homosexuals were most frequently given as an example here, but they weren't the only perceived beneficiaries of Francis' friendliness. (Here's Shirley again: "This current pope is so what I think the Catholic Church needed. He is excellent. I think he's wonderful. I would meet the current pope because I don't think he would put any bias against me being an atheist.") Others were also struck by Francis' pro-science platform. For instance, Melissa was in the midst of telling me how "It totally made sense why my parents felt it so important to protect me from science, because knowledge definitely makes it really impossible or very challenging to buy into [certain evangelical beliefs]." Whereupon, Rhett jumped in: "And now we've got the pope on our side! So, that's good." The use of "now" here is particularly telling, and chimes with Dorothy's ascribing "huge" and "amazing" significance to Francis' affirmation of evolution—that is, as constituting something unprecedentedly new in papal utterances. To be fair to them, this was certainly how the pope's comments in 2014 that "*evolution* in nature is not opposed to the notion of Creation" were reported in the press: "Our New Pro-Science Pontiff," declared a *Washington Post* headline.[29] But this just goes to show how greatly media reporting on Francis shapes, and distorts, public perceptions. For of course there is nothing terribly earth-shattering about a pope making fairly anodyne remarks about the compatibility of evolution and a properly Catholic understanding of creation. They've been doing it, with more or less qualification, since Pope Pius XII in 1950.[30]

Ever since his election in 2013, there has been hopeful talk in Catholic circles of a "Francis Effect" giving a much-needed boost to faltering rates of retention, Mass attendance, and/or vocations. Tangible trickle-down effects from positive papal PR have not, however, been forthcoming.[31] As such, it would probably be more accurate to speak of a Francis *Affect*. The warmth and affection toward him—including among many people who are not merely distant but deliberately *distanced* from religion—is certainly real. Given the types of headlines the US Church has generated over the past few decades, then this is significant in itself. For those trying to attract people to, or keep people in, the Catholic Church, Pope Francis would certainly seem to be a helpful piece of branding.

There's a double-edged aspect to all this, however. In the first place, Francis' critics *within* the Church—despite his generally high approval rating, there's no shortage of these, and they're disproportionately to be found among the more committed—could argue that a pope who polls so strongly among atheists and other nones only does so by mis-selling the fullness of Catholic doctrine and discipline, either directly or (more charitably) via the wishful misinterpretations propagated by the secular media. Second, and more broadly, it is certainly true that the "Pope Francis" my interviewees like so much isn't necessarily the full picture either of him or of the "Catholic Church" they pit him against. For instance, in March 2021 the *Rolling Stone* website carried a story headlined "Guess the Cool Pope Isn't So Cool After All," referring to a recent Vatican statement on the inadmissibility of blessing same-sex unions. Note, first of all, how odd it is for music mags even to notice doctrinal clarifications issued by the Holy See; that's just the strange world we live in these days. For *Rolling Stone*, however, it's personal: having made him their cover star back in 2014, they staked their own cultural credibility on what they termed "Pope Francis' gentle revolution."[32] This new article's opening sentences are worth quoting in full, since they capture perfectly the disjunct between wishful thinking and hard reality.

> Rightly or wrongly, Pope Francis has long enjoyed the reputation as the "cool pope," a view that has been bolstered by, among other things, his public statements in support of the theory of evolution and a 2014 profile in the pages of this magazine. A documentary released last fall even appeared to suggest his emerging support for same-sex pairings.
>
> As it turns out, however, it's pretty difficult to be hip and woke and with-it if you're the face of a retrograde thousands-year-old religious institution, as the Vatican clarified in a statement on Monday that it would not bless same-sex unions on the grounds that God "does not and cannot bless sin."[33]

These mentions of evolution and support for same-sex relationships chime perfectly with the comments of my own interviewees. (As David bluntly put it, in support of Francis' perceived LGBTQ allyship: "Why does God care what hole I'm putting it in?") The "hip and woke and with-it" comment, moreover, says all you need to know about the American media's fanciful projections onto an eighty-four-year-old Argentinian bishop. In retrospect, such crashing disappointment was inevitable. And as the media turn against him, and his failures to recast his "retrograde thousands-year-old religious institution" into a cover version of the Episcopal

Church of America (only with worse music), so too, I suspect, will many of my nones.

Of course, as with evangelicals and Mormons, there's plenty of life left in the US Catholic Church. Having somehow survived without *Rolling Stone's* endorsement since the colonial era, it will no doubt manage to do so still. Immigration may help, as it usually has. But so too, ultimately, will a side-effect of the decades-long process of lapsation and disaffiliation we have traced in this chapter. Paradoxically, the greater the pull of no religion on younger cradle Catholics, the more committed must be the ones who remain *in spite of everything*. This is partly because if they weren't, then they wouldn't have remained in the first place: they'd have left with the rest of their peers (and perhaps siblings). But it's also because the other young Catholics they end up hanging out with, whether at Mass, a college Newman Society, or increasingly online, are also the on-average more committed. Thus they end up forming the kinds of mutually encouraging, "embattled but thriving"[34] subcultures that have helped evangelicals and Latter-day Saints weather the storms of secularization better than other churches.[35] Naturally, as we've seen in Chapters 2 and 6, both groups are also suffering from a bad case of nonversion—though less, and for less long, than Catholics have been. But, as we'll see in the final chapter, this looks set to become a chronic condition for America's religious groups. And as sufferers of such illnesses well know, the debilitating effects of such conditions can be, with careful management and strong therapeutics, if not cured then noticeably mitigated.

Nonvert Nation

European writers have what, for those on the receiving end, must seem an intensely annoying habit: touring around the States for a few weeks or months, before pontificating on The State of American Religion. The French diplomat and political theorist Alexis de Tocqueville, fittingly enough for a Parisian aristocrat, launched the trend in 1831. Lettered luminaries such as the English authors Charles Dickens and G. K. Chesterton, the Dutch theologian and statesman Abraham Kuyper, and the German sociologist Max Weber all followed in his footsteps. If sometimes for very different reasons, each found something distinctive and peculiar—exceptional even—about religious life, thought, and practice in the United States. Thus for Tocqueville, "Christianity rests here on a firmer foundation than in any other country in the world which I know, and I have no doubt but that the religious element influences the political one."[1]

Chesterton's observations, true to form, were more idiosyncratic. He has a particular eye for oddities, such as the reverence with which Americans treat elevators ("Perhaps that flying chapel will eventually be ritualistically decorated like a chapel . . . Perhaps a brief religious service will be held in the elevator as it ascends"), or that "There is in America, I believe, a large religious body that has felt it right to separate itself from Christendom, because it cannot believe in the morality of wearing buttons."[2] There's usually a point behind Chesterton's playfulness—most often a sharp one. Quite what he's getting at with his reverie on elevators, I'm not sure. But the buttons passage comes as part of a wider reflection on the fissiparity of American Protestantism and its sectarian impulse toward ever-greater purity: searching "for truth not by synthesis but by subdivision," in Chesterton's phrase. This, combined with what he perceived as Americans' bloody-minded independence, also lies behind Dickens' views on the unsuitability of religious establishment there: "I think the temper of the people, if it admitted of such an Institution being founded amongst them, would lead them to desert it, as a matter of course, merely because it *was* established."[3] These Chestertonian and Dickensian ideas would later resurface in *The Simpsons*' previously quoted gag about "the one true faith: the Western Branch of American Reform Presbylutheranism."

Weber, too, was interested in the diverse marketplace of American Christianities and was struck by the buoyancy of the religious scene, especially as compared to his native Germany (or at least to the urbane sphere of it he inhabited). Writing in 1906, however, he was confident in prophesying Christian America's impending demise:

> Only the most superficial visitor to the United States could fail to notice the strong growth of community life within the Church here. The permeation by the Church of the whole of life, however, which was an integral part of true "Americanism," is today everywhere being undermined by rapid Europeanization.[4]

This belief is echoed in Weber's famous *Protestant Ethic and the "Spirit" of Capitalism*, where he notes "the general tendency toward 'secularization' in American life, which in a short time will have destroyed the traditional character of this nation and finally changed the ethos of many of the fundamental institutions of the nation."[5] The following century did not, it is fair to say, quite bear out his prediction. Evidently, the "mood of indifference that Europeanization has brought with it"[6] was not quite so powerful as he had supposed. Viewed in retrospect, there is also something a little quaint in Weber's imagining that American culture and society would be taking its cues from Europe over the course of the twentieth century. For Weber, as for many of secularization's subsequent soothsayers, where Europe goes the rest of the ("modern," "civilized") world eventually follows.[7] And since Europe was already getting less religious, and fast, then America would soon be doing so too.

Given this track record, it's no surprise that those *still* predicting the imminent collapse of "American Religious Exceptionalism" should be roundly derided as the Chicken Littles of the sociology of religion. Furthermore, since even some of secularization theory's leading twentieth-century champions—most notably the late, great Peter Berger—have publicly recanted of their follies, those still clinging to some version of it almost seem like those Japanese soldiers in remote Pacific jungles, still fighting World War Two long after it had ended and unable to believe that their side had lost.[8]

Trouble is, religion—and Christianity especially—really *is* less strong in America than it used to be. The upsurge of nonversion over the past few decades is one indicator of this, and an important one. In itself, the shift from ticking one of the Christian boxes on a survey to ticking "no religion" instead might seem of little consequence: hence it is often explained away as mere Christians-in-name-only finally being more honest with themselves and others. But in reality, this is not so. For a start, as the testimonies in the foregoing chapters have amply shown, many of the new nones were once genuinely believing and practicing—even "painfully devout," in Judy's phrase. The data also bear this out. Every ten years or so, the GSS asks a detailed, religion-specific suite of questions. Using these, we can see how nonversion has grown among those who were brought up actually to *practice* their religion. In 1991, only 3% of those saying that they attended religious services weekly or more at the age of twelve (i.e., those therefore raised in committedly religious homes) now identified as nones. By 1998 it was 8%, and by 2008, 10%. In 2018, it had shot up to 18%: roughly the same rate as among all US adults just ten years earlier. There have been similar rises in nonversion among those who, aged twelve, attended religious services either "almost weekly," "2–3 times a month," or "monthly." As Figure 9.1 clearly shows, these trends broadly parallel the rise of the nones in the general population. These were church kids; theirs won't be.

Even *if* growing nonversion was only evidenced among the weakly religious—which it isn't—this too would support the idea

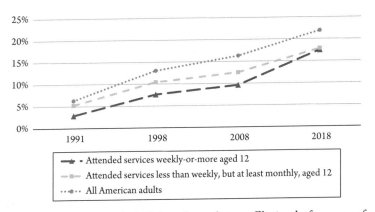

Figure 9.1. Proportion of US adults with no religious affiliation, by frequency of religious practice at the age of 12, and among the general population, over time. *Source: General Social Survey 1991, 1998, 2008, and 2018*

that Christianity's influence is waning in America. Nominal adherence actually tells you a lot about how a certain "brand" is doing. That's why, for example, successful sports teams often have vast numbers of casual fans. These might rarely or never even check the scores, let alone watch games, but they'll still feel a certain tug of pride if "their" team wins the Super Bowl. They'll also likely try to pass this allegiance on to their own children, by buying them the occasional jersey or baseball cap with the team's insignia. Of course, such teams also have a hard core of diehard fans, who will stay loyal even after years of disappointment and decline. They're the sort who'll keep on paying hard-earned cash to feel miserable while watching the team get beaten week in, week out. (I know what this feels like. My soccer team is Nottingham Forest, twice champions of Europe. Never heard of them? Exactly.) But you can bet your vintage Super Bowl ring that after years of failure, the vast majority of nominal fans will have evaporated away and are now buying some other team's merchandise for their children's birthdays.

Of course, if the nones had been rising while most or all other indicators of religious vitality had been hitting ever-new highs, then we might need to rethink some of our assumptions. But this is really not so. Sure, there are relative winners and losers in the American religious marketplace, as there always are. But it's a somewhat smaller market than it used to be.[9] And the growth of the nones is as much a symptom of that fact as it is a contributor.

* * *

America *is* secularizing, but not because of something called "Europeanization." It is perfectly capable of secularizing all by itself, and in its own way. Although it has been traditional to contrast "religious America" to "godless Europe," I'm not so sure it's a very helpful comparison. This is so from both sides of the equation. First off, the USA is a big and varied place. From California to the New York island, as indeed from the Redwood forest to the Gulf Stream waters, this land contains a diverse range of religious climates, and indeed micro-climates. That doesn't mean that it's illegitimate to talk about American religion in the aggregate—*e pluribus unum*, and all that. But it's still an *unum* with a high degree of variation around the mean. The same is even more true, of course, of Europe. Certainly, the Continent contains plenty of countries with high numbers of nones, fairly few practicing Christians, and a generally secular ambience. Britain is one, though it is by no means the only example. But Europe, for all kinds of historical, political, ethnic, and economic reasons, exhibits a great deal of religious diversity too. Several countries, such as Poland and Malta, rival even the most religious of US states. There are also vast swathes of America whose nonreligiosity, on some indicators at least, is well up there with Europe's finest. For example, 33% of adults in America's Pacific states—California, Oregon, Washington, Alaska, and Hawaii—identified as nones in the 2018 GSS. That's roughly the same proportion as one finds in Spain (30%), Sweden (30%), Finland (32%), Slovenia (33%), and Switzerland (35%).[10] Likewise, 38% of New Englanders and 35% of those in the Mountain states (from Idaho and Montana on down) say they "never" attend religious services. That puts them on a rough par with Finns (33%), Germans (33%), Icelanders (38%), and Norwegians (40%). In neither case should we feel the need to posit either a "Scandinaviation" of parts of the United States or a "Seattling" of parts of Europe to account for the parallels.[11]

None of this means that American Christianity is in some terminal death spiral. On the whole, it's still a much more religious country than most of its Western, developed, democratic peers. This is especially true on the hard measure of weekly religious attendance, even allowing for the well-studied phenomenon of overreporting (which is itself evidence *for* the strength of a religious culture rather than decisive proof against it). According to 2018 data from the International Social Survey Programme, 29% of Americans attend religious services on at least a weekly basis, while 29% say that they never do.[12] In Britain, the respective figures are 15% and 57%; in Sweden, 5% and 58%. It's true enough that nonreligiosity is on the rise in the USA, not just in terms of affiliation but by other measures as well. But America's myriad religious congregations, the vast majority of which are Christian churches, possess much greater reserves of resilience than are typically seen elsewhere. (Though there are trend-buckers in these, too. Think Hillsong, the global megachurch and music ministry, started in the Sydney suburbs. Or indeed, the subtle signs of new life springing up among British Catholics. For similar reasons, though it would take us too far off track to explain them here, the Pacific Northwest—long North America's preeminent "none zone"—is home to a good number of thriving megachurches.)[13]

Quite what effect the Covid-19 pandemic will have on all this remains, as I write this, very much an open question. What data we have already, various past precedents, and (perhaps most of all) a heavy dose of personal intuition can and have been spun in all kinds of directions by different observers. My own view is that, in the short to medium term at least, the result will be a fairly significant net loss to American religion. The deaths of a million or more Americans, disproportionately including several groups who tend to be more religious than the national average (that is, older people and minorities), is the most obvious reason.[14] The serious disruption to the churchgoing habits of tens of millions of Americans will also have notable after-effects. Most, of course, will come back— many more eager than ever. But others, perhaps especially those with young families, will have gotten out of the habit for good. They might not know it yet—for they genuinely do mean to start going back regularly, beginning *next* week—but they will. The fall in the collection plate during the pandemic will also mean that churches have fewer resources to fund their mission. Lots, I suspect, will decide that the new "young adult minister" they were planning to recruit two years ago, in order to help stem the growing tide of prodigals, will just have to wait for another few years. Given that regular religious practice in childhood and one's teenage years is the strongest indicator of whether a person grows up to be a religious adult, it remains to be seen what knock-on effects this will have when "Covid kids" come of age.

That's not to say that I don't also anticipate many silver linings for the churches, and indeed other religious groups, too. History shows that times of crisis and anxiety often give rise to religious boom years. This happens for many reasons—proximity to death rendering mortal questions all the more pressing; hopes of eternal peace and rest for loved ones; increased "existential insecurity" brought on by health fears and their economic repercussions; religious groups or individuals stepping in to help in times of need; even the often faith-reinforcing effects of settling down and having kids in the baby boom that frequently follows periods of hardship.[15] One need not look too far into the past to see some or all of these factors plausibly at work. The religious boom of the 1950s, however temporary it turned out to be—the "Indian summer for orthodox belief," as Ross Douthat once memorably put it—would be an obvious candidate.[16] The rebounding of the churches in the wake of the Civil War might also be mentioned.[17] There will certainly be churches and other religious groups who "do well" (so to speak) out of the pandemic. But the bulk of this growth will likely occur at the expense of *other* churches: a product of religious "switching" rather than the converting of the genuinely nonreligious. I don't foresee this making any serious dent in the nones—and perhaps quite the opposite.

One final idea worth floating here, though even more speculatively, is that past crises have often produced a great deal of spiritual experimentation, much of it rather wild in nature. The classic example here is fourteenth-century Europe, where a Great Famine (1315–17), the Black Death (1346–53), and a good deal of political and social tumult besides spawned a profusion of charismatic leaders, apocalyptic movements, and radical communities. (Several of these, suitably domesticated, are still with us today in the form of Catholic religious orders such as the Franciscans and Dominicans.) But there is no shortage of other examples. The Civil War and its aftermath gave rise to Seventh-day Adventism, Theosophy, Christian Science, the Jehovah's Witnesses, the Black Israelites, and many more. Japan underwent a religious boom following the devastation of World War Two.

The pandemic has certainly brought its fair share of conspiracy theories, quack cures, putative revelations of secret knowledge, and fevered apocalypticism. But it is striking how essentially secular in nature most of this has been. Certainly, there are more or less explicitly religious elements within this rich brew—the "QAnon shaman," Marjorie Taylor Greene calling vaccine passports "Biden's mark of the beast," and so on—and these ought not to be ignored. QAnon, especially, samples and remixes several of Christian End-Times speculation's *Greatest Hits* from the past few decades (the New World Order, pedophile cabals, Clinton conspiracies, obsession with Russia, suspicion of vaccinations), easing the passage of a good many Christians into its "big tent." Nevertheless, it is hard to see QAnon as a specifically or primarily *religious* movement, even if it has indeed much in common with some fringe religious groups.

What I mean is that in previous centuries (or even decades) the alleged identity of "Q" would surely have been an angel, Christ reincarnate, the Virgin Mary, or a Native American spirit guide, rather than a whistleblowing government functionary. America's imagined conspirators used to be witches working for the Devil (as at Salem), or else Jesuit priests or Opus Dei assassins in league with the pope (as per Jack Chick and Dan Brown), rather than Big Pharma and Big Tech. And as miracle cures go, intravenous bleach and horse deworming pills are not exactly the faith healer's usual stock in trade.

Writing in 2014, the historian Philip Jenkins argued that the evident waning of America's "spiritual fringe," not least compared to the periodic "cult panics" of earlier decades, "might mark a significant social trend, and perhaps even a bellwether for secularization." His basic point is that more out-there manifestations of religion presuppose and build upon a large and active core of what one might call ordinary religiosity. The bigger the religious market as a whole, the more space it has for a vibrant "long tail" of more extreme offerings.[18] As he has put it more recently, "earlier waves of enthusiasm on the religious margins actually reflected the widespread passion that animated mainstream faith but could not be contained within orthodox boundaries." As such, so-called cult booms such as excited the media and scholars alike in the 1970s are "in some ways a gauge of the nation's thriving spiritual vigor, and the loss of fringe sects is a disturbing sign of secular trends in progress."[19] I see little in the pandemic to suggest otherwise.

* * *

My basic thesis—namely that the rise of the nones, fueled primarily by an extraordinary two or three decades of what I've been calling nonversion, marks a decisive moment in American religious and cultural history—is one that, in its general contours, chimes closely with the insights of several leading religious readers of the signs of the times. Writing in 2017, Charles Chaput, at that time the Catholic Archbishop of Philadelphia (he retired in 2020), directly addressed "the post-Christian world" of the contemporary USA. Exhibit A in his case is the Supreme Court's 2015 *Obergefell* decision in favor of same-sex marriage as proof of America's rapid de-Christianization.[20]

> Obviously *Obergefell* is only one of many issues creating today's sea change in American public life. But it confirmed in a uniquely forceful way that we live in a country very different from that of the past. The special voice that biblical belief once had in our public square is now absent. People who hold a classic under-standing of sexuality, marriage, and family have gone in just twenty years from pillars of mainstream conviction to the media equivalent of racists and bigots.[21]

Chaput ascribes this overarching shift both to the rising tide of nonreligion, especially among younger adults, and to the decades-long weakening of Christianity in American public and private life that laid the groundwork for it. Both, of course, are major themes of this book.

> The reason the Christian faith doesn't matter to so many of our young people is that—too often—it didn't really matter to us. Not enough to shape our lives. Not enough for us to suffer for it. As Catholic Christians, we may have come to a point today where we feel like foreigners in our own country—"strangers in a strange land," in the beautiful English of the King James Bible (Ex. 2:22). But the deeper problem in America isn't that we believers are "foreigners." It's that our children and grandchildren *aren't*.[22]

Chaput is by no means alone in this basic diagnosis. For example, the evangelical theologian Russell Moore, whose views on church scandals were quoted in Chapter 6, has argued that:

> American culture is shifting, it seems, into a different era, an era in which religion is not necessarily seen as a social good. Christianity in its historic, apostolic form is increasingly seen as socially awkward at best, as subversive at worst. This is especially true when it comes to what, at the moment, is perhaps the most offensive aspect of such Christianity: our sexual ethic.[23]

Moore is not, it's worth adding, especially nostalgic for the good old days of Christianity's cultural establishment within society and politics. They were, in his view, a large part of how American Christianity got into its current predicament: "A Christianity that is without friction in the culture is a Christianity that dies. Such religion absorbs the ambient culture until it is indistinguishable from it, until, eventually, a culture asks what the point is of the whole thing."[24] Whatever the cause, however, the consequences are clear enough. "Normal America," at least as it is perceived by large swathes of the population, now has very little overlap with "Christian America."

Completing this ecumenical hat trick, we may also note the views, set out most explicitly in two bestselling books, of the journalist and Orthodox convert Rod Dreher. The central contention of Dreher's 2017 *The Benedict Option: A Strategy for Christians in a Post-Christian Nation* is that in the United States, authentic, worthy-of-the-name Christianity is a rapidly fading—indeed *faded*—force: morally, politically, culturally, socially, artistically.

> The storm clouds have been gathering for decades, but most of us believers have operated under the illusion that they would

blow over. The breakdown of the natural family, the loss of traditional moral values, and the fragmenting of communities . .
. Today we can see that we've lost on every front and that the
swift and relentless currents of secularism have overwhelmed
our flimsy barriers. . . . American Christians are going to have to
come to terms with the brute fact that we live in a culture, one in
which our beliefs make increasingly little sense. We speak a language that the world more and more either cannot hear or finds
offensive to its ears.[25]

Upping the ante, Dreher likens the situation of contemporary
Christians—by whom he means not just his own co-religionists
but all "theologically traditional Protestants, Catholics, and Eastern
Orthodox Christians"[26]—to that of Europe's Christians following
the fall of the Roman Empire. Hence the book's master metaphor of
St. Benedict gathering together the surviving remnants of Christian
practice, morality, and culture under the protective mantle of his
monasteries until times were more hospitable for rebuilding and
re-evangelization.

Accordingly, Dreher's eponymous "Benedict Option" is "a
strategy that draws on the authority of Scripture and the wisdom
of the ancient church to embrace 'exile in place' and form a vibrant
counterculture."[27] These may take myriad concrete forms; Dreher
describes several in some detail, ranging from quasi-monastic
communities to ordinary neighborhoods with high proportions
of committed Christians (which is of course what many American
neighborhoods used to look like, without anyone having to go out
of their way to engineer it). Dreher's injunction to "Secede culturally from the mainstream"[28] does not, in fact, require Christians
sequestering themselves in Amish-esque agrarian communes or
"bunker communities." Rather, at the most basic level, the Benedict

Option simply involves a conscious seeking out of likeminded Christians, and the forming of mutually supportive networks in which being and practicing a serious version of Christianity is the norm. In practice if not in rhetoric, Dreher's prescription is not a million miles away from that proposed by Moore, for whom: "Our call is to an engaged alienation, a Christianity that preserves the distinctiveness of our gospel while not retreating from our callings as neighbors, and friends, and citizens."[29] America's coming generations of Christians must, that is, all hang together or else all hang separately.

Specific diagnoses and prescriptions aside, note above all the mood music here. Chaput, Moore, and Dreher would generally be counted as theological conservatives in today's religious landscape. But they are also more or less mainstream figures, writing books targeted, successfully, at gaining a wide readership within Christian circles. These are not views issuing from the religious fringe. If conservative Christianity were cable news, these folks would be on Fox, not Newsmax.

Against this basic outlook, we may juxtapose that often described as "(White) Christian nationalism," which has attracted a great deal of media and academic attention of late.[30] While it resists easy categorization, the basic package is built out of a "constellation of beliefs" concerning the reciprocal relationship between religion and politics. In very rough terms, one might describe it as the view that (a particular conception of) the Christian God has specially favored—"blessed"—America. And as such, America's legal and political institutions ought therefore to return the compliment. It is, therefore, "a 'deep story' about America's past and a vision of its future. It includes cherished assumptions about what America was and is, but also what it should be."[31] Hence scholars measure it on a scale according to how strongly respondents agree with statements such as "The success of the United States is part of God's plan," and "The federal government should declare the United States a Christian nation"; or disagree with "The federal government should enforce a strict separation of Church and state."[32] White Christian nationalism, so defined (note that one need not be either White or a Christian to score strongly), is argued to be a major explanatory factor in much of America's recent politics and cultural skirmishes.

Such views are nothing new in American society. Their recent prominence stems, rather, from the fact that they have become increasingly challenged and contested. Furthermore, those holding them feel increasingly demographically, economically, culturally, and religiously marginalized.[33] Hence, for many, the desire to "take back our country" or indeed to Make America Great Again. As discussed in earlier chapters, such postures are not ones assumed from a position of taken-for-granted strength and superiority. They are rear-guard actions and are more plausibly viewed as by-products of—and reactions to—secularization, as they are evidence against it.

Both what one might loosely call "MAGA Christianity" and the exile-in-place quietism advocated by Moore, Dreher, and Chaput proceed from the same basic realization: that Christian practice, belief, and cultural standing are now much weaker in America than they used to be. Where the latter differ, however, is in what Christians ought to be doing about it. In what they see as the Brave New World (a literary allusion that is often meant most sincerely) of an increasingly ex-Christian America, the new game plan is for American Christians to form a Moral *Minority* that is worthy of the name. Curiously, much of this aligns with the thought of the Methodist theologian and ethicist Stanley Hauerwas, who fits uneasily within standard depictions of "left" and "right." Hauerwas, who's been pushing the idea that American Christians should see themselves as *resident aliens* in American culture since long before the idea gained its current vogue, is fond of saying, "I say in a hundred years, if Christians are people identified as those who do not kill their children or their elderly, we will have been doing something right."[34]

* * *

The Puritan preacher John Winthrop's famous 1630 injunction that "we shall be as a city upon a hill," echoing Jesus' words in the Gospel of Matthew (5.14), has often been depicted as both promise and prophecy to the whole American enterprise. Its real history is far more complicated than that.[35] *The Model of Christian Charity*, the sermon in which Winthrop coined the phrase, was only really added to the nation's founding canon in the mid-twentieth century: cities built on hills being, one presumes, all the better positioned to scan the horizon for incoming Soviet missiles. Kennedy was the first US president to quote it. Reagan, adding his own embellishment of "shining," would make it his, and many of his countrymen's, own.

Specifics of phraseology notwithstanding, the vision of being called to be a "Christian nation" has exerted powerful sway over key strands of American culture, self-image, and foreign policy for almost four hundred years. Quite what it means for any nation to be *Christian* is, however, notoriously tricky to pin down: is it a matter of founding texts, and/or of their original authors' own intentions; of the grand sweep of social or political history; of ethical or legal norms; or the current identities, beliefs, or practices of its citizenry? While not exclusive to America—witness recent controversies as to the "Christian" nature of various European countries, and indeed of Europe itself—such debates have usually been conducted with greater existential urgency, and visceral emotionality, here than elsewhere.[36]

This book's title speaks not of a Christian America but rather of an *Ex-Christian* one. This could be interpreted in two senses. The first, more minimal one, simply picks out that portion of America made up of people who used to be, or at least consider themselves to be, Christians. In much the same way, one may speak of "Jewish America" or "rural America" or "corporate America," confining one's attention to just those American people, places, or institutions to which the adjective refers. "Ex-Christian America" in this sense is a large, varied, and interesting topic. And I hope that this book has proven worthy of it.

But I also intend the title in a second, more ambitious sense: referring to an "Ex-Christian" quality to America itself. Obviously, the meaningfulness of "Ex-Christian America" in this sense relies, to a large degree, on how one understands "Christian America." In my usage, this is as much about an overarching cultural climate as it is about sociological measures of Christian belonging, believing, or behaving. In such a cultural climate, being a ("normal" type of) Christian is the default setting: one is, unless one has a particular reason not to be, and one may automatically assume others are too (as with Weber's "the inevitable question: 'What church do you belong to?'").[37] Christian symbols, prayers, and invocations don't stand out or require special pleading. Phrases such as "good Christians" or "Christian morality" or "it's the Christian thing to do" can be intended, and understood, as platitudes. Cultures are built up of innumerable, tiny cues such as these, ones that those submerged in them barely notice. Outsiders, however, often do.

"Ex-Christian America" in this more ambitious sense is, then, a claim that this kind of culturally Christian mood music is much quieter in America than previously (and in the many places where it does still exist, it is therefore more conspicuous than it used to be). But it is also the stronger claim that an *Ex*-Christian nation is not simply the same as a *Non*-Christian one. A culture that used to be Christian, just like a person who used to be one, carries much of the past along with it.

Viewed in terms of individuals' biographies, the process of nonversion has often been a slow and gradual process. Taken together, though, and judged by the typical timescales of major social and religious changes at the national level, the nonversion of America itself has been swift. This has been exhilarating for many in society, and profoundly disorienting and distressing for others. As we have seen many times in these pages, these differences of direction and experience have primarily played themselves out not *across* the traditional binaries of American tensions (urban/rural, coast/heartlands, North/South, Democrats/Republicans, White/Black, rich/poor), but deep within them. This will continue for some years to come, before likely coalescing around some new, relative stability.

Futurology is always a risk—just ask Max Weber.[38] Human societies are complex systems, and predictions of how things will look even five or ten years down the line ought always to be qualified with a high margin of error. If physicists struggle to predict how the orbits of three planets interact (the famous "three-body problem") in the long term, mere social scientists ought to be rather humble when speculating about how things will play out among millions of human beings with free will. Note too that when I first had the idea for this book, Britain was still in the EU, President Trump was a *Simpsons* punchline, I'd never heard of Wuhan, and there hadn't been a land war in Europe for a good few years. Things can move fast.

If I had to make a prediction, though, it seems to me that the smart money would be on the eventual emergence of an America in which the nonreligious set (even) more of the cultural and political tone but, having mostly been brought up nonreligiously rather than having had to earn it the nonvert way, they will have the luxury of taking their majority for granted.

That said, the current Christian decline won't continue indefinitely: present trends never do. If Chaput, Moore, Dreher, and others have their way, then many of America's churches will reach a new, resilient normal. There will still be a steady stream of prodigals, since the wider culture will exert a powerful attraction, as it always does. But, significantly helped along by both immigration and birth rate, the overarching religious subculture will both keep enough of its own and attract a good few others (whose nonvert grandparents will be horrified at their abandoning the secular worldview that they themselves had to fight so hard to acquire).[39] They might *even* still justify a latter-day de Tocqueville in affirming that "Christianity rests here on a firmer foundation than in any other country in the [developed] world which I know." But this will be, at least when viewed in the secular eyes of most of their fellow Americans, much closer to a medium town on a fair-sized knoll than it is to a city on a hill, shining or otherwise.

NOTES

Chapter 1

1. Dusty Hoesly, " 'Need a Minister? How about Your Brother?': The Universal Life Church between Religion and Non-Religion," *Secularism and Nonreligion* 4 (2015), art. 12, 1–13.
2. While Mormonism is very much considered an "American" religion, in the 19th century somewhere around 100,000 Mormons emigrated to the United States, many of them from England.
3. Cf. "The phenomenon of being an ex is sociologically and psychologically intriguing since it implies that interaction is based not on current role definitions but, more important, past identities that somehow linger on and define how people see and present themselves in their present identities" (Robert K. Merton, "Foreword," in Helen Rose Fuchs Ebaugh, *Becoming an Ex: The Process of Role Exit* [Chicago: University of Chicago Press], xiii). Ebaugh's book, drawing partly on her own experiences as an "ex-nun," is the classic study of the topic, and much of her thinking lurks in the background of my own ideas on the topic.
4. Following Durkheim, I mean here such things as customs, norms, conventions, which have an objective reality over and above individuals' beliefs in, agreement with, or acceptance of them. While there is much more that could be said, this is not a historical treatise on social theory. Durkheim's own maxim is, though, always worth bearing in mind: "The first and most basic rule is *to consider social facts as things*": see Émile Durkheim, *The Rules of Sociological Method*, trans. W. D. Hall (New York: Free Press, [1895] 1982), 60.

5. See Darren E. Sherkat, *Changing Faith: The Dynamics and Consequences of Americans' Shifting Religious Identities* (New York: New York University Press, 2014), 24–9.

6. Aristotle, *Politics*, I, 1253a. Later quoted with approval by Thomas Aquinas (*Summa Theologiae*, II-I, q. 95, a. 4).

7. Christopher D. Bader and Scott A. Desmond, "Do as I Say and as I Do: The Effects of Consistent Parental Beliefs and Behaviors upon Religious Transmission," *Sociology of Religion* 67/3 (2006), 313–29; Vern L. Bengtson, Norella M. Putney, and Susan C. Harris, *Families and Faith: How Religion Is Passed Down across Generations* (New York: Oxford University Press, 2013).

8. Rodney Stark and William Sims Bainbridge, "Networks of Faith: Interpersonal Bonds and Recruitment to Cults and Sects," *American Journal of Sociology* 85/6 (1980), 1376–95; Sean Everton, *Networks and Religion: Ties That Bind, Loose, Build Up, and Tear Down* (Cambridge: Cambridge University Press, 2018), chap. 3.

9. Cf. Robert Wuthnow, *Rough Country: How Texas Became America's Most Powerful Bible-Belt State* (Princeton, NJ: Princeton University Press, 2014); Patricia O'Connell Killen and Mark Silk (eds.), *Religion and Public Life in the Pacific Northwest: The None Zone* (Walnut Creek, CA: Altamira Press, 2004); Laurence Iannaccone and Michael D. Makowsky, "Accidental Atheists? Agent-Based Explanations for the Persistence of Religious Regionalism," *Journal for the Scientific Study of Religion* 46, 1–16.

10. See Ryan T. Cragun, Christel Manning, and Lori L. Fazzino (eds.), *Organized Secularism in the United States: New Directions in Research* (New York: De Gruyter, 2017); David Niose, *Nonbeliever Nation: The Rise of Secular Americans* (New York: Palgrave Macmillan, 2012).

11. Out of a vast and voluminous literature see, for example: Karen Hwang, "Atheism, Health, and Well-Being," in Stephen Bullivant and Michael Ruse (eds.), *The Oxford Handbook of Atheism* (Oxford: Oxford University Press, 2013), 525–26; T. J. VanderWeele, S. Li, A. C. Tsai, and I. Kawachi, "Association between Religious Service Attendance and Lower Suicide Rates among US Women," *JAMA Psychiatry* 73/8 (2016), 845–51; Stephen M. Merino, "God and Guns: Examining Religious Influences on Gun Control Attitudes in the United States," *Religions* 9/6 (2018), 1–12; and Phil Zuckerman, Luke W. Galen, and Frank L. Pasquale, *The Nonreligious: Understanding Secular People and Societies* (New York: Oxford University Press, 2016), 128–45 and 174–96.

12. For those readers who find an endnote reference preceded by the words "boring reasons," too great a temptation to pass up:

    In short, each wave of surveys the GSS conducts is based on face-to-face interviews with a national sample of 2,000–3,000 American adults. Its response rate is typically around 50%, which is much higher than typically achieved by phone or internet polling. (This is potentially significant, since it may well be the case that certain types of people are systematically likely to be reachable, or to agree to be surveyed —a phenomenon known as "nonresponse bias.") The responses of those who do answer are then "weighted" to ensure that the survey sample is an adequate proxy for the national adult population as a whole, at least according to a small set of demographic indicators (e.g., sex, age, region), which are known with a reasonably high degree of confidence (e.g., due to the Census).

For full methodological details of the GSS, including sampling and weighting criteria, please see: Tom W. Smith, Peter V. Marsden, and Michael Hout, *General Social Surveys, 1972–2014: Cumulative Codebook* (Chicago: National Opinion Research Center, 2015). On the whole thorny topic of US religious polling, see Robert Wuthnow, *Inventing American Religion: Polls, Surveys, and the Tenuous Quest for a Nation's Faith* (Oxford: Oxford University Press, 2015) is unmatched. A good explainer on contemporary (political) polling is Dan Cassino, "How Political Polling Works," *Harvard Business Review*, August 1, 2016, available online: https://hbr.org/2016/08/how-tod ays-political-polling-works.

13. Stephen Bullivant, "Explaining the Rise of 'Nonreligion Studies': Subfield Formation and Institutionalization within the Sociology of Religion," *Social Compass* 67/1 (2020), 86–102.

Chapter 2

1. This type of arrangement is a common and long-standing one in states with high local concentrations of Mormons, such as Utah, Idaho, Nevada, and Arizona. According to the LDS's own statistics, in 2013 around 125,000 American high-schoolers were enrolled in this type of "released-time" semi-nary program ("five hours a week of more church," as one of my interviewees put it). Young Mormons at schools where this isn't an option typically follow the same curriculum but in another format, such as gathering at a seminary teacher's home for an hour every day before school.

2. Nomenclature in this field, as in most others, can be a complicated issue. For the avoidance of doubt, I use "Mormon" colloquially to refer to a member of the Church of Jesus Christ of Latter-day Saints (as did my interviewees). This, which I typically abbreviate to "LDS Church" or "the LDS," is by far the largest of several denominations tracing their foundings back to Joseph Smith. Likewise, mentions of Mormonism, Mormon Church, Latter-day Saints, or Saints should be taken as referring to the LDS Church and its members, unless otherwise stated.

3. Most notable here is the much-discussed Rodney Stark, "The Rise of a New World Faith," *Review of Religious Research* 26/1 (1984), 18–27, and the

updated version in Rodney Stark, *The Rise of Mormonism*, ed. Reid L. Nielson (New York: Columbia University Press, 2005), chap. 7.

4. Kenda Creasy Dean, *Almost Christian: What the Faith of Our Teenagers Is Telling the American Church* (New York: Oxford University Press, 2016), chap. 3; Stephen H. Webb, *Mormon Christianity: What Other Christians Can Learn From the Latter-day Saints* (New York: Oxford University Press, 2016), chap. 1.

5. Clear overviews of LDS doctrine and practice can be found in Richard Lyman Bushman, *Mormonism: A Very Short Introduction* (Oxford: Oxford University Press, 2008), chap. 5; and Ryan T. Cragun and Rick Phillips, *Could I Vote for a Mormon for President? An Election-Year Guide to Mitt Romney's Religion* (Washington, DC: Strange Violin Editions), chaps. 9–13.

   For data on what actual Mormons actually believe, see Pew Research Center, *Mormons in America: Certain in Their Beliefs, Uncertain of Their Place in Society* (Washington, DC: Pew Research Center, 2012), section 2.

6. Leland A. Fetzer, "Tolstoy and Mormonism," *Dialogue* 6/1 (1971), 13–30; David Feltmate, *Drawn to the Gods: Religion and Humour in* The Simpsons, South Park, *and* Family Guy (New York: New York University Press, 2017), chap. 5.

7. Zane Grey, *Riders of the Purple Sage* (New York: Harper and Brothers, 1912), chap. 3. Murderous Mormons feature heavily in the very first Sherlock Holmes story, *A Study in Scarlet* (1887). Jules Verne's *Around the World in Eighty Days* (1873) devotes an uncomplimentary chapter to Mormon history and practice.

8. *The Week* Staff, "Mitt Romney: 'Boring' by Design?" *The Week*, December 1, 2011.

9. Mathew Bowman, *The Mormon People: The Making of an American Faith* (New York: Random House, 2012), Conclusion. On a similar theme, see the entertaining and insightful Stephen J. Mansfield, *The Mormonizing of America: How the Mormon Religion Became a Dominant Force in Politics, Entertainment, and Pop Culture* (Brentwood, TN: Worthy Books, 2012).

10. On these types of irreligious experiences, positive and negative, see Stephen Bullivant, "Introducing Irreligious Experiences," *Implicit Religion* 11/1 (2008), 7–24.

11. Edward L. Kimball, "Confession in LDS Doctrine and Practice," *BYU Studies* 36/2 (1996), 7–73.

12. "Cult" is (former member) Brandon's own description of the group, a relatively small New Age-y self-improvement group focused—like so many—on "Enlightenment" and spiritual maturity. It is worth noting here that, among scholars of such groups, "cult" is considered a contested and controversial term. Most prefer more neutral phrases like New Religious Movements, alternative religions, or minority religions (for a good historical introduction to the debate, see Thomas Robbins and Philip Charles Lucas, "From 'Cults' to New Religious Movements: Coherence, Definition, and Conceptual Framing in the

Study of New Religious Movements." in James A. Beckford and N. J. Demerath III [eds.], *The SAGE Handbook of the Sociology of Religion* [London: SAGE, 2007], 227–47). Such items of sociologese have not, however, exactly caught on among the media and wider public—or, despite my best efforts, my own undergraduates.

13. Grey, *Riders*, chap. 9.

14. See Jana Riess, *The Next Mormons: How Millennials Are Changing the LDS Church* (New York: Oxford University Press, 2019), 4–7; Darren E. Sherkat, *Changing Faith: The Dynamics and Consequences of Americans' Shifting Religious Identities* (New York: New York University Press, 2014), 59–71. For earlier studies of Mormon deconverts, see Stan L. Albrecht and Howard M. Bahr, "Patterns of Religious Disaffiliation: A Study of Lifelong Mormons, Mormon Converts, and Former Mormons," *Journal for the Scientific Study of Religion* 22/4 (1983), 366–79; and Howard M. Bahr and Stan L. Albrecht, "Strangers Once More: Patterns of Disaffiliation from Mormonism," *Journal for the Scientific Study of Religion* 28/2 (1989), 180–200.

15. Riess, *The Next Mormons*, 7.

16. An interesting elaboration of the below basic themes, from a well-regarded sociologist of religion who is himself an ex-LDS nonvert, can be found in Ryan T. Cragun, *What You Don't Know about Religion (But Should)* (Durham, NC: Pitchstone, 2011), chaps. 4, 5, 10, and 11. See also Rick Phillips, "Sources of Mormon Religious Activity in the United States: How Latter-day Saint Communities Function Where Mormons Predominate, and Where They Are Sparse," *Journal of the Utah Academy of Sciences, Arts and Letters* 91 (2015), 259–76.

17. Rick Phillips, "Demography and Information Technology Affect Religious Commitment among Latter-day Saints in Utah and the Intermountain West," *Journal of the Utah Academy of Sciences, Arts, and Letters* 95 (2018), 317–32.

18. C. Smith, K. Longest, J. Hill, and K. Christofferson, *Young Catholic America: Emerging Adults in, out of, and Gone from the Church* (Oxford: Oxford University Press, 2014), 27. On Mormons specifically, see also Vern L. Bengtson, Norella M. Putney, and Susan C. Harris, *Families and Faith: How Religion Is Passed Down across Generations* (New York: Oxford University Press, 2013), 166–71.

19. "First LDS men serve as priests within their own families. Family home evening is conducted by the father and is partly devotional, partly focused on family activities together, and partly given to exploring any problems in the family. Second, these same men serve as priests to one another's families through their role as monthly visitors" (Stark, *Rise of Mormonism*, 126).

20. What else are endnotes even *for* if not for giving unsolicited LDS romcom recommendations? *The Singles Ward* (2002) and *The 2nd Singles Ward* (2007) are the classics of the genre. Plotwise, imagine the *American Pie* franchise, but where the "goal" is a chaste courtship followed by a happy (eternal) marriage

with seven kids. *The R.M.* (2003), meanwhile, centers on the hapless efforts of the eponymous Returned Missionary to pick up the pieces of his life. Like my brother always says of mawkish *Hallmark*-esque Christmas movies, "They all follow the same formula, but it's a brilliant formula." What can I say? I'm a fan.

As to singles wards themselves, see Riess, *The Next Mormons*, chap. 4.

21. Pew, *Mormons in America*, section 3.
22. Conor Friedersdorf, "Mitt Romney: My Conscience Won't Allow Me to Vote for Trump or Clinton," *The Atlantic*, June 29, 2016.
23. Timothy Egan, "Mormons to the Rescue?" *New York Times*, October 11, 2019.
24. On all these topics, see R. Marie Griffith, *Moral Combat: How Sex Divided American Christians and Fractured American Politics* (New York: Basic Books, 2018).
25. Melissa J. Wilde, *Birth Control Battles: How Race and Class Divided American Religion* (Berkeley: University of California Press, 2019). On the respectability of eugenic ideas and social policy in and before this period, see also Thomas Sowell, *Intellectuals and Race* (New York: Basic Books, 2013), chap. 3.
26. The phrase comes "from a discourse given by Joseph Smith on Jan. 21, 1844, in Nauvoo, Illinois" (*Teachings of Presidents of the Church: Joseph Smith* [Salt Lake City, UT: Church of Jesus Christ of Latter-day Saints, 2011], 473).

Chapter 3

1. Glenn M. Vernon, "The Religious 'Nones': A Neglected Category," *Journal for the Scientific Study of Religion* 7/2 (1968), 219–29; Frank L. Pasquale, "Unbelief and Irreligion, Empirical Study and Neglect of," in Tom Flynn (ed.), *The New Encyclopedia of Unbelief* (Amherst, NY: Prometheus, 2007), 760–6.
2. On other "cultural costs" of nonreligiosity experienced by minority millennials, see Aprilfaye Manalang, "Millennials and Disaffiliation from Religious Communities: Not Belonging and the Cultural Cost of Unbelief," *Interdisciplinary Journal of Research on Religion* 17 (2021), 1–24.
3. Lois Lee, *Recognizing the Non-Religious: Reimagining the Secular* (Oxford: Oxford University Press, 2015), 132, 153. See also Lois Lee, "Secular or Nonreligious? Investigating and Interpreting Generic 'Not Religious' Categories and Populations," *Religion* 44/3 (2014), 466–82.
4. Robert Wuthnow, *Inventing American Religion: Polls, Surveys, and the Tenuous Quest for a Nation's Faith* (Oxford: Oxford University Press, 2015), chap. 5.
5. See Chapter 2's discussion of the "Is Mormonism a type of Christianity?" debate. Whether, and how, a Mormon option gets included in polls very much depends on where they're being asked and how detailed a religious picture is desired. For example, a poll in Utah and Idaho that *didn't* include a Mormon option in its religious affiliation options would be poorly thought through. The

same poll fielded in, say, Delaware might well not bother, unless one was specifically after a sufficiently large and fine-grained dataset to pick up relatively tiny religious minorities. The GSS, for instance, includes several Mormon options (i.e., the LDS plus various much smaller groups descended from Joseph Smith) on a list among other highly specific sub-categories of "Protestant."

6. The quest to corral American Christianity's "endless forms" into usably bigger categories, while avoiding misleading oversimplification, is a long and tortuous one, generating a sizable literature of its own. See, for competing "solutions," Brian Steensland et al., "The Measure of American Religion: Toward Improving the State of the Art," *Social Forces* 79/1 (2000), 291–318; Robert D. Woodberry et al., "The Measure of American Religious Traditions: Theoretical and Measurement Considerations," *Social Forces* 91/1 (2012), 65–73; Derek Lehmann and Darren E. Sherkat, "Measuring Religious Identification in the United States," *Journal for the Scientific Study of Religion* 57/4 (2018), 779–94. And for a small, still voice of calm, see Conrad Hackett et al., "Choose the Method for Aggregating Religious Identities That Is Most Appropriate for Your Research," *Journal for the Scientific Study of Religion* 57/4 (2018), 807–16.

   Specific discussion of how I'm defining "mainline Protestants" and "evangelicals" in this book—i.e., fast and loosely by the some of the above standards—will be given in the relevant chapters.

7. Ideally, a religious organization wants *both* to keep a high percentage of cradle members *and* to attract large numbers of new recruits. In practice, that can be a very difficult trick to pull off. For various reasons, groups that are good at keeping people are often less effective at luring new members, and vice versa. Walls that stop people from leaving also stop others from joining; open doors make it easy to enter or exit.

8. This was a dedicated survey of atheists and agnostics in six different countries. Some of our initial findings can be found in Stephen Bullivant, Jon Lanman, Miguel Farias, and Lois Lee, *Understanding Unbelief: Atheists and Agnostics around the World: Interim Findings from 2019 Research in Brazil, China, Denmark, Japan, the United Kingdom, and the United States* (Twickenham: Understanding Unbelief and Benedict XVI Centre for Religion and Society, 2019).

9. The problem is this. On the one hand, there are people who seriously identify as practitioners of something called "Jediism," building upon ideas presented in the *Star Wars* films. This goes further than simply being a fan of the franchise. While acknowledging that the movies are fictional, such real-world Jedis generally regard their teachings about the Force as expressing something fundamentally true about the universe, which in turn entails a specific outlook and morality ("the Jedi Code"). They are also, naturally enough, fond of dressing up in hooded robes and dueling with toy light sabers. Sci-fi cosplaying aside, the theology and practices of Jediism are not a galaxy far, far away from various

forms of contemporary meditation, mindfulness, and human-potential spirituality. In common with other religious groups, there are a number of competing
denominations of Jediism, several of which offer legally recognized wedding
"ministers."

On the other hand, in several countries whose national censuses (unlike
the US's) ask about religion, there have been well-publicized campaigns encouraging people to write in "Jedi" as their own religious affiliation. In the
UK's 2001 Census, for example, around 390,000 people did just that. Clearly,
not all of these are practicing Jedi Knights, in the above sense. But what *does*
identifying oneself as a Jedi amount to? It's hard to say; for most, I'm sure, it's
simply a funny prank. It seems to me, though, one could certainly interpret a
tongue-in-cheek avowal of Jediism as a form of nonreligious "protest vote": as
in, "I'm not any of these, and besides, all religions are silly and made up." As
it happens, I once lived next-door to a "census Jedi," and certainly for him it
had been a choice between jokingly writing that or seriously ticking the "no
religion" box. This at least made me feel a bit more justified in having once
created a "No religion+" category for a presentation analyzing data from the
2016 Irish Census. This included all those who had ticked the official "No religion" box as well as those writing in various avowedly nonreligious alternatives
such as "Atheist" and "Agnostic," along with the 2000 or so "Jedis" and fully
92 "Pastafarians" (i.e., followers of the satirical Church of the Flying Spaghetti
Monster, popular within New Atheist subcultures, especially online).

For those eager to read more about Jediism and the interesting questions it
raises for religion scholars, see Markus Altena Davidsen, "From Star Wars to
Jediism: The Emergence of Fiction-Based Religion," in Ernst van dem Hemel
and Asja Szafraniec (eds.), *Words: Religious Language Matters* (New York:
Fordham University Press, 2016), 376–89; and Teemu Taira, "The Category
of 'Invented Religion': A New Opportunity for Studying Discourses on
'Religion,'" *Culture and Religion* 14/4 (2013), 477–93.

10. Abby Day and Lois Lee, "Making Sense of Surveys and Censuses: Issues in
Religious Self-identification," *Religion* 44/3 (2014), 345–56; Conrad Hackett,
"Seven Things to Consider When Measuring Religious Identity," *Religion* 44/3
(2014), 396–413.

11. Pew Research Center, *A Portrait of Jewish Americans* (Washington, DC: Pew
Research Center, 2013), chap. 3.

12. For further background on this topic, I heartily recommend C. Lim, C.
A. MacGregor, and R. D. Putnam, "Secular and Liminal: Discovering
Heterogeneity among Religious Nones," *Journal for the Scientific Study of
Religion* 49/4 (2010), 596–618; and Michael Hout, "Religious Ambivalence,
Liminality, and the Increase of No Religious Preference in the United States,
2006–2014," *Journal for the Scientific Study of Religion* 56/1 (2017), 52–63.
On Catholics specifically, see Stephen Bullivant, *Mass Exodus: Catholic*

Disaffiliation in Britain and America since Vatican II (Oxford: Oxford University Press, 2019), 78–82.

13. Pew Hispanic Center, *When Labels Don't Fit: Hispanics and Their Views of Identity* (Washington, DC: Pew Hispanic Center, 2012).

14. Further methodological details for GSS 2021 can be found in NORC at the University of Chicago's *2021 GSS (Cross-Section Study) Methodological Primer*, Release 1, available online at: https://sda.berkeley.edu/sdaweb/docs/gss21/DOC/2021XSECR1MethodologicalPrimer.pdf.

    Note that this specifically cautions that: "While the data will contribute to our understanding of society, any changes in public opinion seen in the 2021 GSS data could be due to either changes in actual opinion and/or changes the GSS made in the methodology to adapt to COVID-19. We caution that when users employ 2021 GSS data to examine trends over time, they carefully consider if changes in the GSS methodology may be impacting the analysis." This is why, while the GSS 2021 is included as a valuable datapoint in Figure 3.1, it is excluded from analyses based on the GSS 1972–2018 series. Using the 2018 dataset as the basis for the rest of this chapter also means that we need not be concerned by any potentially temporary pandemic "blips" (which is not to say that the pandemic won't have significant long-term effects, as will be discussed in Chapter 9).

15. See also Joel Thiessen and Sarah Wilkins-Laflamme, *None of the Above: Nonreligious Identity in the US and Canada* (New York: New York University Press, 2020), chap. 2.

16. The precise birth-year brackets here follow those used by Pew: Michael Dimock, "Defining Generations: Where Millennials End and Generation Z Begins," *Pew Fact Tank*, January 17, 2019, available online at: https://www.pewresearch.org/fact-tank/2019/01/17/where-millennials-end-and-generat ion-z-begins/.

17. Phil Zuckerman, "Secular 'Values Voters' Are Becoming an Electoral Force in the US—Just Look Closely at 2020's Results," *The Conversation*, December 21, 2020, available online: https://theconversation.com/secular-values-vot ers-are-becoming-an-electoral-force-in-the-us-just-look-closely-at-2020s-resu lts-151953.

18. Ryan P. Burge, "The 2020 Vote for President by Religious Groups—The Nones," *Religion in Public*, April 6, 2021, available online at: https://religioni npublic.blog/2021/04/06/the-2020-vote-for-president-by-religious-groups-the-nones/; Ryan P. Burge, "The Nones May Be the Reason That Joe Biden Is the President Elect," *Religion in Public*, November 20, 2020, available online at: https://religioninpublic.blog/2020/11/20/the-nones-may-be-the-rea son-that-joe-biden-is-the-president-elect/. On the growing political signifi cance of the nones in general, see David E. Campbell, Geoffrey C. Layman,

and John C. Green, *Secular Surge: A New Fault Line in American Politics* (New York: Cambridge University Press, 2020).

19. See also Joseph O. Baker, "The Many Meanings of the Secular," in James L. Heft and Jan E. Stets (eds.), *Empty Churches: Non-Affiliation in America* (New York: Oxford University Press, 2021), 56–78.

20. Kune Biezeveld, Theo de Boer, Marjoleine de Vos, and Gijs Dingemans (eds.), *In Iets geloven: Ietsisme en het christelijk geloof* (Kampen: Kok, 2006).

21. Stephen Bullivant, *The "No Religion" Population of Britain: Recent Data from the British Social Attitudes Survey (2015) and the European Social Survey (2014)* (Twickenham: Benedict XVI Centre for Religion and Society, 2017), 15.

22. See Elizabeth Drescher, *Choosing Our Religion: The Spiritual Lives of America's Nones* (New York: Oxford University Press, 2016); Kaya Oakes, *The Nones Are Alright: A New Generation of Believers, Seekers and Those in Between* (Maryknoll, NY: Orbis, 2015); Tara Isabella Burton, *Strange Rites: New Religions for a Godless World* (New York: PublicAffairs, 2020); and Thiessen and Wilkins-Laflamme, *None of the Above*, 60–77.

23. Stephen Bullivant, Jon Lanman, Miguel Farias, and Lois Lee, *Understanding Unbelief: Atheists and Agnostics around the World: Interim Findings from 2019 Research in Brazil, China, Denmark, Japan, the United Kingdom, and the United States* (Twickenham: Understanding Unbelief and Benedict XVI Centre for Religion and Society, 2019), 15. See also the excellent and entertaining Christopher D. Bader, F. Carson Mencken, and Joseph O. Smith, *Paranormal America: Ghost Encounters, UFO Sightings, Bigfoot Hunts, and Other Curiosities in Religion and Culture* (New York: New York University Press, 2010).

24. Cf. Kelley D. Strawn, "What's Behind the 'Nones-Sense'? Change over Time in Factors Predicting Likelihood of Religious Nonaffiliation in the United States," *Journal for the Scientific Study of Religion* 58 (2019), 707–24; Burge, *Nones*, 70.

25. See Cass R. Sunstein, *Conformity: The Power of Social Influences* (New York: New York University Press, 2019); Tina Rosenberg, *Join the Club: How Peer Pressure Can Transform the World* (New York: Norton and Co., 2011).

26. E.g., James R. Lewis, Sean E. Curry, and Michael P. Oman-Reagan, "The Religion of the Educated Classes Revisited: New Religions, the Nonreligious, and Educational Levels," *Journal for the Scientific Study of Religion* 55/1 (2016), 91–104.

27. Bullivant, *"No Religion" Population*, 11; David Voas and Siobhan McAndrew, "Three Puzzles of Non-religion in Britain," *Journal of Contemporary Religion* 27/1 (2012), 29–48.

28. Tina Block and Lynne Marks, "Atheism and Unbelief in the Pacific Northwest, 1880–2001," in Michael Ruse and Stephen Bullivant (eds.), *The Cambridge History of Atheism*, vol. 2 (Cambridge: Cambridge University Press, 2021), 932–51; Patricia O'Connell Killen and Mark Silk (eds.), *Religion and Public*

Life in the Pacific Northwest: The None Zone (Walnut Creek, CA: Altamira Press, 2004).

Chapter 4

1. See James Hudnut-Beumler, "Introduction," in James Hudnut-Beumler and Mark Silk (eds.), *The Future of Mainline Protestantism in America* (New York: Columbia University Press, 2018). 2018 data here are based on my own analysis of the GSS. Here as elsewhere, I've adopted the commonly used RELTRAD classification for defining the mainline, as originally set out in Brian Steensland et al., "The Measure of American Religion: Toward Improving the State of the Art," *Social Forces* 79/1 (2000), 291–318. For details of the precise coding used, please see Ed Setzer and Ryan Burge, "Reltrad Coding Problems and a New Repository," *Politics and Religion* 9/1 (2016), 187–90.

2. For reference, the original "Seven Sisters," as coined by William Hutchison, were: the Episcopal Church, the Evangelical Lutheran Church of America, the United Methodist Church, the Congregationalist Church, the American Baptist Convention, the Presbyterian Church, and the Disciples of Christ. The best discussion of the Mainline is Jason S. Lantzer, *Mainline Christianity: The Past and Future of America's Majority Faith* (New York: New York University Press, 2012). See his Introduction, in particular, for a thorough walk-through of the various issues around definition.

3. Margaret Bendroth, *The Last Puritans: Mainline Protestants and the Power of the Past* (Chapel Hill: University of North Carolina Press, 2015).

4. "She of Little Faith," *The Simpsons*, Series 13, Episode 6 (first broadcast: December 16, 2001).

5. See David Feltmate, *Drawn to the Gods: Religion and Humor in* The Simpsons, South Park, *and* Family Guy (New York: New York University Press, 2017); and "The Humorous Reproduction of Religious Prejudice: 'Cults' and Religious Humor in *The Simpsons, South Park*, and *King of the Hill*," *Journal of Religion and Popular Culture* 24/2 (2012), 201–16.

6. Joseph Bottum, *An Anxious Age: The Post-Protestant Ethic and the Spirit of America* (New York: Image, 2014), 10.

7. Ibid., 11.

8. See Fenggang Yang, *Chinese Christians in America: Conversion, Assimilation, and Adhesive Identities* (University Park: Pennsylvania State University Press, 1999).

9. So much so, that there's a whole collection of his Lutheran-centric writings and monologues: Garrison Keillor, *Life among the Lutherans*, ed. Holly Harden (Minneapolis, MN: Augsburg, 2010).

10. Max Weber, "'Churches' and 'Sects' in North America: An Ecclesiastical and Sociopolitical Sketch" (1906), in *The Protestant Ethic and the "Spirit" of Capitalism and Other Writings*, trans. Peter Baehr and Gordon C. Wells (London: Penguin, 2002), 203–20, 205.

11. Ibid.

12. E.g., Valerie A. Taylor, Diane Halstead, and Paula J. Haynes, "Consumer Responses to Christian Religious Symbols in Advertising," *Journal of Advertising* 39/2 (2010), 79–92; W. H. Henley, M. Philhours, S. K. Ranganathan, and A. J. Bush, "The Effects of Symbol Product Relevance and Religiosity on Consumer Perceptions of Christian Symbols in Advertising," *Journal of Current Issues & Research in Advertising* 31/1 (2009), 89–103.

13. Christel Manning, *Losing Our Religion: How Unaffiliated Parents Are Raising Their Children* (New York: New York University Press, 2015), chap. 5.

14. Rory Sutherland, *Alchemy: The Surprising Power of Ideas That Don't Make Sense* (London: Penguin, 2019), 163–4.

15. Wade Clark Roof and William McKinney, *American Mainline Religion: Its Changing Shape and Future* (New Brunswick, NJ: Rutgers University Press, 1987), 80; Maren Freudenberg, *The Mainline in Late Modernity: Tradition and Innovation in the Evangelical Lutheran Church in America* (Lanham, MD: Lexington Books, 2018), 120.

16. Robert N. Bellah, "Civil Religion in America," *Daedalus* 96/1 (1967), 1–21, 3–4.

17. E.g., Dale McConkey, *United Methodists Divided: Understanding Our Differences over Homosexuality* (Rome, GA: Global Parish Press, 2018). On the impact of women's ordination debates across the whole US church ecosystem, see Mark Chaves, *Ordaining Women: Culture and Conflict in Religious Organizations* (Cambridge, MA: Harvard University Press, 1997).

18. E.g., John Shelby Spong, *Why Christianity Must Change or Die: A Bishop Speaks to Believers In Exile* (San Francisco: Harper, 1998).

19. Cf. Freudenberg, *Mainline in Late Modernity*, 156.

20. Bendroth, *The Last Puritans*, 1. For a similar assessment, see also Ross Douthat, *Bad Religion: How We Became a Nation of Heretics* (New York: Free Press), 89–94.

21. Melissa J. Wilde, *Birth Control Battles: How Race and Class Divided American Religion* (Berkeley: University of California Press, 2019).

22. While the full tale is too long, complex, and interesting even to try summarizing here, see Miranda K. Hassett, *Anglican Communion in Crisis: How Episcopal Dissidents and Their African Allies Are Reshaping Anglicanism* (Princeton, NJ: Princeton University Press, 2007). This in itself is but a single subplot in the splintering of US Episcopalianism over the past several decades. For the bigger story, I highly recommend Alfred Bess, *Divided We Stand: A History of the Continuing Anglican Movement* (Berkeley, CA: Apocryphile Press, 2006).

23. Randall Balmer, *Grant Us Courage: Travels along the Mainline of American Protestantism* (New York: Oxford University Press, 1996), 148.

24. Rodney Stark, *The Triumph of Faith: Why the World Is More Religious Than Ever* (Wilmington, DE: ISI Books), chap. 5.

25. On the history of the changing priorities (and fortunes) of the American missionary endeavor over the course of the twentieth century, see David A. Hollinger, *Protestants Abroad: How Missionaries Tried to Change the World but Changed America* (Princeton, NJ: Princeton University Press, 2017).

26. "As important as the converts made by these efforts, the year and a half or two years in the mission field discipline the missionaries themselves, adding immense strength to LDS society" (Claudia L. Bushman, *Contemporary Mormonism: Latter-day Saints in Modern America* [Westport, CT: Prager, 2006], 4). For an excellent, in-depth study of LDS returned missionaries, see Garrett Stone, "Return with Honor: An Investigation of the Reentry Experiences and Discourses of Returning Missionaries in the Church of Jesus Christ of Latter-day Saints" (2018), PhD thesis, Clemson University, South Carolina.

Chapter 5

1. Max Weber, "'Churches' and 'Sects' in North America: An Ecclesiastical and Sociopolitical Sketch" (1906), in *The Protestant Ethic and the "Spirit" of Capitalism and Other Writings*, trans. Peter Baehr and Gordon C. Wells (London: Penguin, 2002), 203–20, 205.

2. US Bureau of the Census, *Population of the United States, Trends and Prospects: 1950–1990* (Washington, DC: US Government Printing Office, 1974), 98. See also Mark Chaves, *American Religion: Contemporary Trends*, 2nd ed. (Princeton, NJ: Princeton University Press, 2017), 15–16.

3. For other well-researched and insightful accounts, see Phil Zuckerman, "The Rise of the Nones: Why More Americans Are Becoming Secular, and What That Means for America," in Anthony B. Pinn (ed.), *Theism and Public Policy: Studies in Humanism and Atheism* (New York: Palgrave Macmillan, 2014), 37–52; Joseph O. Baker and Buster G. Smith, *American Secularism: Cultural Contours of Nonreligious Belief Systems* (New York: New York University Press, 2015), 66–88; and Ryan P. Burge, *The Nones: Where They Came From, Who They Are, and Where They Are Going* (Minneapolis, MN: Fortress Press, 2021), 32–69.

4. E.g., Glenn T. Stanton, *The Myth of the Dying Church: How Christianity Is Actually Thriving in America and the World* (New York: Worthy, 2019), chap. 4; Kenneth Newport, *God Is Alive and Well: The Future of Religion in America* (New York: Gallup Press, 2012), 12–17. Note that Newport's figures for those

identifying with no religion in historical Gallup data in fact combine those stating "no religion" with those answering "don't know"—hence giving higher figures than those I've quoted above.

5. Christopher P. Scheitle, Katie E. Corcoran, and Caitlin Halligan, "The Rise of the Nones and the Changing Relationships between Identity, Belief, and Behavior," *Journal of Contemporary Religion* 33/3 (2018), 567–79.

6. My thinking about identity, and its centrality to religion and a great deal else, has been sharpened in significant ways by the work of several important theorists. Helpful works in this field include: Helen Rose Fuchs Ebaugh, *Becoming an Ex: The Process of Role Exit* (Chicago: University of Chicago Press, 1988); Abby Day, *Believing in Belonging: Belief and Social Identity in the Modern World* (Oxford: Oxford University Press, 2011); Francis Fukuyama, *Identity: The Demand for Dignity and the Politics of Resentment* (London: Profile Books, 2018); Helen Pluckrose and James Lindsay, *Cynical Theories: How Universities Made Everything about Race, Gender, and Identity—And Why This Harms Everybody* (London: Swift Press, 2020); and Bradley Campbell and Jason Manning, *The Rise of Victimhood Culture: Microaggressions, Safe Spaces, and the New Culture Wars* (London: Palgrave Macmillan, 2018).

7. See Laurence R. Iannaccone and Michael D. Makowsky, "Accidental Atheists? Agent-Based Explanations for the Persistence of Religious Regionalism," *Journal for the Scientific Study of Religion* 46 (2007), 1–16.

8. *Sacramento Bee*, June 2, 1927, 12; *Poughkeepsie Eagle-News*, April 22, 1926, p. 12; *Los Angeles Times*, June 10, 1927 (pt. 2), p. 1; *Brooklyn Daily Eagle*, March 3, 1926, p. 2.

9. Edward J. Larson's Pulitzer-winning *Summer for the Gods: The Scopes Trial and America's Continuing Debate over Science and Religion* (New York: Basic Books, 1997) remains the definitive historical study.

10. Quoted in Cecilia DeMille Presley and Mark A. Vieira, *Cecil B. DeMille: The Art of the Hollywood Epic* (Philadelphia, PA: Running Press, 2014), chap. 3.

11. Charles Dickens, *American Notes for General Circulation* (London: Chapman and Hall, 1850), 17.

12. Cf. Will Herberg, *Protestant, Catholic, Jew: An Essay in American Religious Sociology* (Garden City, NY: Doubleday, 1955).

13. As he put it, "In my opinion the State Department, which is one of the most important government departments, is thoroughly infested with communists." All quotations from the speech are taken verbatim from the transcript provided by the University of Houston's Digital History Project, online at: https://libe ralarts.utexas.edu/coretexts/_files/resources/texts/1950%20McCarthy%20 Enemies.pdf.

14. Haynes Johnson, *The Age of Anxiety: McCarthyism to Terrorism* (New York: Houghton Mifflin Harcourt, 2005), 21.

15. Quoted in Martin E. Marty, *Modern American Religion. Volume 3: Under God, Indivisible, 1941–1960* (Chicago: University of Chicago Press, 1996), 300.

16. Richard Gribble, "Anti-Communism, Patrick Peyton, CSC and the C.I.A.," *Journal of Church and State* 45/3 (2003), 535–58.

17. George M. Docherty, "Under God," February 7, 1954, preached at New York Avenue Presbyterian Church, Washington, DC. Quotations taken from the transcript provided at: http://www.christianheritagemins.org/articles/ UNDER%20GOD.pdf. See also R. Laurence Moore and Isaac Kramnick, *Godless Citizens in a Godly Republic: Atheists in American Public Life* (New York: Norton and Co., 2018), chap. 5; and Stephen Bates, "'Godless Communism' and Its Legacies," *Society* 41 (2004), 29–33.

18. Rep. Eugene Siler (Kentucky), January 5, 1957, *Congressional Record: Vol. 103, Part 1—Extensions of Remarks*, 234.

19. U.S. House of Representatives' Committee on Un-American Activities, *100 Things You Should Know about Religion and Communism: The Second of a Series on the Communist Conspiracy and Its Influence in This Country as a Whole, on Religion, on Education, on Labor, and on Our Government* (Washington, DC: U.S. Government Printing Office, 1948), 3.

20. Clive F. Field, *Britain's Last Religious Revival? Quantifying Belonging, Behaving, and Believing in the Long 1950s* (Basingstoke: Palgrave Macmillan, 2015), 18.

21. "Comparisons" because (among other reasons) Anglophone, heavily influenced by US popular culture, on same sides in WW2 (with none occupied), highly developed, liberal democracies. Only "quasi" ones because, well, there's nowhere *really* like America, now, is there?

22. *Leader-Telegram* (Madison, WI), May 28, 1963, p. 5; *Los Angeles Times*, May 24, 1964, p. 10.

23. Kendrick Oliver, *To Touch the Face of God: The Sacred, the Profane, and the American Space Program, 1957–75* (Baltimore, MD: Johns Hopkins University Press, 2013), 143–63.

24. *LIFE*, June 19, 1964, 91–4.

25. William J. Murray, *My Life without God* (Cave Junction, OR: WND Books, 2012).

26. E.g., "National Survey Shows the Teen-agers Flunk Religion," *Daily Republic* (Mitchell, SD), December 19, 1957, p. 5; "The State of Religion in America," *Miami Herald*, April 18, 1965, p. 19.

27. Callum G. Brown, *Religion and the Demographic Revolution: Women and Secularisation in Canada, Ireland, UK and USA since the 1960s* (Woodbridge: Boydell Press), 60–70.

28. Google's NGram analytic tool tells an interesting story here. The term *un-churched*, used throughout the 1800s, began climbing in usage from the 1880s until the 1920s when it began to tail off. It then grew in relative popularity again, more or less annually, from around 1971 till the early noughties.

29. Cf. Ross Douthat, *Bad Religion: How We Became a Nation of Heretics* (New York: Free Press, 2012).

30. Michael Hout and Claude S. Fischer, "Explaining Why More Americans Have No Religious Preference: Political Backlash and Generational Succession, 1987–2012," *Sociological Science* 1 (2014), 423–47, at 423. On similar lines, see also: Michael Hout and Claude S. Fischer, "Why More Americans Have No Religious Preference: Politics and Generations," *American Sociological Review* 67/2 (2002), 165–90; Robert D. Putnam and David E. Campbell, *American Grace: How Religion Divides and Unites Us* (New York: Simon & Schuster), 100–33; Chaves, *American Religion*, 16–17.

31. Cf. Ezra Klein, *Why We're Polarized* (New York: Avid Reader Press, 2020).

32. E.g., Penny Edgell, Joseph Gerteis, and Douglas Hartmann, "Atheists as 'Other': Moral Boundaries and Cultural Membership in American Society," *American Sociological Review* 71/2 (2006), 211–34; Ryan T. Cragun, Barry Kosmin, Ariela Keysar, Joseph H. Hammer, and Michael Nielsen, "On the Receiving End: Discrimination toward the Non-Religious in the United States," *Journal of Contemporary Religion* 27/1 (2012), 105–27.

33. Christopher Hitchens, "The Zeitgeist Shifts," *Free Inquiry* 27/5 (August/ September 2007), 17–18. See also Stephen Bullivant, "The New Atheism and Sociology: Why Here? Why Now? What Next?" in Amarnath Amarasingam (ed.), *Religion and the New Atheism: A Critical Appraisal* (Leiden and Boston, MA: Brill), 109–24.

34. E.g., "Madalyn Murray O'Hair Urges Atheists to Come out of Closet," *Indianapolis Star*, February 15, 1992, p. 31.

35. See Richard Cimino and Christopher Smith, *Atheist Awakening: Secular Activism and Community in America* (New York: Oxford University Press, 2010); Teemu Taira, "New Atheism as Identity Politics," in Mathew Guest and Elisabeth Arweck (eds.), *Religion and Knowledge: Sociological Perspectives* (Farnham: Ashgate, 2012), 97–113; and Steven Kettell, "Faithless: The Politics of New Atheism," *Secularism and Nonreligion* 2 (2013), 61–72.

36. Michael Ruse, "I'm an Atheist, but Thank God I'm Not a New Atheist," *Premier Christian Radio*, September 2018, available online: https://www.premierchr istianradio.com/Shows/Saturday/Unbelievable/Unbelievable-blog/I-m-an-atheist.-But-thank-God-I-m-not-a-New-Atheist; Chris Steadman, "I'm an Atheist, But I Had to Walk Away from the Toxic Side of Online Atheism," *Washington Post*, November 7, 2017; Yessica Hernandez-Cruz, "I'm an Atheist, But I'm Not . . . ," *BuzzFeed*, December 28, 2015.

37. Writing these paragraphs in early 2021, and thus just a few weeks after the US Capitol was stormed, brings no shortage of examples to mind. Prior to the internet, if you had an inkling that perhaps forest fires were caused by space lasers, you would probably have to go a very long way out of your way to find anyone else who might take you seriously. Now, you're just a couple of clicks

away from a community of others who not only think you're onto something, but make *you* feel like the normie: "I mean, I only believe in space lasers . . . it's not like I'm one of those *Jewish* space laser crazies in, um, Congress."

On the general point, see Chris Anderson, *The Long Tail: Why the Future of Business Is Selling Less of More* (New York: Hyperion, 2006); Seth Godin, *We Are All Weird: The Rise of Tribes and the End of Normal* (London: Penguin, 2015).

38. True Bronies will, of course, realize that my timeline here is utterly fanciful. Rainbow Dash was only introduced in MLP Gen 4—i.e., with the "Friendship Is Magic" series—which itself marks the beginning of real Bronydom. Since Gen 4 only debuted in 2010, it has always been a digital native, and in fact much of its success was driven by social media (including, curiously enough, on 4chan). This means that the hypothetical scenario I'm sketching here is just that. If it helps, think of it as existing in some *Equestria Girls*–esque parallel universe.

On the influence of 4chan in driving various aspects of internet "tribal" culture, see Angela Nagle, *Kill All Normies: Online Culture Wars from 4chan and Tumblr to Trump and the Alt-Right* (London: Zero Books, 2017); and Cole Stryker, *Epic Win for Anonymous: How 4chan's Army Conquered the Web* (New York: Overlook Press, 2011).

39. Within a burgeoning scholarly literature, see especially: Patrick Edwards, Daniel P. Chadborn, Courtney N. Plante, Stephen Reysen, and Marsh Howze Redden, *Meet the Bronies: The Psychology of the Adult My Little Pony Fandom* (Jefferson, NC: McFarland, 2019).

40. Robert D. Putnam, *Bowling Alone: The Collapse and Revival of American Community* (New York: Simon & Schuster, 2000), 172. I've discussed this idea at greater length in Stephen Bullivant, "I Call You (Facebook) Friends: New Media and the New Evangelization," in Martin Lintner (ed.), *God in Question: Religious Language and Secular Languages* (Brixen: Verlag Weger, 2014), 461–73.

41. Richard Cimino and Christopher Smith, *Atheist Awakening: Secular Activism and Community in America* (New York: Oxford University Press, 2010), 85–117; Phil Zuckerman, Luke W. Galen, and Frank L. Pasquale, *The Nonreligious: Understanding Secular People and Societies* (New York: Oxford University Press, 2016), 219–21; and Christopher Smith and Richard Cimino, "Atheisms Unbound: The Role of the New Media in the Formation of a Secularist Identity," *Secularism and Nonreligion* 1 (2012), 17–31.

On contemporary involvement in such groups, see Sarah Wilkins-Laflamme and Joel Thiessen, "Religious Socialization and Millennial Involvement in Organized and Digital Nonbelief Activities," *Secularism and Nonreligion* 9/2 (2020), 1–15.

42. See, in particular, Cass R. Sunstein, *Going to Extremes: How Like Minds Unite and Divide* (Oxford: Oxford University Press, 2009). For recent, arresting explorations of what this kind of online radicalization can look (and *feel*) like in practice, see Julia Ebner, *Going Dark: The Secret Social Lives of Extremists* (London: Bloomsbury, 2020); Anna Errelle, *In the Skin of a Jihadist: Inside Islamic State's Recruitment Networks* (San Francisco: HarperCollins, 2015); and Laura Bates, *Men Who Hate Women: From Incels to Pickup Artists, the Truth about Extreme Misogyny and How It Affects Us All* (London: Simon & Schuster, 2020).

43. Connoisseurs of sociological theory will note here the influence of Peter Berger and Thomas Luckmann's work on "plausibility structures," most especially as presented in: Peter Berger and Thomas Luckmann, *The Social Construction of Reality* (Harmondsworth: Penguin, [1966] 1971); and Peter Berger, *The Heretical Imperative: Contemporary Possibilities of Religious Affirmation* (London: Collins, 1980). I have applied this idea to American religion at length, with particular reference to Catholicism, in Stephen Bullivant, *Mass Exodus: Catholic Disaffiliation in Britain and America since Vatican II* (Oxford: Oxford University Press, 2019).

44. Paul K. McClure, "Tinkering with Technology and Religion in the Digital Age: The Effects of Internet Use on Religious Belief, Behavior, and Belonging," *Journal for the Scientific Study of Religion* 56/3 (2017), 481–97, at 481, 491; Allen B. Downey, "Religious Affiliation, Education, and Internet Use" (2014), *ArXiv*, available online: https://arxiv.org/abs/1403.5534. Also relevant here is: Paul K. McClure, "Faith and Facebook in a Pluralistic Age: The Effects of Social Networking Sites on the Religious Beliefs of Emerging Adults," *Sociological Perspectives* 59/4 (2016), 818–34.

45. Cf. Steve Silberman, *NeuroTribes: The Legacy of Autism and How to Think Smarter about People Who Think Differently* (London: Allen & Unwin, 2015), 440–56.

Chapter 6

1. I'm a Cawker man, through and through.
2. By the by, this was my opening to recover some street cred after Power Team-gate. Not only had I heard of PM, many years ago I took a pilgrimage to the Precious Moments Chapel and Giftstore in Carthage, Missouri: the Mecca, as I'm sure they don't describe it, for Christian girls and their figurine-loving moms everywhere.
3. Though for state-of-the-art attempts, see Thomas S. Kidd, *Who Is an Evangelical? The History of a Movement in Crisis* (New Haven, CT: Yale University Press, 2019), esp. 1–7; Mark A. Noll, "What Is 'Evangelical'?" in

Gerald R. McDermott (ed.), *The Oxford Handbook of Evangelical Theology* (New York: Oxford University Press, 2010), 19–32; and Timothy Larsen, "Defining and Locating Evangelicalism," in Timothy Larsen and Daniel J. Treier (eds.), *The Cambridge Companion to Evangelical Theology* (New York: Cambridge University Press, 2007), 1–14.

4. See especially James K. Wellman, Katie Corcoran, and Kate Stockly, *High on God: How Megachurches Won the Heart of America* (New York: Oxford University Press, 2020); and Anne C. Loveland and Otis B. Wheeler, *From Meetinghouse to Megachurch: A Material and Cultural History* (Columbia: University of Missouri Press, 2003), 114–53.

5. Cf. Chrissy Stroop, "Now Defunct: Confessions of a Former Short-Term Youth Missionary to Russia," in Chrissy Stroop and Lauren O'Neal (eds.), *Empty the Pews: Stories of Leaving the Church* (Indianapolis, IN: Epiphany Publishing, 2019), 157–72, at 160.

6. Kimon Howland Sargeant, *Seeker Churches: Promoting Traditional Religion in a Nontraditional Way* (New Brunswick, NJ: Rutgers University Press, 2000), 5–6; Maren Freudenberg, *The Mainline in Late Modernity: Tradition and Innovation in the Evangelical Lutheran Church in America* (Lanham, MD: Lexington Books, 2018).

7. For an absorbing history of this movement, see Alan Schreck, *A Mighty Current of Grace: The Story of the Catholic Charismatic Renewal* (Frederick, MD: The Word Among Us Press, 2017).

8. Cf. George Weigel, *Evangelical Catholicism: Deep Reform in the 21st-Century Church* (New York: Basic Books, 2013).

9. E.g., Christian Smith, *How to Go from Being a Good Evangelical to a Committed Catholic in Ninety-Five Difficult Steps* (Eugene, OR: Cascade Books, 2011), 73–4; Joseph Bottum, *The Gospel according to Tim* (Kindle Single, 2012); Dave Cullen, *Columbine* (New York: Twelve, 2009), chap. 32.

10. Christian Smith, *American Evangelicalism: Embattled and Thriving* (Chicago: University of Chicago Press, 1998). For this subcultural approach, see also Randall Balmer, *Mine Eyes Have Seen the Glory: A Journey into the Evangelical Subculture in America*, 5th ed. (New York: Oxford University Press, 2014).

11. Andrew Mall, *God Rock, Inc.: The Business of Niche Music* (Oakland: University of California Press, 2021), 14–16. For background, see Larry Eskridge, *God's Forever Family: The Jesus People Movement in America* (New York: Oxford University Press, 2013), chap. 10.

12. Clinton Heylin, *Trouble in Mind: Bob Dylan's Gospel Years—What Really Happened* (Pontefract: Route, 2017).

13. Among no shortage of examples, consider Hal Lindsay's *The Late, Great Planet Earth* (1970), Billy Graham's *Angels: God's Secret Agents* (1975), Frank Peretti's *This Present Darkness* (1986), Tim LaHaye and Jerry B. Jenkins' *Left Behind* (1995) and multiple sequels and prequels, Bruce Wilkinson's *The Prayer of*

Jabez (2000), Rick Warren's *The Purpose-Driven Life* (2002), William P. Young's *The Shack* (2007), Todd Burpo's *Heaven Is for Real* (2010)—all million-sellers, often several times over. On this whole topic, see Daniel Vaca, *Evangelicals Incorporated: Books and the Business of Religion in America* (Cambridge, MA: Harvard University Press, 2019).

14. Popularized by the scholar, activist, and freelance journalist Dr. Chrissy Stroop, the term "exvangelical" has taken on a life of its own in only a short span of time. See, for example, Josiah Hesse, " 'Exvangelicals': Why More Religious People Are Rejecting the Evangelical Label," *The Guardian*, November 3, 2017. For an illuminating collection of exvangelical (and other nonvert) testimonies, see Chrissy Stroop and Lauren O'Neal (eds.), *Empty the Pews: Stories of Leaving the Church* (Indianapolis, IN: Epiphany Publishing, 2019).

15. Smith, *American Evangelicalism*, 50–1.

16. Strictly speaking, I understand, "continuous revolution" is now the preferred English translation of the idea in Mao's thought—to distinguish it from an earlier and different idea in Marx and Trotsky. However, since I first learned the phrase from an episode of *The West Wing* where it's attributed to Mao, and since I suspect that series is more familiar to most readers than the minutiae of Marxist theory, the attribution here can stand.

17. Within a vast literature, see especially Mary L. Eberstadt, *Adam and Eve After the Pill* (San Francisco: Ignatius Press, 2012), and Mark D. Regnerus, *Cheap Sex: The Transformation of Men, Marriage, and Monogamy* (New York: Oxford University Press, 2017).

18. E.g., Mark D. Regnerus, *Forbidden Fruit: Sex and Religion in the Lives of American Teenagers* (New York: Oxford University Press, 2007), 53–4; Mark D. Regnerus and Jerry Uecker, "Finding Faith, Losing Faith: The Prevalence and Context of Religious Transformations during Adolescence," *Review of Religious Research* 47 (2006), 217–37; Sara A. Vasilenko and Eva S. Lefkowitz, "Changes in Religiosity after First Intercourse in the Transition to Adulthood," *Psychology of Religion and Spirituality* 6/4 (2014), 310–15.

19. On this, see Donna Freitas, *Sex and the Soul: Juggling Sexuality, Spirituality, Romance, and Religion on America's College Campuses* (New York: Oxford University Press, 2008), 75–92; Sara Moslener, *Virgin Nation: Sexual Purity and American Adolescence* (New York: Oxford University Press, 2015), 109–53.

20. The body of work I'm drawing on here is based around the idea of "Credibility Enhancing Displays" (CREDs), principally associated with the psychologist Joseph Henrich. See especially Joseph Henrich, "The Evolution of Costly Displays, Cooperation and Religion: Credibility Enhancing Displays and their Implications for Cultural Evolution," *Evolution and Human Behaviour* 30 (2009), 11–28; and Joseph Henrich, *The WEIRDest People in the World: How the West Became Psychologically Peculiar and Particularly Prosperous* (London:

Allen Lane, 2020), chap. 4. Also foundational for my thinking on this topic are Jonathan A. Lanman, "The Importance of Religious Displays for Belief Acquisition and Secularization," *Journal of Contemporary Religion* 27 (2012), 49–65; and Hugh Turpin, Marc Andersen, and Jonathan A. Lanman, "CREDs, CRUDs, and Catholic Scandals: Experimentally Examining the Effects of Religious Paragon Behavior on Co-religionist Belief," *Religion, Brain and Behavior* 9/2 (2019), 143–55.

21. Coined by the law professor Glenn Reynolds, on whose blog (www.pfmedia. com/instapundit) it's been a consistent catchphrase since at least 2007. On this topic, see also George Marshall, *Don't Even Think about It: Why Our Brains Are Wired to Ignore Climate Change* (New York: Bloomsbury, 2014), chap. 37.

22. A popular trope in the evangelical subculture, Proverbs 31:10–31 provides a detailed wish list for the ideal wife, beginning with the line: "A capable wife who can find? She is far more precious than jewels. . . ."

23. See, e.g., Wellman et al., *High on God*, chap. 14.

24. *Psycho-logic* is a term I'm borrowing from Rory Sutherland: *Alchemy: The Surprising Power of Ideas That Don't Make Sense* (London: Penguin, 2019), Intro (while he uses it in a very different context, the basic sense is the same).

25. Russell Moore, "Enraged by Ravi (Part 1): The Wreckage of Ravi Zacharias," February 15, 2021, available online: https://www.russellmoore.com/2021/ 02/15/enraged-by-ravi-part-1-the-wreckage-of-ravi-zacharias/.

26. Kidd, *Who Is an Evangelical?*, 143.

27. Not that there's been any shortage of them thus far. Those I've read, learning much from each of them, include: Stephen J. Mansfield, *Choosing Donald Trump: God, Anger, Hope, and Why Christian Conservatives Supported Him* (Grand Rapids, MI: Baker Books, 2017); James Roberts and Martyn Whittock, *Trump and the Puritans: How the Evangelical Religious Right Put Trump in the White House* (London: Biteback, 2020); Andrew L. Whitehead and Samuel L. Perry, *Taking America Back for God: Christian Nationalism in the United States* (New York: Oxford University Press, 2020).

28. See Chrissy Stroop, "5 Key Moments from the Year of the 'Exvangelicals,'" *Rewire News*, December 26, 2018; Nina Burleigh, "Evangelical Christians Helped Elect Donald Trump, but Their Time as a Major Political Force Is Coming to an End." *Newsweek*, December 13, 2018.

29. Philip Gorski, "Why Evangelicals Voted for Trump: A Critical Cultural Sociology," *American Journal of Cultural Sociology* 5/3 (2017), 338–54, at 338.

30. Elizabeth FitzGerald, *Evangelicals: The Struggle to Shape America* (New York: Simon & Schuster, 2017), 291–318.

31. In addition to the studies cited in Chapter 5, see these nuanced additions to the literature: Paul A. Djupe, Jacob R. Neiheisel, and Anand E. Sokhey, "Reconsidering the Role of Politics in Leaving Religion—The Importance of Affiliation," *American Journal of Political Science* 62/1 (2018), 161–75; and Paul

A. Djupe, Jacob R. Neiheisel, and Kimberly H. Conger, "Are the Politics of the Christian Right Linked to State Rates of the Nonreligious? The Importance of Salient Controversy," *Political Research Quarterly* 71/4 (2018), 910–22.

32. Alex Ayris, "'They'd Vote against Jesus Christ Himself': Trump's 'White Evangelicals,' the Construction of a Contested Identity, and the Need for a New Narrative," *Journal of Church and State* 63/4 (2021), 648–70; Dante J. Scala, "The Skeptical Faithful: How Trump Gained Momentum among Evangelicals," *Presidential Studies Quarterly* 50 (2020), 927–47.

33. See Ross Douthat, *Bad Religion: How We Became a Nation of Heretics* (New York: Free Press, 2012); Rod Dreher, *The Benedict Option: A Strategy for Christians in a Post-Christian Nation* (New York: Sentinel, 2017); Rod Dreher, *Live Not by Lies: A Manual for Christian Dissidents* (New York: Penguin Random House, 2020); and Russell Moore, *Onward: Engaging the Culture without Losing the Gospel* (Nashville, TN: B&H Publishing, 2015).

34. The classic statement of this is, of course, Smith, *American Evangelicalism*. On Christian schools and colleges as key components of the evangelical subculture, see Jeffrey Guhin, *Agents of God: Boundaries and Authority in Muslim and Christian Schools* (New York: Oxford University Press, 2020); and Adam Laats, *Fundamentalist U: Keeping the Faith in American Higher Education* (New York: Oxford University Press, 2018).

35. See Ryan Burge, "Think US Evangelicalism Is Dying Out? Well, Define Evangelicalism . . ." *The Conversation*, January 26, 2021, available online: https://theconversation.com/think-us-evangelicals-are-dying-out-well-def ine-evangelicalism-152640.

36. Paul A. Djupe and Ryan Burge, "Exvangelicals—A Note on Size and Sources," *Religion in Public*, March 1, 2021, available online: https://religioninpublic. blog/2021/03/01/exvangelicals-a-note-on-size-and-sources/. On the wider point about politics driving religious identification, see Michele Margolis, *From Politics to the Pews: How Partisanship and the Political Environment Shape Religious Identity* (Chicago: University of Chicago Press, 2018).

37. Gregory A. Smith, "More White Americans Adopted Than Shed Evangelical Label during Trump Presidency, Especially His Supporters," Pew Research Center, September 15, 2021, available online: https://www.pewresearch.org/ fact-tank/2021/09/15/more-white-americans-adopted-than-shed-evangeli cal-label-during-trump-presidency-especially-his-supporters/.

38. Kidd, *Who Is an Evangelical?*, 126.

Chapter 7

1. Donald C. Reitzes and Elizabeth J. Mutran, "Lingering Identities in Retirement," *Sociological Quarterly* 47/2 (2006), 333–59. On the whole topic

of "ex-" identities, see Helen Rose Fuchs Ebaugh, *Becoming an Ex: The Process of Role Exit* (Chicago: University of Chicago Press, 1988).

2. William Faulkner, *Requiem for a Nun* (London: Vintage, [1951] 2015), 85.

3. On US converts to Catholicism, see Mark Gray, "Portrait of the American Catholic Convert: Strength in New Numbers," *Center for Applied Research in the Apostolate*, April 2014, available online: http://nineteensixty-four.blogs pot.co.uk/2014/04/portrait-of-american-catholic-convert.html.

4. Note that this is slightly below the 23% figure we've been quoting for 2018 itself, since we're here giving the mean figure across the 2014, 2016, and 2018 waves.

5. Yinxuan Huang, "How Christian Upbringing Divides the Religious Nones in Britain: Exploring the Imprints of Christian Upbringing in the 2016 EU Referendum," *Journal of Contemporary Religion* 35/2 (2020), 341–62.

6. D. R. Van Tongeren, C. N. DeWall, Z. Chen, C. G. Sibley, and J. Bulbulia, "Religious Residue: Cross-Cultural Evidence That Religious Psychology and Behavior Persist following Deidentification," *Journal of Personality and Social Psychology* 120/2 (2021), 484–503.

7. Philip Schwadel, Sam A. Hardy, Daryl R. Van Tongeren, and C. Nathan DeWall, "The Values of Religious Nones, Dones, and Sacralized Americans: Links between Changes in Religious Affiliation and Schwartz Values," *Journal of Personality* 89 (2021), 867–82.

8. For a full and absorbing study of nonreligious parenting, see Christel Manning, *Losing Our Religion: How Unaffiliated Parents Are Raising Their Children* (New York: New York University Press, 2015).

9. This observation is based on what, if this were a sociology journal article, I'd describe as "intensive fieldwork utilizing a range of digital ethnography methodologies." During—and for a good while after—the recent presidential campaign, I caught most of the main monologues and culture or politics-related segments, along with much else besides, from the following: Tucker Carlson and Sean Hannity (Fox News); Stephen Colbert (CBS); Trevor Noah (Comedy Central); John Oliver (HBO); *Saturday Night Live*, Seth Meyers, Amber Ruffin (NBC); Liz Wheeler (OAN); and Michael Moore ("Rumble").

10. See Ezra Klein, *Why We're Polarized* (New York: Avid Reader Press, 2020); and Robert D. Putnam with Shaylyn Romney Garrett, *The Upswing: How We Came Together a Century Ago and How We Can Do It Again* (New York: Simon & Schuster, 2015).

11. See, e.g., Hugh Urban, *The Church of Scientology: A History of a New Religion* (Princeton, NJ: Princeton University Press, 2011). A very engaging account of what this looks like in practice is Leah Remini, *Troublemaker: Surviving Hollywood and Scientology* (New York: Ballantine, 2015).

12. Richard Dawkins, *The God Delusion* (London: Bantam Press, 2006), 1.

13. For an overview of this whole topic, see Jay Wexler, *Our Non-Christian Nation: How Atheists, Satanists, Pagans, and Others Are Demanding Their Rightful Place in Public Life* (Stanford, CA: Stanford University Press, 2019).

14. Heather L. Weaver, "The Supreme Court Will Decide Whether the Government Can Display a 40-Foot Latin Cross," *ACLU*, November 6, 2018, available online: https://www.aclu.org/blog/religious-liberty/government-promotion-religion/supreme-court-will-decide-whether-government.

15. *American Legion v. American Humanist Association*, 139 S. Ct. 2067 (2019).

16. E.g., "First Amendment—Establishment Clause—Government Display of Religious Symbols—*American Legion v. American Humanist Ass'n*," *Harvard Law Review* 133/1 (2019), 262–71; Ira Lupu and Robert Tuttle, "Symposium: A Splintered Court Leaves the Bladensburg Cross Intact," *SCOTUSblog*, June 21, 2019, available online: https://www.scotusblog.com/2019/06/symposium-a-splintered-court-leaves-the-bladensburg-cross-intact/ (April 15, 2021).

17. On the institutional ecology of organized secularism in the USA, see Ryan T. Cragun, Christel Manning, and Lori L. Fazzino (eds.), *Organized Secularism in the United States: New Directions in Research* (Boston: De Gruyter, 2017).

18. Shane Bugbee, "Unmasking Lucien Greaves, Leader of the Satanic Temple," *Vice*, July 30, 2013. For a full history and exploration of the Satanic Temple, see Joseph P. Laycock, *Speak of the Devil: How the Satanic Temple Is Changing the Way We Talk about Religion* (New York: Oxford University Press, 2020). Also check out the 2019 documentary *Hail Satan?*.

19. Laycock, *Speak of the Devil*.

20. The Satanic milieu is more varied than one might think. TST itself is a rival of the older Church of Satan, founded in 1960s San Francisco. Both groups have also given rise to schismatic splinter groups. See Laycock, *Speak of the Devil*, chap. 3.

21. See Steve Bruce, "Late Secularization and Religion as Alien," *Open Theology* 1/1 (2014), 13–23; Linda Woodhead, "The Rise of 'No Religion' in Britain: The Emergence of a New Cultural Majority," *Journal of the British Academy* 4 (2016), 245–61.

Chapter 8

1. I exaggerate here, though only a little. See Andrew Greeley, "The 'October Count' of Mass Attendance Is Misleading Indicator," *Religion News Service*, January 1, 1997; see also Ken Untener, *The Practical Prophet: Pastoral Writings* (Mahwah, NJ: Paulist Press, 2007), 39.

2. Vatican II, *Sacrosanctum Concilium* (1963), art. 11.

3. See Carrie Gibson, *El Norte: The Epic and Forgotten Story of Hispanic North America* (New York: Grove Atlantic, 2019); Adrienne LaFrance, "A Skeleton, a Catholic Relic, and a Mystery about American Origins," *The Atlantic*, July 28, 2015.

4. This is not, I might add, simply a function of "averaging out" between separate, racially distinct churches catering exclusively to, say, White evangelicals, Black evangelicals, or Latino/a evangelicals—though that is certainly a factor.

5. I do not say that this is a *good* thing, either theologically or sociologically. But it is a thing nonetheless.

6. Fates that have separately befallen two of my friends.

7. Though see Jill Peterfeso, *Womanpriest: Tradition and Transgression in the Contemporary Roman Catholic Church* (New York: Fordham University Press, 2020); Michael W. Cuneo, *The Smoke of Satan: Conservative and Traditionalist Dissent in Contemporary American Catholicism* (Oxford: Oxford University Press, 1997); Patricia Walsh Chadwick, *Little Sister: A Memoir* (Nashville, TN: Post Hill Press, 2019).

8. On this and much else, see Massimo Faggioli, *Joe Biden and Catholicism in the United States* (Worcester, MA: Bayard, 2021).

9. As Stef, one of my Portland interviewees, describes her own fairly traumatic experiences: "With Jehovah's Witnesses, there's a lot of very black-and-white thinking: you're either in or you're out. I feel like sooner or later it comes to a head. You're either in or you're out; you either have a relationship [with your JW relatives] or you don't. The really rigid belief structure seems to force that separation *or* inclusion. It's really difficult to fall anywhere in the middle once you've decided that you don't want to be a Jehovah's Witness anymore."

10. Graham Greene, Evelyn Waugh, and G. K. Chesterton all leap immediately to mind here. No doubt there are American analogues, too.

11. E.g., Brandon Vogt, *Return: How to Draw Your Child Back to the Faith*, 2nd ed. (Chicago: Word on Fire, 2021); Sebastian Walshe, *Always a Catholic: How to Keep Your Kids in the Faith for Life—And Bring Them Back If They Have Strayed* (El Cajon, CA: Catholic Answers Press, 2021); Nicolette Manglos-Weber and Christian Smith, *Understanding Former Young Catholics: Findings from a National Study of American Emerging Adults* (South Bend, IN: Institute for Church Life, 2015).

12. Cf. David Yamane, *Becoming Catholic: Finding Rome in the American Religious Landscape* (Oxford: Oxford University Press, 2014).

13. Since I haven't given a film recommendation in these endnotes for a chapter or two, here's one. Netflix's *The Polka King* can best be described as a true-crime comedy biopic set deep inside the Polish American subculture. It's brilliant. If not for the unsurpassable *School of Rock*, it'd be the best film Jack Black's ever made.

14. As a general rule, names of people have been changed to protect interviewees' confidentiality. However, I feel confident that the original Philo Taylor Farnsworth (1826–1887), who had thirty children from four wives, had a sufficiently large number of "great-great-great-great-great" nieces and nephews as not to risk outing anybody here. Information garnered from: https://familypedia.wikia.org/wiki/Philo_Taylor_Farnsworth_(1826–87). His grandson was indeed an early television pioneer, and also made important contributions to research into nuclear fusion.

15. The phenomenon of children no longer going to Mass as the catalyst for parents to stop doing so too has been noted in other studies of non-practicing Catholics. See Stephen Bullivant, Catherine Knowles, Hannah Vaughan-Spruce, and Bernadette Durcan, *Why Catholics Leave, What They Miss, and How They Might Return* (Mahwah, NJ: Paulist Press, 2019), 3–8.

16. Stephen Bullivant, *Mass Exodus: Catholic Disaffiliation in Britain and America since Vatican II* (Oxford: Oxford University Press, 2019).

17. Own analysis, using pooled GSS 2010–18 data. Out of the 1,907 who said they were brought up Catholic in these five waves, 192 (i.e., 10%) identified as a current Catholic who attends religious services "weekly" or "several times a week." In contrast, 407 (21%) identified as a none.

18. Michael J. Pfeifer, *The Making of American Catholicism: Regional Culture and the Catholic Experience* (New York: New York University Press, 2021).

19. See Tricia Colleen Bruce, *Parish and Place: Making Room for Diversity in the American Catholic Church* (Oxford: Oxford University Press, 2017).

20. See Secretariat of State of the Holy See, *Report on the Holy See's Institutional Knowledge and Decision-Making Related to Former Cardinal Theodore Edgar McCarrick (1930 to 2017)*, November 10, 2020, available online: https://www.vatican.va/resources/resources_rapporto-card-mccarrick_20201110_en.pdf. On the wider context, see Stephen Bullivant and Giovanni Radhitio Putra Sadewo, "Power, Preferment, and Patronage: Catholic Bishops, Social Networks, and the Affair(s) of Ex-Cardinal McCarrick," working paper 2020, available online: https://arxiv.org/abs/2007.06606; and Stephen Bullivant and Giovanni Radhitio Putra Sadewo, "How McCarricks Happen," *Catholic Herald*, April 18, 2021.

21. See Jason Berry, *Lead Us Not into Temptation: Catholic Priests and the Sexual Abuse of Children* (Urbana: University of Illinois Press, [1992] 2000).

22. The Pennsylvania Grand Jury report was the culmination of a two-year investigation into child sex abuse within six of the state's eight Catholic dioceses. To quote from its opening paragraphs:

We, the members of this grand jury, need you to hear this. We know some of you have heard some of it before. There have been other reports about child sex abuse within the Catholic Church. But never on this scale. For many of us,

NOTES

those earlier stories happened someplace else, someplace away. Now we know the truth: it happened everywhere.

[. . .] We heard the testimony of dozens of witnesses concerning clergy sex abuse. We subpoenaed, and reviewed, half a million pages of internal diocesan documents. They contained credible allegations against over *three hundred* predator priests. Over *one thousand* child victims were identifiable, from the church's own records. We believe that the real number—of children whose records were lost, or who were afraid ever to come forward—is in the thousands. (p. 1)

See Office of Attorney General [of the] Commonwealth of Pennsylvania, *Report I of the 40th Statewide Investigating Grand Jury* (2018), available online: https://www.attorneygeneral.gov/wp-content/uploads/2018/08/A-Report-of-the-Fortieth-Statewide-Investigating-Grand-Jury_Cleland-Redactions-8-12-08_Redacted.pdf. For real-time reporting on the multiple scandals rocking the Catholic Church in 2018, see Christopher R. Altieri, *Into the Storm: Chronicle of a Year in Crisis* (Charlotte, NC: TAN Books, 2020).

23. David Feltmate, *Drawn to the Gods: Religion and Humour in* The Simpsons, South Park, *and* Family Guy (New York: New York University Press, 2017), chap. 4.
24. See Investigative Staff of the Boston Globe, *Betrayal: The Crisis in the Catholic Church*, updated ed. (London: Profile, [2002] 2015).
25. Though see Evan Lenow, "Protestants and Contraception," *First Things*, January 2018.
26. I'm not saying here that there haven't been pedophilia-related crimes in evangelicalism, or drugs-and-prostitutes scandals in the Catholic Church (or that one is more prevalent in either: I've no idea). My point is simply that when people think "Catholic scandals" they automatically think of one thing, and when they think "evangelical scandals" they automatically think of another. *And* that the former are widely considered (including by the legal system, in terms of sentencing) as graver than the latter. So that however much popular perception of "evangelical scandals" is damaging to evangelicalism, it's reasonable to think this applies *a fortiori* in the case of popular perceptions of "Catholic scandals."
27. On Francis' approval ratings in US polls, see Justin Nortey and Clare Gecewicz, "Three-Quarters of U.S. Catholics View Pope Francis Favorably, Though Partisan Differences Persist," *Pew Research Center*, April 3, 2020, available online: https://www.pewresearch.org/fact-tank/2020/04/03/three-quarters-of-u-s-catholics-view-pope-francis-favorably-though-partisan-differences-persist/.
28. Ross Douthat, *To Change the Church: Pope Francis and the Future of Catholicism* (New York: Simon & Schuster, 2018), 66.

29. Chris Mooney, "Our New Pro-Science Pontiff: Pope Francis on Climate Change, Evolution, and the Big Bang," *Washington Post*, December 31, 2014. The pope's full remarks can be read here: "Address of his Holiness Pope Francis on the Occasion of the Inauguration of the Bust in Honour of Pope Benedict XVI," Plenary Session of the Pontifical Academy of Sciences, October 27, 2014, available online: http://www.vatican.va/content/francesco/en/speec hes/2014/october/documents/papa-francesco_20141027_plenaria-accade mia-scienze.html.

30. See Pius XII, *Humani Generis* (1950). On this whole topic, including media misperceptions of it, I recommend Louis Caruana (ed.), *Darwin and Catholicism: The Past and Present Dynamics of a Cultural Encounter* (London: T. & T. Clark, 2009); and James R. Riley, "Popes, Papers & Publics: Media Representations and Public Perceptions of Catholicism and Evolution in England" (2019), PhD thesis, University of Birmingham, UK.

31. Tim O'Malley, "Stop Looking for a Francis Effect," *Church Life Journal*, December 17, 2019, available online: https://churchlifejournal.nd.edu/artic les/the-francis-effect-isnt-about-numbers/; Bullivant, *Mass Exodus*, 232.

32. Mark Binelli, "Pope Francis: The Times They Are A-Changin'," *Rolling Stone*, January 28, 2014.

33. E. J. Dickson, "Guess the Cool Pope Isn't So Cool after All," *Rolling Stone*, March 15, 2021.

34. Cf. Christian Smith, *American Evangelicalism: Embattled and Thriving* (Chicago: University of Chicago Press, 1998).

35. This phenomenon is more clearly evident in countries where secularizing factors have bitten much harder and deeper than they have (or quite possibly will) in the United States. For a more detailed rundown of the sociological factors in play here, with reference to recent British data, see Ben Clements and Stephen Bullivant, *Catholics in Contemporary Britain: Faith, Society, Politics* (Oxford: Oxford University Press, 2022). I am currently working toward another book, specifically structured around "deep dives" into various signs of growth within British Catholicism, which my colleagues and I hope to publish in 2024.

Chapter 9

1. Alexis de Tocqueville, "Letter to M. de Kergorlay," June 20, 1831, in *Memoir, Letters, and Remains of Alexis de Tocqueville* (London: Macmillan and Co., 1861), 304–13, at 309.

2. G. K. Chesterton, *What I Saw in America* (London: Dodd, Mead, and Co., 1922), 25, 171.

3. Charles Dickens, *American Notes for General Circulation*, vol. 2 (London: Chapman and Hall, 1842), 299.

4. Max Weber, "'Churches' and 'Sects' in North America: An Ecclesiastical and Sociopolitical Sketch" (1906), in *The Protestant Ethic and the "Spirit" of Capitalism and Other Writings*, trans. Peter Baehr and Gordon C. Wells (London: Penguin, 2002), 203–20, at 203.

5. Max Weber, "The Protestant Ethic and the 'Spirit' of Capitalism" (1905), in Baehr and Wells, *The Protestant Ethic and the "Spirit" of Capitalism*, 1–202, at 129.

6. Weber, "Churches and Sects," 208.

7. Cf. Grace Davie, *Europe: The Exceptional Case: Parameters of Faith and Society in the Modern World* (London: Darton, Longman and Todd, 2002).

8. On the apparent discrediting of secularization theory in general, see Peter Berger, "The Desecularization of the World: A Global Overview," in Peter Berger (ed.), *The Desecularization of the World: Resurgent Religion and World Politics* (Grand Rapids, MI: Eerdmans), 1–18; Rodney Stark, "Secularization, RIP," *Sociology of Religion* 60/3 (1999), 249–73.

9. I'm aware that I'm trespassing on a rather fraught area of scholarly debate here, with the reality and/or extent of US secularization having been (once again!) keenly contested in the pages of various technical journals in the past few years. Two key opening salvos here are David Voas and Mark Chaves, "Is the United States a Counterexample to the Secularization Thesis?," *American Journal of Sociology* 121/5 (2016), 1517–52; and Landon Schnabel and Sean Bock, "The Persistent and Exceptional Intensity of American Religion: A Response to Recent Research," *Sociological Science* 4 (2017), 686–700. Each duo has since published responses to the responses in *Sociological Science*. My own views are, as should be clear from this book, rather nearer to those of Voas and Chaves. For other statements of the case for American religious decline, see also Steve Bruce, *Secularization: In Defense of an Unfashionable Theory* (Oxford: Oxford University Press, 2011), 157–76; Kevin McCaffree, *The Secular Landscape: The Decline of Religion in America* (New York: Palgrave Macmillan, 2017); Steve Brauer, "The Surprising Predictable Decline of Religion in the United States," *Journal for the Scientific Study of Religion* 57 (2018), 654–75; and Allen Downey, "The Retreat from Religion Is Accelerating," *Open Data Science*, November 12, 2017, available online: https://opendatascience.com/the-retr eat-from-religion-is-accelerating/.

10. European figures based on my own analysis of 2018 data from the International Social Survey Programme, of which the GSS forms a part.

11. On the related idea of "multiple secularities," see Monika Wohlrab-Sahr and Marian Burchardt, "Multiple Secularities: Toward a Cultural Sociology of Secular Modernities," *Comparative Sociology* 11/6 (2012), 875–909.

12. Although the ISSP "piggybacks" on top of the GSS survey in the United States, it asks a slightly different question on regularity of religious service attendance. This, unlike the GSS, doesn't include an "almost weekly" option. This means that the ISSP records a higher rate of "weekly or more" attenders than does the GSS: 29% compared to 23%. Since my purpose here is to draw international comparisons, I've used the ISSP's figures.

13. James K. Wellman, *Evangelical vs. Liberal: The Clash of Christian Cultures in the Pacific Northwest* (New York: Oxford University Press, 2008).

14. At the time of writing, March 2, 2022, the *New York Times'* online tool was reporting 953,134 total Covid deaths, with the toll rising by around 1,800 each day: https://www.nytimes.com/interactive/2021/us/covid-cases.html.

15. On the religious (and other) impacts of the pandemic, see Nicholas Christakis, *Apollo's Arrow: The Profound and Enduring Impact of Coronavirus on How We Live* (New York: Little, Brown, 2020), chap. 7. My own modest contribution to the soon-to-be-vast "Covid and religion" literature, written very early into the pandemic, is *Catholicism in the Time of Coronavirus* (Park Ridge, IL: Word on Fire, 2020), available for free download here: https://www.wordonfire.org/covid/.

16. Ross Douthat, *Bad Religion: How We Became a Nation of Heretics* (New York: Free Press, 2012), 180.

17. See Roger Finke and Rodney Stark, *The Churching of America, 1776–2005: Winners and Losers in Our Religious Economy*, 2nd ed. (New Brunswick, NJ: Rutgers University Press, 2005), chap. 5.

18. Cf. Chris Anderson, *The Long Tail: Why the Future of Business Is Selling Less of More* (New York: Hyperion, 2006).

19. Philip Jenkins, "Where Have All the Cultists Gone?," *Anxious Bench*, June 27, 2014, available online: https://www.patheos.com/blogs/anxiousbench/2014/06/where-have-all-the-cultists-gone/; Philip Jenkins, *Fertility and Faith: The Demographic Revolution and the Transformation of World Religions* (Waco, TX: Baylor University Press, 2020), 109.

20. For context, see R. Marie Griffith, *Moral Combat: How Sex Divided American Christians and Fractured American Politics* (New York: Basic Books), 273–310.

21. Charles J. Chaput, *Strangers in a Strange Land: Living the Catholic Faith in a Post-Christian World* (New York: Henry Holt, 2017), 3.

22. Ibid., 7.

23. Russell Moore, *Onward: Engaging the Culture without Losing the Gospel* (Nashville, TN: B&H Publishing, 2015), 4.

24. Ibid., 8.

25. Rod Dreher, *The Benedict Option: A Strategy for Christians in a Post-Christian Nation* (New York: Sentinel, 2017), 8–9, 12.

26. Ibid., 5.

27. Ibid., 18.

28. Ibid., 98.
29. Moore, *Onward*, 8.
30. E.g., Katherine Stewart, *The Power Worshippers: Inside the Dangerous Rise of the Religious Right* (New York: Bloomsbury, 2020). On this topic, see also Andrew L. Whitehead and Samuel L. Perry, *Taking America Back for God: Christian Nationalism in the United States* (New York: Oxford University Press, 2020); and Christian Smith, *Christian America? What Evangelicals Really Want* (Berkeley: University of California Press, 2000).
31. Philip S. Gorski and Samuel L. Perry, *The Flag and the Cross: White Christian Nationalism and the Threat to American Democracy* (New York: Oxford University Press, 2022), 3.
32. Ibid., 15.
33. See Robert P. Jones, *The End of White Christian America* (New York: Simon and Schuster, 2017); Robert Wuthnow, *The Left Behind: Decline and Rage in Small-Town America* (Princeton, NJ: Princeton University Press, 2018).
34. Quoted here from Stanley Hauerwas, "Love, Suffering, and Theology," a 2017 interview available online at: https://cct.biola.edu/love-suffering-theol ogy. However, it has become almost a catchphrase of his, so plenty of other variants, with slightly different wordings, also exist. See also Stanley Hauerwas and William Willimon, *Resident Aliens: Life in the Christian Colony* (Nashville, TN: Abingdon Press, 1989).
35. Abram C. Van Engen, *City on a Hill: A History of American Exceptionalism* (New Haven, CT: Yale University Press, 2020). See also Richard M. Gamble, *In Search of the City on a Hill: The Making and Unmaking of an American Myth* (New York: Continuum, 2012).
36. Cf. Olivier Roy, *Is Europe Christian?*, trans. Cynthia Schock (London: Hurst, 2019).
37. Weber, "Churches and Sects," 204.
38. For an entertaining look at failed prophecies, see Dan Gardner, *Future Babble: Why Expert Predictions Fail and Why We Believe them Anyway* (London: Virgin, 2011).
39. For various reasons, religious parents tend to have more children than do the nonreligious. For a detailed exploration of the evidence, explanations, and implications of this trend, see Philip Jenkins, *Fertility and Faith: The Demographic Revolution and the Transformation of World Religions* (Waco, TX: Baylor University Press, 2020).

INDEX

For the benefit of digital users, indexed terms that span two pages (e.g., 52–53) may, on occasion, appear on only one of those pages.